OTHER BOOKS BY TREVOR K BELL:

Ten for the Devil: *A whodunit set on a remote Hebrides Island*
Gothic Ghost Stories: A Study in Horror

Website: trevorkbell.co.uk

THE COAST TO COAST WALK

A TRAVELOGUE

TREVOR A K BELL

The Book Guild Ltd

First published in Great Britain in 2021 by
The Book Guild Ltd
9 Priory Business Park
Wistow Road, Kibworth
Leicestershire, LE8 0RX
Freephone: 0800 999 2982
www.bookguild.co.uk
Email: info@bookguild.co.uk
Twitter: @bookguild

Typeset in 11pt Adobe Garamond Pro

Printed and bound by CPI Group (UK) Ltd, Croydon, CR0 4YY

ISBN 978 1913551 445

British Library Cataloguing in Publication Data.
A catalogue record for this book is available from the British Library.

This book is dedicated to the memory of Brian Wilkinson, Warden of Black Sail Youth Hostel, who gave so much and asked so little.

ACKNOWLEDGEMENTS

This travelogue is based on the route described in *A Coast to Coast Walk by A. Wainwright,* © *Michael Joseph 1992*. I express my gratitude for permission to use some of the pen-and-ink drawings from Paul Hannon's *Coast to Coast Walk,* © *Paul Hannon 1992, 1994*. I am also grateful for permission to use Caroline A. Metcalfe-Gibson's drawings of Kirkby Stephen and Sunbiggin Tarn, and to David Woodthorpe for his photograph of Castle Rock, Borrowdale. Inexpressible thanks are due to Ann Schuberth for her suggestions and for checking the manuscript. For obvious reasons, some names in the book have been changed.

FOREWORD

This book is a partly anecdotal account of walking Wainwright's Coast to Coast route across northern England, from Robin Hood's Bay in the North Riding of Yorkshire, to St Bees in Cumbria. Among topics covered on the journey include the mines, churches and monasteries visited by the author. Also referenced are the flora and folklore, the fells and waterfalls, historic seats and stone circles. He pays particular attention to the trail's political, industrial and social history; its towns, villages and people. The geology and geography of the area traversed is often remarked upon. His travelogue is told with a light, often humorous, touch, which He hopes the travelogue will encourage the walking reader to lace up his boots and follow in the author's footsteps.

The walk, undertaken by the author in the early '90s, crosses three national parks: the North Yorkshire Moors, the Yorkshire Dales, and the Lake District, and is illustrated with many evocative old pictures (some of which are in colour) and many sketches. The many attractive line drawings evoke a sense of nostalgia for an England that is fast disappearing.

PART ONE

ROBIN HOOD'S BAY TO RICHMOND

Whitby, by J M Turner (© Tate Gallery London, by permission)

I suppose there are many reasons why one embarks on a long distance journey on foot. In my case, no single reason stands out, though I'd been working hard and felt in need of a change, the pressures of work making me feel tired and jaded. I definitely wanted to get out into the restorative, natural world; to fill my soul again with unfiltered raw experience.

There are, of course, always reasons to put off embarking upon such a challenge: the need to earn money being one, for the cost of thirteen nights' accommodation – the number of nights I'd decided upon for the trip, even staying in youth hostels, is considerable. I'd planned to walk, on average, fifteen miles a day. I knew I would be missed by my family – and I would miss them – but salved my conscience at forsaking them by bringing them across to Whitby for a few days' holiday before I set off. When the family had gone, I confess to feeling rather dejected, knowing I would not see their smiling faces again until I reached St Bees.

So, as I set off that April day, for St Bees in Cumbria, a distance of some 190 miles, carrying only essential equipment, I got into my stride as the quiet town of Robin Hood's Bay fell behind. Looking out over the sea-panorama, from the clifftops, a small fishing vessel a half a mile offshore kept pace with me. It seemed almost to suggest that it would come to my rescue should I decide to retrace my steps.

But such thoughts were far from me on that day, as the pale blue and white clouds drifted beneath a thin sun, the light coruscating over the surface of the water. How many moods, I wondered, idly, did the sea have? How many stormy days, how many benign ones? Today it was tempting seafarers to go out upon its shiny surface. But I know, when sailors are far from land, the sea can become a bullying ruffian, capsizing and crushing boats, breaking them into pieces on rocky shores. It tends to throw a tantrum when least expected. It is rather like a horse which, just as its rider thinks he has mastery of it, throws him to the ground. Personally, I've had most trouble with the sea in the supposed 'boating lake' of the Ionian Sea. A strong wind crashed down on us from a mountain range, disturbing the sea so much that we struggled to make port. As Odysseus found, the sea is unpredictable and tempestuous, and it delayed his voyage homeward from Troy.

Main Street, Robin Hood's Bay

But this odyssey was to be on land, and I soon congratulated myself on having started the walk in April, heading westerly. The long-range weather forecast threatened only a dusting of snow mid-way through the trek, with an easterly wind behind me. I had decided to walk the trail from east to west, instead of in the 'correct' direction, from west to east, in order to complete the walk in the Lake District. Once there, I could dispense with map and compass, focusing on the Lakes' natural beauty. In my opinion, the Lakes are incomparable, though a Yorkshire man will tell you that the Yorkshire Moors, or dales, are just as, if not more, attractive. There is no doubt that each national park through which the trail passes, are areas of outstanding national beauty, with their own special character. The only drawback would be, I thought, wrongly, as I travelled westward, that I'd be lonely, walking in the opposite direction to eastbound travellers, providing few opportunities of jaunty companionship.

But before finding true freedom, I had chosen to perform an act of kindness by promising the landlady of my overnight B&B in Robin Hood's Bay, whose house had a 'coffin' window above the door to enable coffins to be removed, that I would call in with a letter to a Mrs Brownlee, who lived in a caravan site overlooking the sea, a few miles further up the coast. 'It will save me a stamp!' she explained.

Arriving at her van, the dear lady must have been expecting me, for, as I approached, she flung open the caravan door and embraced me like a long-lost relative, almost smothering me in her bosom.

'Playing postman for Mrs Sidebottom, are you?' she beamed, obviously tipped off that I would be calling. She gave me a python-like hug, from which I struggled to escape, and looked searchingly into my eyes, as if trying to recall the last occasion she had seen me. 'It is good of you to call, young man!' she said, eventually, 'Come in for a cup of tea!' The dear lady didn't seem particularly interested in the letter I continued to hold out in front of her, but rather more interested in giving me a cup of tea and persuading me to stay. I began to suspect she had an ulterior motive for my visit, and that I wouldn't be leaving as quickly as I had arrived.

'Well, alright,' I said, , anticipating a longer stay than I had intended, 'but I'm doing the Coast-to-Coast, westbound, so I can't stay long. It's just that Mrs Sidebottom asked me to drop this letter off to you, to save her a stamp, and I was happy to do it as you were on my route.'

'Yes of course!' Mrs Brownlee exclaimed, as if there were no need at all for explanations. 'But, you know, I don't get many visitors here these days, so I'll put the kettle on… it won't take a jiffy! I'm sure you could do with a cuppa!'

She was a stout, weighty woman with a round face, greying hair and a generous smile. I wondered if it would be so easy to free myself once inside her caravan, for it's been my experience some jiffy's can take a very long time. I had the feeling that this was going to be another of them. As a matter of fact, I do rather like talking to old people except, but on this occasion, I was pressed for time.

'Thank you,' I said. As I entered the van and sat down, a large cup of tea quickly appearing in front of me. 'Just a quick cup then and I must be off.'

'Of course,' she promised, without a hint of sincerity, 'you'll be on your way in a jiffy!'

That word again.

It was then that I noticed the many gnomes inside her caravan, as well as those I'd passed on my way in, and, as I sipped my tea, they seemed to look pityingly down at me, as though they had foreknowledge of my fate. Rivers of tea flowed from her enormous brown teapot into my cup faster than I could drink the liquid. My 'No thanks' were brushed aside, and my rucksack looked wistfully up at me like a faithful dog wanting to be off.

Bursting with tea, I was just summoning up the strength to announce my departure, when the dear lady produced a huge plate of cream cakes. I began to lose the will to live. Cajoled into eating one, every time I took a cake from the pastry mountain Mrs Brownlee immediately restored the pile to its original height.

'What would we do without tea and cakes?' she asked, rhetorically, pushing the plate ever closer to me, threatening me again with the teapot. 'Do have more than one cake,' she beamed, 'they'll only go to waste! Tea dilates the capillaries you know,' and she pointed to a framed testimony by William Gladstone on the wall, extolling the virtues of the liquid.

> *'If you are cold,*
> *Tea will warm you.*
> *If you are too heated,*
> *It will cool you.*
> *If you are depressed,*
> *It will cheer you.*
> *If you are excited,*
> *It will calm you.'*

That was her cue to top up my cup again. I noticed the strength in her arms, for she could pour from the heavy pot single-handed. I calculated, frighteningly, that there were at least half a dozen more cups remaining in the huge pot. As the level of the liquid in the pot dropped and cooled, she asked:

'Shall I make another pot of tea?'

God forbid! I thought, for I had now been in the van for forty-five minutes, eaten two cakes to her one, and was ahead of her by three cups to one in the tea stakes.

'It's very kind of you,' I said politely, 'but I've had sufficient. I really must be going. I've got to keep to my schedule.'

I stood up.

She looked downcast, as if my announcement of imminent departure had mortally wounded her.

'Surely you've time for one more cup?' she cajoled. 'There are still these cream cakes left, and I do so seldom have visitors. I pretended not to notice the moisture creeping into her eyes. I picked up my rucksack, determinedly. 'I'm sorry, but I must go,' I said, throwing it on to my shoulder.

'Oh, very well!' she capitulated, 'But take a cake for the road, I shan't eat any more.'

As she escorted me to the door, I thanked her for the refreshments and set off down the path, closing the gate firmly behind me. It was a few hundred yards before I felt it was safe to look back. When I looked Mrs Brownlee was dabbing her eyes with a white handkerchief. I must say the sight of her made me feel remorseful, for, I suppose, she must have been very lonely. In a way, my brief visit had reminded her of the fact. Hopefully, she did have some friends on the caravan site and wasn't entirely bereft of company.

Whitby Abbey

Later, shortly after a signpost gave me the choice of either Whitby or Fyling Dales, I arrived at the village of Hawsker and headed for my overnight accommodation, which, I'm bound to say, had a very peaceful – if not an altogether pleasant – feel to it, so much so that I wondered if, at some time, it had been a funeral parlour. I discovered later, on the wall of an obscure passage, a sign which read 'Chapel of Rest'. I wondered if, perhaps, some of its former inhabitants had yet to leave. The proprietor – a tall gaunt man, but pleasant enough – showed me to my room. I placed my toilet bag and pyjamas on the bed ready for slumber. Later, after a bite to eat, I went down to the sitting room and, not long afterwards, a fellow traveller came in, rather flushed and agitated.

'Come far?' I ventured in casual greeting. He settled himself in to an easy chair opposite.

'RAF Fyling Dales,' he answered abruptly, as if there was nowhere else he could have been. 'I've been at the protest.' He gushed: 'It's provocative to have an Early Warning System at an RAF base. It just invites the Ruskies to lob a nuclear bomb on us.' He took an immoderate gulp from the bottle of Newcastle Brown Ale in his hand and continued: 'Just imagine,' he said, 'you're in the Kremlin and you're thinking of who to blast first with your nuclear weapons. Who would you go for?'

'I don't know,' I said.

'I do,' he said, 'the Ruskies would say to themselves, let's lob a bomb on them smug buggers in Yorkshire – the ones with the Early Warning System. We'll clout those golf balls so hard they'll fly all the way across the Atlantic to the U.S.A. That'll upset the Americans. Then what? Well, of course, the Yanks will press a button in retaliation, and that'll be the end of everything.' He looked at me, as if daring me to disagree with him and, I must confess, I thought it better not to do so, partly because I was unsure of how much his attitude was based on his strong political views, and how much on the Newcastle

Brown Ale. He was also beginning to slur his words. With some alarm, I noticed he had several more bottles in a bag by the side of his chair.

'That's what would go through their minds,' he repeated, more to himself than to me. 'You see, it would be a propaganda victory for them.'

'It would be more than that, surely?' I commented.

Ignoring my question, he took another glug from the bottle.

'Now we can't sleep at night in case some Russian's got an itchy trigger finger and presses the button. It's obvious we've got to dismantle Fyling Dales before it's too late!'

I nodded, unable to think of anything else to say. I hadn't really thought about it. A few seconds later, I was spared a response, as he switched to talking, with some garrulity, about the demise of the fishing industry in the North Sea – and the herring in particular. I wondered why he had abandoned his original topic in favour of this new one. Was he, I wondered, a perpetual supporter of causes?

Of course he was right about the herring. From Lowestoft to Northumbria, small boats which had once put out to sea on their precarious business of hooking and netting the white-bellied fish, piling them up on the deck of the Cobles (the local fishing boats), mixing them with salt, enduring untold privations as the seas swept over them, are now mostly all gone. In their traditional twin-keeled boats, sheltering under a tarpaulin stretched between the thwarts, with only a penknife and, perhaps, a little transistor radio for company (making scratching sounds like pebbles being dragged backwards along the shore), they spent many solitary hours at sea.

Their fishing lives have almost come to an end. Hardly ever now, is heard the rhyme they sang, illustrating the central place of herring in their Northumbrian lives.

A fishing coble

'Dance for your daddy
My little laddie,
Dance for your daddy
Hear the mammy sing,
Thou shalt have a fishy
On a little dishy,
Thou shall have a fishy
When the boat comes in.'

But the boat no longer 'comes in'. The place where the fishermen left the world behind has vanished; vanished with the dying gasp of the herring they sought to catch. Coastal fishing in small boats no longer affords a living. Worse, no-one seems interested in the fishermen's fate, or their cultural legacy. Their boats, for the most part, are now hauled ashore and lie like rotting sea creatures in the salty air, victims of over-fishing, pollution, and the invasion of foreign trawlers. The effect is considerable on what fish remain. They have developed strange deformities – caused no doubt by the mountains of fertilizers and heavy metals which flow down our rivers into the sea every day. In some cases the fish have strange protuberances, such as female fish having male sexual organs, so that the mating of various species results not in offspring, but in a macabre dance of infertility. This is not only happening in the North Sea, of course, but along many of our coasts. Our seas and oceans are being poisoned and much of humanity seems unaware, or disinterested, in the outcome. Herrings have abandoned their usual routes through the sea. Their vast shoals no longer blow in. Even when they are present, they are cruelly caught, their gills entangled in nets. No-one can know what the herring feels in death, though it protests its demise by glowing for a few days afterwards with a strange kind of phosphorescence. The scene Oswald Harland recalls is now one of nostalgia:

> *'All down the coast from Saltburn to Filey and beyond, the village folk live in fierce detached shyness. Their Viking blood is still strong-running. They are a silent dour people, busy among shore wrack and sea junk, nets, crab-pots, tackle and such.'*

Later that night, before I drifted off, I recalled an image of a *Fiskehelse* in Norway which I had once visited. There, on vast racks, like gallows, hung countless thousands of cod woven like grotesque ties in scaly gold. The wracks are similar to those upon which kippers are still hung in the smoke houses, notably at Seahouses, Northumberland, and in other places along the east coast.

Early down for breakfast the following day, I set off for May Beck across a mud-churned soggy field, a herd of bullocks eyeing me warily as I squelched across Sneaton Low Moor, descending to the stream near Beck Farm. A mizzle rain began to fall and, for lack of anything else to think about, my mind returned to the conversation with the protester of the previous evening.

The Early Warning System established at Fyling Dales was designed by the U.S.A. to give radar coverage for intercontinental missile attacks from the Soviet Union. But many people do not know that the place had an equally important function; namely, to track space objects, including the thousands of active satellites, flakes of paint and tool boxes dropped by careless astronauts. Even small items of space debris, when they are travelling at 25,000 miles an hour, can cause a surprising amount of damage.

First mooted in the mid 1980s, during the time of the Greenham Common protests, Fyling Dales was mistakenly thought by some, to be a potential base for 'Star Wars'. But, in 2005, it tracked the space shuttle *Discovery* because NASA was worried about a tile falling off the vehicle, in case such article became a threat to later space missions. Since then, its role has become ever more vital; for example, by 1957, there were 16,000 objects orbiting planet Earth – about the time *Sputnik* was launched. How many there are now is anyone's guess [1]. The famous 'golf balls' are now long gone, replaced by, what looks like, a misshapen Egyptian pyramid that looms up out of the moor like a giant spaceship.

But returning to life in Robin Hood's Bay, the story is of a running fight between the villagers and the sea; of a brave, industrious people, cousins of the oarsmen who came over from Scandinavia looking for land, and who now pursue the sought-after Bay Lobster, and, in season, delicious sea trout. But in the 19th century, the coastal fisherman would have been busy barrelling cod and ling.

Other ways of making a living in the area was through

---

1   There are plans to employ 'hunter satellites' to capture debris.

The Golf Balls at Fyling Dales Moor

illegal imports, and the bulk of 18th century smuggling on the Yorkshire coast took place, as it turns out, at Robin Hood's Bay. This was because of its isolation, and because it was protected by marshy moorland on three sides – one of which I was in the process of tramping across. Local history is rife with tales about old free-traders and their wealthy patrons: highly organised gangs of landsmen with connections to Continental traders. As a result, in those days, often would be seen the square-bearded mariner carrying a cask of smuggled brandy on his shoulders across the moor. Though I kept a sharp eye out for him, no-one was carrying a cask of the liquid on the day of my crossing!

But the coast's Jurassic legacy is still there. And it is said, if you spend thirty minutes searching the beach at Robin Hood's Bay, you'll find an ammonite – as I did – but not quite as quickly. If you are exceptionally lucky, you may find, as some university students did in 1961, a giant-like fossil of a plesiosaurus, or other similar creature. These fossils are many millions of years old and the cliffs between Raven Hall and File Bay are some of the most fossiliferous in Britain. The fossils at Ravenscar were, in fact, formed 220 million years ago when swamps in the area were forming coal deposits. At that time, the swamps were home to all manner of strange creatures, like small crocodiles and large newts. Many fossils of them can be found in the alternate beds of limestone and blue shale which make up the Scar.

Superstitious folk of the Middle Ages thought the fossils they found were the remains of creatures petrified by St Hilda: the abbess and Princess Saint Hilda of Whitby. Her abbey was destroyed 200 years after its foundation, and was not rebuilt for another 200 years. Its ruins, of course, still stand on the headland and can be visited. The fossilized ammonites are named after the classical Roman god, Jupiter Ammon, which died out over sixty million years ago; though a close cousin, the pearly Nautilis, a relative of the octopus and the cuttlefish, continues to live in the warm waters of the Indian Ocean.

Stone Age man is known to have lived around Whitby. Flint axes, dating back 6000 years, as well as many barrows and tumuli are found in the coastal hinterland. A Bronze Age urn (1400-800BC) was found on Fyling Dales Moor. It can be viewed

Whitby Harbour

at the Scarborough Museum. A Bronze Age axe was found at Hawsker, where I stayed the previous evening. But, just about everywhere you place your foot along this coast, you are treading on history, and it sticks to your boots as firmly as mud.

At May Beck, I felt at last that I'd thrown off the trappings of civilisation. Now I was spared the drone of the internal combustion engine. Now I heard the tinkling little stream and the gentle 'swish' of the overhead canopy. I could hear birdsong! A huge Crack willow, pale and creamy-brown, its ragged grey bark exposed like the ribs of some giant, leaned towards me in friendly greeting. A White willow, often used by farmers for making household and dairy utensils, as well as for plaiting hurdles and repairing gaps in fences, intermittently kissed the stream with its branches, its dappling foliage catching the sunlight on the water. A coal tit was busy scavenging for insects on a fallen log.

Then the rain lifted. The scene was so sublime that I threw off my rucksack and sat down on the bank with biscuit and flask, gazing upon the scene. A quote from Jane Austen came to mind:

'To sit in the shade on a fine day is the most perfect refreshment'.

I sat there for a full half hour in blissful contemplation. Even now, with that inward eye, I look back on that sublime moment.

After my break, it was not long before I came up on Midge Hall, which stands almost halfway between May Beck and Little Beck. It squats, toad-like, on one side of the stream, the trees and vegetation rising up on either side. It is a derelict shell and, as it seemed to me on that day, so dark and foreboding that I could not escape the thought that it was watching me. I was

Midge Hall

transfixed as I looked at it, and it reminded me of something Ibsen said:

'If you stare into the abyss long enough, the abyss will stare into you'.

It seemed a place, I thought, which you must either pass by quickly or go inside. A lump rose up in my throat as I entered the building, wondering if there was a boggle inside, or, rather – as they call them in Yorkshire – a *grimwith,* a place inhabited by a ghost or goblin. My research informed me that, hereabouts, some still hold that such things exist, and the likelihood of such things, as I looked up at the glassless windows and at the stones covered with green moss and lichen, did not seem too much of a stretch of the imagination. The building, shaded in the wood, emitted an eerie glow and, I must confess, I was only able to go briefly inside before feeling an overwhelming desire to come out of it again.

Incidentally, before I forget, I should mention the delightful little Portofino-type harbour of Staithes, further up the coast from Whitby, where the famous Captain Cook served

Falling Foss

his apprenticeship in a house in Gape Lane, and took from his master's till a shilling and ran away to sea. Returning to grimswith's, Runswick Bay, further south, just north of Whitby, from which you can see Kettleness Point, is the reputed home of the 'Yorkshire Bogies'. Runswick Bay includes Hob Hole, the abode of 'Hob Thrush', a spirit whose locals invoked to cure whooping-cough. There may be lots of Hobs, as some folk believe, curing different ailments.

But behind Midge Hall, I wandered over to Falling Foss, a tributary sheet of water which joins the main stream, tumbling over a step in the river behind the wall. It really is a place worth visiting, and quite mesmerising to watch the water falling. But I still had an uneasy feeling about the building and, coming back up past the hall, to continue along the path, I glanced at it over my shoulder. Imagine my consternation when I saw a male figure peering at me round the corner of the front doorway. Who was he? And more importantly, where had he been when I'd gone inside? I confess, upon seeing him? My heart somersaulted into

/ m

Runswick Bay

my mouth, for I had no desire to make his acquaintance. Indeed I felt, should I do so, that some harm would befall me. I'm not generally given to flights of fancy, but I was several hundred yards along the track before the prickles on the back of my neck began to subside. For some time afterwards, I kept checking the trail behind, just in case I *was* being followed. The most disconcerting aspect of the visit was that I was unable to imagine where the figure had been standing when I went inside. He (or it) should have been easily visible. To this day, I still wonder if I saw a *grimwith*. The reader will make up his own mind.

Continuing along the stream, the descent to Little Beck offers wide views down the wooded Esk, and the hamlet itself is a real gem. Within its environs are a wood carver and a converted mill. Further along are the low Bride Stones, originally circles thirty feet in diameter. The meaning of the stones has been lost to antiquity, but I was reminded of The Lords' Stones, which are a group of three 'boundary stones' found at the southern end of Green Dyke on Fyling Dales. Two of the stones are very

The Lords' Stones, North Yorkshire Moors

similar, but the third is very different. The inscription on the latter is on the flat top of a natural boulder, firmly embedded in a small Bronze Age barrow, standing in what is now Stationdale territory. The inscription consists of a well-cut letter 'H', followed by a puzzling cipher, which might be described as an elongated double 'E' – with the possibility that the letters are conjoined back to back. Perhaps they marked the boundary of land belonging to Sir Thomas Hoby who held Harkness from 1596 to 1640. But the speculation is unproven. The meaning of these stones, as with other inscriptions, including those on stone circles further along the trail, is far from clear. Neither, I suspect, will their meaning become any clearer with the passage of time.

Thinking about such stones set off an internal dialogue in my mind; namely, what does history consist of? And the answer, at least to my mind, is that history is a record of the misfortune and troubles that afflict every one of us; so that, in all our days on Earth, we know few moments when we are genuinely at peace and free from apprehension. For example, do chance happenings, such as the one just described at Midge Hall, occur more often than we suspect? I think it is likely. We all do seem to move, one after the other, along the same path; and literally so in the case of the Coast to Coast path. I fancy that the ghost of repetition, or déjà vu, as it is more often referred to, can sensitize us to future events, just as I was sensitized to them after my Midge Hall experience. For that feeling now afflicts me every time I go into an old deserted building, drawing my mind back, if subliminally, to the experience at the hall.

But if it it is nothing else, history is a timeline. The questions is: does it exist only in the shape of our present ~~apprehensio~~ns and hopes, of which the past is merely a memory? The philosophical schools of Tlön believe that the world and everything in it is a complete, yet illusory history of things created only moments ago. Another idea is that we are presently in the cul-de-sac of time, created by an eternal god, in which we see things 'as through a glass darkly', to quote the bible, waiting, albeit not unpleasantly, for death, at which point we enter into another state of existence, a Hell or Heaven, depending perhaps upon one's moral conduct; or, from an evangelical point of view, a sacrificial belief in a saviour. Yet another idea is that time itself does not pass, but curves around us rather like space-time, so that the past and the future are simultaneous. Or, as seems possible in quantum theory, every event is replicated immediatley elsewhere, the moment it happens. Time may perhaps be an illusion. But whichever is the case, it does seem that our natural state is to be deeply suspicious of optimism. It is almost as if we believe there is a gorilla waiting for us round the corner. Our mindsets seem set in a negative direction.

I was still pondering this question when I walked into Grosmont, a pleasant village dominated in the 19th century by ironstone mining (of which the scars remain). Grosmont once supported an abbey of the little known Grontimontine Order, which was dissolved in 1536. It was also the birth place of one Nicholas Postgate, an English Catholic priest, nicknamed 'The Martyr of the Moors', who trained ecclesiastically in France and spent many post-reformation decades working in this oddly Catholic district of Yorkshire. Betrayed by an excise man from Whitby, for conducting a baptism at Red Barns Farm, near Ugglebarnby, he was executed on the Knaves Mire in York, in 1675, for his troubles, becoming one of eighty-five English Catholic priests, or martyrs. Posterity, you will not be surprised to hear, has taken a different view of his work. Every one of these murdered priests was beatified by Pope John Paul II in 1987. Poor Nicholas, I'm sure you would like to know, was hung, drawn and quartered for his religious pains, following the Popish Plot of 1678. His portable altar stone still hangs at the front of the altar in Saint Joseph's Catholic Church, Pickering. He was undoubtedly a 'Good Samaritan' but, as is often the case in political or religious matters, his good works counted for nothing.

As I walked by the stream that day, I imagined poor Nicholas had also walked beside this same peaceful salmon-river on his way to Glaisdale, a place truly caught up in the 19th century iron ore boom. It is surrounded by lovely woods and rolling moors, which hug us close as the River Esk gurgles and whispers on its way. It must also have whispered to Nicholas Postgate on his sojourns.

Thankfully, nurturing was also the order of the day at the Anglers' Arms, surely misnamed now the Coast to-Coast gives it most of its trade. Not having passed a single walker all day, in either direction, upon entering the establishment I immediately beatified the landlady when she greeted me with a cup of tea. Such simple acts of kindness are not frequently experienced by the solo traveller. I went to bed that night, comfortable and satiated after a meal of chicken and chips, washed down by a couple of pints. I felt pleased that I'd chosen the right distance for the leg and looking forward to the morrow. At least I could be sure of a friendly welcome in the morning!

But, before I succumbed to the arms of Hypnos, I again began to entertain the idea that I *had* seen a ghost at Midge Hall; or at least a spirit which sought to commune with the living. I am not alone in considering such beliefs; Charles Dickens, for example, considered that we feel such fancies. It is easy to pass off such experiences as hallucinations, or delusions, or some other form of mental aberration, but it seems to me that far too many sober, sensible, people report seeing 'ghosts' for them to be entirely fictitious. And another curious thing is that such sightings are often related to the historical setting in which they take place. For example, here in the North Riding of Yorkshire, the ghosts of Cavaliers are frequently reported, and this fits in with the historical narrative of the area; namely, the clash between Royalists and Parliamentarians. Indeed, I spoke to a young woman at a very small inn in Osmotherley (shown in the image below), who told me she often saw an apparition of a Cavalier about the place. Such coincidences, for many, promote belief in these experiences.

According to the folklore of the North York Moors, many inhabitants believed, and some may still believe, that every dale has its own hobgoblin. For example at Levishorn, north of Pickering, they consider it essential to keep the fire lit at the Saltergate Inn, to avert catastrophe. Near Sleights, a village passed on the way up Eskdale, Ralph de Percy was out hunting

The Village of Osmotherly

one day and chased a boar into the chapel at Eskdaleside, killing the creature on the chapel alter. For some unknown reason, he attacked the hermit who lived there, and now the hermit's ghostly apparition haunts the place. There are plenty of other examples from other parts of the country.

At Glaisdale we see the Beggars Bridge, built by one Tom Ferris, an amorous man enraptured of his true love, Agnes, who lived on the opposite bank. Having almost drowned swimming the turbulent river to visit her, he did not forget his experience and, after a prosperous return to his native village, fulfilled his vow to build a bridge across the water in which he had been forced to swim – presumably to help other men with similar amorous intentions. (Some say his frame still casts a shadow upon the water.) An interesting caveat to the story is that the squire, who originally forbade Tom to marry Agnes, because of poverty, granted him permission to marry when Tom went to Whitby, after distinguishing himself as a sailor/by helping to capture a Spanish galleon. Coming home with his share of the plunder, he took Agnes to Hull, where he grew rich, becoming mayor. At last, he received the desired permission from the squire to marry Agnes. Tom died in 1631. The bridge is his memorial.

The Beggars Bridge

As I climbed out of the valley, picking up the pace across Glaisdale Rise, said goodbye to the wooded valley and cultivated land below. Crossing the Danby, Westerdale and Greenhow moors, I saw less of the pied flycatchers, sparrow hawks and wood warblers; and began to hear the call of the ring ouzel, lapwing and curlew. Red grouse flew round my heels that day, and on many others which followed, protesting my invasion of their territory – the bogs and patches of bilberries upon which they feed. As the weather began to change, my boots left a crisp trail in the falling snow. Visibility across to where the trees feathered the moors on this cold day, was sufficient for navigation. The wind kept behind me, as it did for most of my journey. The route is exposed to strong winds, and I was grateful for the rucksack keeping my back warm.

Descending from the moors, after some twenty-seven miles, chilled and tired, I was glad to reach the Wainstones Hotel in Great Broughton, where I enjoyed a pint by a warm fire, and later busied myself writing up my journal for the day.

Here, in Great Broughton is the Jet Miners Arms, a reminder of the local rocks once mined for alum, ironstone, sandstone and jet, particularly between Scarborough and Saltburn. Most of these rocks were worked in huge quantities all over the North York Moors, and most conveniently along the coast. Before the railways were developed, shipping was the best form of transport, the sea a convenient dumping ground for mining spoil.

Before the advent of synthetics, incidentally, alum was used for fixing dyes, most notably in the 14th century. The mineral consists of aluminium sulphate. Ammonium or potassium sulphate has been used for tanning leather, fire-proofing and in the manufacture of parchment and candles. In the 15th and 16th centuries, the Vatican controlled most of the world's alum supply, and the mineral commanded a very high price. The shale, from which the alum is extracted, was first burned and then leached in large tanks of water, the resulting liquid being boiled over a coal fire. Afterwards, it was mixed with potash or burnt seaweed – as a source of ammonium. A more convenient source of ammonium was urine, which, believe it or not, was collected in jars left out on doorsteps by the local population – an example of productive recycling at its best! The collection of the urine from doorsteps gave rise to the now well-known phrase, 'taking the piss'.

The commodity, the coal potash, burnt seaweed and urine, had to be transported to the quarries in Whitby where it sparked an important ship-building industry. The alum workers were poorly paid, often waiting months for their wages. Sometimes, itinerant workers were provided with a house and enjoyed grazing rights for their cattle. Following the development of an efficient means of obtaining alum from colliers' waste, the industry died out but, between 1600 and 1871, there were at least twenty-five quarries actively mining the stuff.

Whitney jet first appeared about 5,500 years ago, in the Neolithic era. It became popular during mourning for George IV, who died in 1830, and by the time of the 1861 census, half the town was employed in the industry. The jet industry grew further during the 19th century, peaking when Queen Victoria chose to wear a broach made of the mineral during her period of mourning for Prince Albert. As a result, to the detriment of the industry, articles made from alum later became associated with death and funerals. Jet is a hard, black, coal-like mineral in appearance, rather like Obsidian. It is easily carved and can be very highly polished. Jet was formed when pieces of monkey-puzzle trees, common in the area 150 million years ago, floated out to sea and became fossilized. The best jet, though, which is found throughout Europe and America, comes from Whitby. The mineral was highly regarded by the early inhabitants of the area, and jet beads have been found in 5000-year-old Bronze Age barrows along the coast, and in stunning articles of Roman jewellery. The brittle mineral has to be worked by picks, because it is destroyed by explosives, and is therefore a difficult substance to mine. Today only a handful of jet workers remain, but, in 1850, there were over fifty workshops in Whitby alone. There are now plenty of fakes about, and antique shops sell the jewelry to customers unaware both parties have been duped. Genuine Whitley jet comes only from fossilised wood found on a 7.5 mile stretch of coastline. This black gemstone is more stable than other jets, and polishes to a mirror shine

Chilled after my long leg, I went early to bed and slept soundly until breakfast, waking to slanting rain. This was my day to cross the remainder of the moors before descending to the Vale of Mowbray, an extension of the Vale of York. I knew I was in for a soaking as I climbed back up Clay Bank, turning right on to the Cleveland Way with intermittent views below.

The Wainstones

As I scrambled up to the Wainstones, a jumble of boulders and rock outcrops, the weather momentarily clearing, I was rewarded by some panoramic views of the patchwork of fields below the dramatic cliffs, and saw a number of circling hang-gliders. Onwards across Cold Moor (well-named) to Cringle Moor, with its tempting Jet Miners' track heading off to the right, I descended to Scarth Wood, down by the boundary of Arncliffe Wood. Though increasingly soaked by the rain, I diverted to Mount Grace Priory, having promised myself a visit whatever the weather.

Mount Grace is one of several 11th and 12th century monasteries established on the Yorkshire Moors, at Whitby, Rievaulx and Byland, being a Carthusian Monastery, founded about 1084 by a group of monks (Christ's Poor Men) who wanted to emulate the harsh contemplative lives of the early Christian hermits. This new monastic order spread from near Grenoble in France and, in common with other Carthusian churches, Grace Priory is a small and relatively plain structure. It is the only Carthusian priory in Yorkshire, and only one of nine in England,

Mount Grace Priory

28

founded by a nephew of Richard the Second, Thomas Holland, who became Duke of Surrey and who was subsequently executed at Cirencester for conspiring against Henry the Fourth. The lives of the monks who lived there were simple and plain, spending most of their daily lives in their cells – except for matins, mass and vespers – receiving very few visitors. They resided in the eastern part of the church, while the lay brothers, who served the monks, and were subject to the same monastic discipline, used the knave. There is a Great Cloister, and the shields on the label-stops of the cells bear the arms of Archbishop Richard Scrone, who endowed the place – though he died before he saw it rebuilt in stone. Each of the cells received fresh water through lead pipes from a water source in the grounds. The place is currently under the care of English Heritage.

As you approach Mount Grace today, the view is not original, and you are confronted by an arts and crafts manor house, built by Thomas Lascelles in 1654, which forms part of the 'ruins' of a 15th century guest house. His initials can be seen over the entrance of the two-storey porch. It is set on a terrace above a beautiful garden, and the house has many mullioned windows, walls with battlements and gables, and a pan-tiled roof with dormers.

The current extended building is largely the country house that Sir Lothian Bell, a wealthy industrialist, built at the turn of the century. But many of the features of the Lascelles' house, and its medieval predecessor are still present. The strict discipline imposed on the monks in former times may be envisaged by examining the priory prison – for recalcitrant monks. At the moment, the monastery has a very peaceful and relaxing atmosphere. I can imagine that staying there would be a very spiritual experience, and somewhat more comfortable than in days gone by.

Equally uncomfortable, I imagine, was the place that I would pass a few miles further away to the west, on my way to my overnight stop. It was here that the Battle of the Standard took place in 1138, a few miles north of Northallerton, just across from the Great North Road. On this moor, the Scottish forces, led by King David 1st of Scotland, unwisely took on the troops of King Stephen of England, commanded by William of Aumale, King Stephen being away at the time fighting rebel forces in southern England. The English Army consisted mainly of local militia and baronial retinues from Yorkshire and the north Midlands, whereas the Scottish Army comprised 'wild' Glaswegian infantry, who proved no match for the well-armoured English knights and Men-at-Arms. Though William's men were outnumbered, they managed to cut down King David's men after assaulting them with an English arrow storm.

The Battle of the Standard was the first major engagement between the English and Scots since the Norman Conquest; King David of Scotland had entered England to support Matilda, his niece, who had lodged a claim to the English throne against that of Stephen (who was married to another niece, of the same name). On the English side, Archbishop Thurstan of York had 'exerted himself greatly' in raising troops, preaching vigorously that to withstand the Scots

The Battle of the Standard

was to do God's work. At the centre of the English position during the battle, was a mast carrying the consecrated host and the banners of York, Beverley and Ripon minsters; hence the name, 'Battle of the Standard'.

Arriving thoroughly soaked at my selected ~~hostelry~~ refuge for the night, my sodden clothes were taken from me by the farmer's wife, who, I wrongly assumed, would dry them overnight. I was shown to a pleasant, recently refurbished, warmly radiated room and, after writing up my journal, I climbed into bed and slept soundly until morning. Dinner that night was a Mars bar and a packet of peanuts. Fortified by, I must say, a splendid breakfast, I was ready to face the day when, horror of horrors, the farmer's wife handed me back my sodden waterproofs and boots in exactly the same ringing wet state as I had given them the previous evening. I just could not believe that a farmer's wife, who, one might have expected would appreciate the need for dry outdoor clothing, could have done such a thing. Thinking about this afterwards, I realised the dear lady had probably taken my wet clothes from me because she didn't want them dripping all over her newly refurbished room. But I paid a high price for this negligence as I squelched, in wet boots and socks, all the way to Richmond.

As it turned out, this particular farmer's wife had been to school with a girl I'd played with as a young boy, on a Lincolnshire farm, and I had rather lost my heart to this delightful creature. Indeed, whenever I visited the farm, I sought her out. My everlasting memory ~~of her~~ is of her sitting on a fence under a huge elm tree, laughing and giggling at the game we'd played together, the sun lighting up her delightful countenance and golden hair. Discussing her with the farmer's wife the previous evening, had brought back this bitter-sweet memory of unrequited love, and I tried to work out why the regret was so painful on such short acquaintance. But it does seem to me that it is always the lost 'love' we regret, rather than ache for a love 'yet to be'. As I squelched on towards Richmond, I cheered myself with the thought that the hotel which I had booked would/at least/produce a hearty meal, a dry bed and a good pint. Surely the crowns which adorned the title of the establishment guaranteed it?

I couldn't have been more wrong.

The first sign that all might not be well was the observation that I appeared to be the only person staying in the establishment. As I came down to dinner, I was further alarmed to find there was no-one else in the dining room. The waitress, who seemed also to be the barmaid and receptionist, ~~understandably perhaps,~~ had forgotten my dinner order taken at the bar. After three-quaters of an hour, my meal finally showed up, heralded by the proud voice, 'It's ready!' By ~~this~~ *which* time, of course, being ravenously hungry, I had drunk three pints of ale and, stomach rumbling, had devoured a whole packet of KP nuts waiting for the fabled meal to arrive. How could I know that eating the nuts would prove to be far more enjoyable than the forthcoming meal!

I have, several times, gone over the episode in my mind in search of error.

The first culinary mistake I made, in retrospect, was in ordering the fish. This poor creature, lying prostrate on the plate before me might well have lain entombed in a freezer since Roman times. As a species of its kind, it was almost unrecognisable, its breadcrumb armour-plating partially singed by the grill, proved difficult to penetrate. In the revelation that followed, I found the creature to be little more than an empty shell, almost devoid of flesh. Indeed I would not have been surprised to learn that it had starved to death, or else had weakly surrendered just before it was killed. After attacking it for several minutes, my post-mortem revealed a sorry mess lying between two plastic sachets of tartar sauce, and the remains of a teaspoonful of bullet-hard green peas, together with, what looked like, parsnips. Several soggy chips, gleaming with fat, lay like unburied coffins alongside the creature, as if mourning its death. I finished my 'meal', put down my knife and fork, and waited.

An interminable time later, the waitress, obviously one of life's finest multi-taskers, scurried out from the shadows to clear away the detritus. Smiling at me in expectation of some kind of compliment, I found myself unable to speak. It was a near-fatal moment (for her) when she asked if I had enjoyed my meal, but I like to think that my facial expression halted further enquiry. I was proud of a self-restraint I thought was beyond me, and kept silent. All I can remember about the dear lady now was the deep freckles running from below her neckline almost up to her chin; and a jangling collection of silver pigs on a bracelet around her wrist, which she'd managed to trail through the tartar sauce. The reader will not be surprised that I decided not to risk a sweet but went up to the sanctuary of my room. Once there, I devoured my emergency pack of whole-wheat biscuits and two squares of chocolate. Hardly satiated, I comforted myself with the thought of a good night's sleep.

But that wasn't to be, either.

At two o'clock in the morning I was woken by some dirge-like music coming from a room along the corridor. I waited ten minutes, in the hope of an adjustment to the volume or, in God's mercy, for it to cease altogether, but, after such time period elapsed, with no audible change, I pulled on my trousers and padded along the landing, knocking firmly on the offending door. To my surprise, it was opened by a young woman in a night dress, affecting to cover, with little success, her ample bosom. An empty bottle of red wine stood on her dressing table. Another stood half full beside it. Presumably the alcohol she had drunk had made her careless of strangers, for not only was she inebriated, she seemed rather depressed. I explained to her that her music was making it difficult for me to sleep. Could she turn the volume down? Imagine my surprise when, instead of acknowledging the disturbance, she invited me in, smiling provocatively from the doorpost. As I had realised by then, I was not in the most salubrious of establishments, I wondered if she thought I was some well-known acquaintance, or other regular client. Entering a strange woman's bedroom in the early hours of the morning, however pleasantly invited, was definitely not on my agenda. I muttered some kind of polite refusal and returned to my room wondering what I had done to deserve her favour, still trying to sleep. The volume of the music did, thankfully, decrease; though, not long afterwards, it rose again. This time, however, I pulled the blankets over my head, fearing I might be even more severely compromised if I were to make a second visit. Eventually, overwhelmed with fatigue, I drifted off.

Market Place, Church and Culloden Tower at Richmond

The historic market town of Richmond is overlooked by the Culloden Tower which declares the defeat at Culloden of the Jacobite Army of Charles Edward Stuart, on 16th April 1746, by the Duke of Cumberland. It was also here, in 1664, that Prince Rupert and his men rested after their defeat at Marston Moor and where, four years later, Oliver Cromwell halted on his way south from Scotland. The town boasts several famous sons, including Henry Greathead, the inventor of the lifeboat, and Samuel Buck, the engraver. At Hill House lived Fanny I'Anson who inspired the song '*The Lass of Richmond Hill*'.

The town is described by Betty James as 'the most romantic place in the whole of the North-East'. Perhaps the woman in the bedroom had read this? It was founded after the Norman Conquest and stands at the entrance to Swaledale, on the edge of the Yorkshire Dales National Park, coming complete with a castle constructed in 1086 by Alan Rufus (Alan the Red), on land given him by William the Conqueror. The said Earl Alan, called his castle 'Richemunde' meaning 'strong hill', and Richmond duly became the capital of Richmondshire. The fourth Earl of Richmond married the heiress of a Breton dukedom and became both Earl and Duke. His son, Conan, built the massive keep which now crests the precipice above the River Swale, and married Margaret, sister of Malcolm IV of Scotland, whose daughter is held to be Lady Constance in Shakespeare's *King John*, the mother of Arthur and Eleanor. Below the castle the beautiful River Swale swirls on a rocky bed around the hill, upon which the castle stands. Underneath the castle, King Arthur and his knights are said to lie 'spellbound' in mysterious sleep until England needs them once more.

At the end of the 18th century, some soldiers seeking to enter the castle, found an entrance to a small tunnel underneath the keep, into which they inserted a drummer boy, together with an instruction to him to keep drumming as he progressed along the tunnel, to ascertain the length of the tunnel – presumably for invasion purposes. Alas, the tunnel caved in on top of the poor lad and, unsurprisingly, the drumming stopped. The entrance to the tunnel is still there and, it is said, on a cold winter's night, if one listens carefully, can still be heard the faint sound of the boy's drumming below the marker stone in the castle grounds, where the drumming stopped.

The town itself preserves a medieval aspect, particularly with the chapel of Holy Trinity in the wide cobbled market place (once the un-cobbled castle yard), and is ringed with houses and shops. It has a Georgian Theatre in Frenchgate. A riverside walk from Richmond takes you to the Premonstratensian abbey of St Agatha, Easby (founded in 1152 by Roald, Constable of Richmond Castle). The cannons who lived there (as opposed to monks) wore white habits; hence they were known as the White Cannons. Within the precinct of the abbey there is still an active parish church, displaying 13th century wall paintings. The town has suffered, somewhat from frequent Scottish raids during the Middle Ages, as well as from the billeting of the English Army there on its way to the Battle of Nevilles Cross. Incidentally, further along the trail, is Shap Abbey, in Cumbria,

HOSPITAL OF ST NICHOLAS, NEAR RICHMOND, YORKSHIRE.

which is also a Premonstratensian abbey – though its stones have largely been absorbed into adjoining farms. In the Middle Ages, however Richmond dominated this part of Swaledale. Near Applegarth, in the vale, was the New Forest, where the Earls of Richmond once hunted. Now denuded of trees, it is a wild, bleak, highland. In this area there also lived such families as the FitzHughs, Scropes and other followers of the Earls – some fighting at the above-mentioned Battle of the Standard. Others joined the Crusades and went to Jerusalem. There is an excellent research library in the town, should one wish to make further historical enquiries.

There is an old hospital near Richmond (St Nicholas's) which, though I didn't have time to visit, was founded in the 12th century by Queen Mary until finally dissolved by Queen Elizabeth I. In the Civil War, it was the headquarters of the Scottish Army. In 1813 it was tastefully restored by Ignatius Bonomi, the Durham architect, and there are 19th and early 20th century additions to the structure. The main two-storey house is, apparently, not visible from the road. Overall, I understand, it has the appearance of being a 17th century construction, though some of the building ascribed to Bonomi is older. Around 1900, the Honourable Robert James laid out the gardens, which were the inspiration for the famous Hidcote

Gardens in Gloucestershire. The Clenby Rose, Bobbie James, is named after him. He died in 1960, the house being maintained by his widow, Lady Serena James, who herself died at the age of ninety-nine, in the year 2000. I understand that the gardens are occasionally open to the public. But, having tarried too long in this charming town, and conscious of the many miles of lovely moorland yet to traverse, I stepped westwards out of Richmond and into the valley of the Swale.

RICHMOND TO KIRKBY STEPHEN

Swaledale

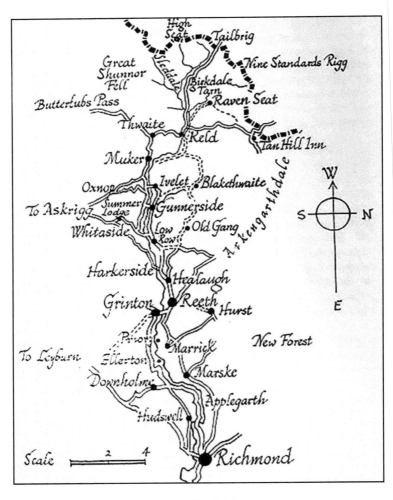

Map of Swaledale

As one travels west up this enchanting valley, the Swale gives vista after vista of magnificent trees and foliage, before dropping down to the deep glen hiding the village of Marske, resting in a sequestered hollow. Tree-protected, I could almost imagine it as a fairy dell. In the autumn, apparently, the woods turn russet and golden and, as one approaches, one sees the remains of a common field system. Until the last war, the place had a smithy. Its church, which looks down on a fine 13th century bridge, is of the 12th century. It boasts a 17th century restoration, lending it an old-fashioned air. Inside the building can be found box-

Marske Hall

pews, a squire's pew, and a pulpit from a two-decker. The bell cot is medieval.

Cascades of water flow under the trees here and run through the beautiful lawns and gardens of Marske Hall. Clipped yew hedges and a magnificent lime tree avenue can be seen. One of the trees in the grounds is an Austrian pine, about twenty feet in circumference, and seventy feet high. The ornamental grounds below the hall give the place the air of an estate village.

The Huttons, who once owned Marske Hall, have long since sold the place. They claimed the rare distinction of having had two archbishops in the family: Matthew Hutton, Archbishop of York (from 1595 to 1600), and a later Hutton, who became Archbishop of Canterbury (in 1757). The obelisk in the park, rising to sixty feet, is a memorial to Captain Mathew Hutton, who died just before the battle of Waterloo. Marske Hall and Clints Hall (now demolished) are less than a mile from each other.

Glad to be out of the town, with the gurgling river for company, I went up on to the purple moor, thick with pheasant and grouse, whose breeding territory I had long invaded. Black-faced and Swaledale sheep stared at me warily. *Who is this interloper?* The fleeces of these sheep, incidentally, are used in the manufacture of Harris Tweed.

The silvery Swale, on my way to Reeth, was sometimes a more distant friend, at other times much closer. My other friend was the curlew, its trilling song calling me towards some invisible place (or so I thought). How its song haunts the moors, serenading the ewes and the feeding lambs. At Hollins Farm, a fox had been taking advantage of these newborn lambs. A shepherd told me he was again waiting up with a gun that night to kill it, as the red vagabond had taken two lambs the previous evening. It's the job of the fox to hunt, and that of the farmer to protect his lambs. But it doesn't matter how man makes his mark on the landscape, wild things, like foxes will have their way.

'Three Blind Mice'

Not long afterwards, I sat down on a grassy bank above the river, threw off my sack and dived for the cheese sandwiches I'd bought in the town. As usual, in this part of the world, my cheese was grated, which generally means less cheese between the bread. As I lay munching on my sandwiches on the sunlit grass, I found myself entering into that semi-conscious state where one is neither in the here-and-now, nor in the dream world. My disturbed sleep of the previous night, and the soporific gurgle of the river, seduced me into thinking again about my visit to the sleepless lady of the previous night. I began to wonder what had happened to her, and, for some reason, it became important to me to know that she had greeted the following day with greater optimism. Immediately thereafter, in some kind of dream state, my super-ego accused me of a total disregard for her welfare, even though it was *she* who had woken *me* from my slumber. Never mind! I was convicted of a guilty conscience and, in my dream, escorted her to an imaginary house from which she had been missed, and where she was eagerly welcomed back into the bosom of her

Reeth Village

family. I, *the hero of the hour*, was lavishly toasted for bringing her safely home. Nevertheless, when I woke, my subconscious mind did its best to convince me that I really had returned her to her family but, as I discovered later, the guilty Hydra had still not been slain and it kept rearing up accusingly over the next few days.

Hoping that the hostelry which awaited me at the Arkleside Hotel would be more welcoming and satisfying than my last, my hope was quickly realised. The convivial proprietors could not do enough for me and, by the time I left, I considered Richard and Dorothy my friends. Alas, Richard, a stalwart of the village society, has now passed on but Dorothy still lives nearby, an exceedingly pleasant and affable woman. Bidding farewell, I again pointed my boots westward and headed further up the valley.

From Maske, incidentally, the Swale boasts a wooded valley, with a prominent limestone scar a mile long, watered by the Marske Beck and its many tributaries. Here, during the Ice Age, the Stainmore glacier overflowed into Swaledale, carving out the river's deep channel. The result is a delightful place on a spring evening, as the westerly sun lights up the yew-fringed scars and splashing waterfalls.

Marrick Priory

A little south-west of the farm, at Orgate, you find large mounds lining the beck. Here once stood Clints Smelt Mill, from which lead was taken in the 18th century. On either side of the river stand the Marrick and Ellerton Priories.

Westwards again, visiting the debris of lead mines worked from Roman times to the end of the 19th century, a Roman pig of lead, now lost – possibly stolen – had been discovered in the old workings at Hursh lead mines which stand below a desolate moor. They further discovered a horde of Roman military scrap, now in the York Museum, found on Fremington Hagg.

But Romans weren't the only inhabitants of the area. Angles, coming from the east established themselves at Reeth, Grinton and Fremington; Norsemen, arriving from the west, reached down to the south side of Feethon while, on the wild upland road to Askrigg, can still be seen the ruins of the ling-thatched houses and barns that were once the miners' small holdings. Here, the Haverdale Beck cuts down the hillside and plunges into a wooded ravine; while, further up, at Sommer Lodge Pastures, is a cave – the Fairy Hole – out of which one of the tributaries of the Haverdale Beck flows. Another tributary flows down Bloody Vale, supposedly the scene of a clash between Scots raiders and the men of the dale. It is certainly the case that battleaxes and pieces of armour have been found nearby at Crackpot – not to be confused with Crackpot Hall which leans drunkenly further up Swaledale.

Although it may not be easy to recognise now, the theme of Swaledale is the lead mines. Its history is shot through with greed, philanthropy and poverty. Rievaulx Abbey, for example, had mines at the head of the dale, its lead used for the roofs of Bridlington Priory, which competed even with the renowned lead roofs of Jervaulx Abbey, which came from Grinton.

By the end of the century, 1,000 to 2,000 men were engaged in mining, producing 6,000 tonnes of lead annually. Slowly, however, the woods burnt as fuel in the smelt mills was used up, and the mining was also affected by the Napoleonic wars. In the 1880s, the whole great bubble collapsed, owing to a slump in prices caused by foreign imports. The men who descended the shafts by the crude, and dangerous, wooden ladders became few. Their seldom dry groove clothes, often frozen on to them in winter, died out. Most returned home to live lives shortened by the breathing in of poisonous fumes. The industry gradually faded over the last twenty years of the 19th century, wounded by foreign imports at a time when all the easily accessible lead had been won. Instead, the folk of the dale threw themselves into 'religious' revivals, and organised horse-races and hound trails. Those who still preferred mining left for the Durham coal fields, others for the Lancashire cotton mills. Some went to Spain. Those that remained adjusted themselves to the life of a farming community and, gradually, the fresh air of Swaledale swept away the unhealthy fumes of the smelt mills and dusty mines, the remaining mining skeletons proof of their endeavours.

The Old Gang Smelt Mine

At Gunnerside Gill, for example, shattered by hushing (a method of exposing lead ore by releasing water from a dam down a hillside), is still seen the devastation wrought by lead mining. The Gill cleaves a majestic purple and black fell, slashed with rushes, spring turf and grey outcrops of limestone. The only sound now is the tinkle of a peaty stream, the whistle of a shepherd to his dog, the cries of moor birds, and the bleating of sheep and their lambs.

The lead mines, notably the Smelt Mill and the Old Gang Mines, are as much a part of Swaledale as the waterfalls of Keld. The ruins of Blakethwaite Smelt Mill, from which one man in the 18th century raised lead worth £120,000, stands on a spit of land at a fork of deep heather-clad gullies; monuments to their endeavours.

Westwards, at the top of Botcher Gill is Moss Dam which, by long races supplied water to Swinner Gill on the one side, and the mines of Gunnerside on the other. Black-headed gulls, rising from their nests, screeched at me as I approached. Sharp gusts of wind reminded me of the bitter cold of winter in these exposed places, and the tough conditions faced by the mining men.

Blakethwaite Smelt Mill

Further up, at the head of Swinner Gill, is a cave known as Swinner Gill Kirk, where endeavours of a different kind took place; for it was here each Sunday, Dissenters (or 'yet to be legitimised' Methodists or Quakers) climbed up for secret worship, hiding in the Kirk if strangers approached. At a time of religious intolerance, in the 1670s and 1680s, this is where they held their meetings, and the place is testimony to the strength of the dale men's religious beliefs. At the cave entrance, dark mosses have made a habitat for ferns, maiden hair and green spleenwort. I also saw Hard Shield fern and brittle bladder. A liverwort with green flat lobes grows in the waterfall.

It was below here, in 1761, that John Wesley preached at Low Row and Blades, finding 'an earnest, loving and simple people' in whom he was able to sow the first seeds of Methodism. Further along the hillside, built in 1691 by Philip Lord Wharton (more of which later), also a Dissenter, was a public meeting house for Protestants, it was replaced in 1809 by Low Row Congregational Church.

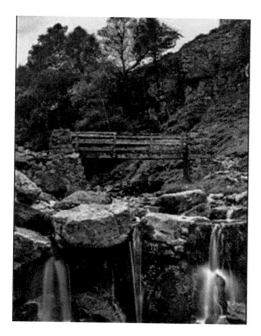

Swinner Gill

Further down the dale, at a place known as Red Hurst – so called from the discoloured waters of a chalybeate spring that surfaces there – legend has it that a passing traveller, snatched by a guardian spirit, dyed the well red with his blood. Villagers tarrying there to pray for his soul, were said to have seen a vision of the Virgin Mary. Methodists held meetings at the well on Trinity Sunday – the day associated with the legend. It is a wild place, gazing down the dramatic curving gorge of Swaledale, surrounded by the remnant of a medieval deer forest, and the forlorn, treeless legacy of lead-mining.

A few steps further on I looked down upon Crackpot Hall (not to be confused with Crackpot near Low Row), built by Lord Wharton for his keeper. The latter looked after the red deer that roamed here in the 17th century. Alas, it was made uninhabitable by mining subsidence, though its glorious views down the Swale are unaltered.

It was here, in the 1770s, that a tremendous border dispute occurred between the Earl of Pomfret and Thomas Smith, the lord of the manor, which split the dale into factions. The final result was a victory for the said Smith, who, unfortunately, died shortly afterwards. Perhaps, in divine retribution, the Earl of Pomfret, who had dissipated his fortune in the above dispute, was imprisoned for debt in the Tower of London – a sad end to a sad business.

The name Crackpot, incidentally, is derived from a mining term denoting a hole or chasm in the ground, and not a description of a mentally disturbed person who lived there. The hall was once a farm-house, and a cottage stood there before the present hall was built. It was the home of the famous Alice, 'the wild girl of the dales', whose speech was so strong in dialect that strangers thought it a foreign tongue. The wild girl was regularly lost, and subsequently found, in a gully or in a hayfield, far from the hall. It was lived in up until the 1920s. Alice, the farmer's four-year-old daughter, was once described as having 'the madness of the moors about her', with all their wariness and mocking, and her chuckling laugh as untamed as her lonely house. Large animals, such as sheep, couldn't be kept at the hall, because they suffered from lead poisoning; though the rabbits, apparently, were unaffected. Now the place is the haunt of crows, its twisted window frames bearing witness to its subterranean torture. As for wild Alice, she has passed into dales' folklore.

Half a mile further on, near Keld, is the renowned waterfall of Kisdon Force, occupying a steep limestone gorge cut by torrents of glacial melt water. It flows past a large pinnacle of rock almost detached from the cliff face, that looks as if it will give way at any moment. In the gorge itself, the differing rock strata of the Yoredales is revealed. The falls themselves are approached across a former landslip, and great care needs to be taken during the approach. On the bright sunlit day I passed

Alice of Crackpot Hall, with her kitten, and Moss, the farm's dog.

Kisdon Force

by, a hardy soul was jumping into the lower pool, and it must make a refreshing dip on a hot day.

The pool, however, can be approached from a few hundred yards further downstream, allowing for a more gradual immersion – if one doesn't fancy jumping into the unseen depths. One can climb up out of the lower pool to the top of the fall, without too much difficulty. Incidentally a track over Kisdon Hill was used as a corpse road before 1580, before Muker acquired its own church and burial ground. The pall bearers had a two-day trek to Grinton Church down the valley, carrying the coffin in a wicker basket, resting their burden on strategically placed coffin stones. These stones can still be seen at Gunnerside and Ivelet Bridge.

Ascending from Muker to Keld, including the chasm containing Kisdon Force, the Swale is a yawning abyss shut in by the steep sides of desolate fells. The Swale and the beck almost make an island of Kisdon – which is a lofty 1636 feet above sea level. As the road goes through the hamlets of Ivlet and Gunnerside it forms a triple cascade down Yew Scar, falling 100 feet. The church at Muker, whose font was once buried under its floor, looks out over the roofs of houses to the little beck which runs under its one-arched bridge before joining the Swale. A member of the Gant family gave a vast pasture to Rivelaux Abbey, which eventually became the Manor of Muker. And 12th century Maud, daughter of Count Stephen of Brittany, brought 'Swaledale' as a dowry to her husband, Walter of Gant. The charming village of Muker is one of the last stops before ascending over the moors towards Kirkby Stephen.

To the south of the village, the mountain road runs between Great Shunner Fell and Lovely Seat, linking Muker with Hawes in Wenslydale. The Butter Tubs, which gives its name to the road that ascends over Butter Tubs Pass, is a dramatic series of shafts sunk into the limestone, to a depth of between fifty to 100 feet. It is the birthplace of Cliff Beck, which runs below the road to join Muker Beck.

From Keld you climb up Whitsundale, passing the isolated farm of Raven Seat, on the right. The farmer here has been known to drive his Land Rover over the ancient packhorse bridge (below) in an emergency; that is, when the river is too deep to ford, and it is a pleasant place to linger.

Muker, Swaledale

As one climbs up to Raven Seat, we can, if in need of refreshment, or of a hostelry, turn right towards the Tan Hill Inn which dates to the 17th century. Its earlier name, The Kings Pit, reflects its use as a hostelry for workers digging coal pits during the 18th century. It was previously surrounded by miners' cottages, but these buildings were demolished when the pits closed. The pub remains open due to the patronage

Raven Seat

Packhorse Bridge

of local farmers and the advent of the motor car. There is a good swimming pool, on the left, as you climb up to Tan Hill, should you fancy immersion on a hot day.

The desolate countryside surrounding Tan Hill

Tan Hill, in the parish of Muker, incidentally is a high point on the Pennine Way, close to the Durham-Cumbria border. In the hinterlands, /containing carboniferous strata, shallow pit shafts, produced coal for Richmond Castle. The coal is of poor quality but, mixed with peat, it gave a satisfying glow and would smoulder all night, to be revived the following morning. Most of the easily accessible seams of coal were worked out before the start of the industrial revolution. By the 17th century, the poor-quality coal was being converted into coke (known locally as 'cinders') in beehive kilns, and used in lead and iron smelting.

Onwards and upwards is the trail, over the desolate moors, to Nine Standards Riggs towards Kirkby Stephen. No-one actually knows who constructed the remarkable cairns that is Nine Standards Riggs, but the first known reference goes back to 1325. From the valley bottom they look like standing stones, yet they are dry-stone columns made of limestone blocks, from six to ten feet in height, beehive in shape.

Approaching them for the first time, the atmosphere is one of awe and mystery. Something fundamental to the soul shouts out at you. It is a remarkable place. Suggestions have been

Nine Standards Riggs

made about its origin. One is that they were route markers for shepherds. But I can't imagine any shepherd needing to make reference to them. And why are there nine of them? Another suggestion is that they were built to scare off the invading Scots. If so, it didn't work: the invading Scots swept down nearby Mallerstang Vale, destroying Pendragon Castle, the occasional home of Lady Ann Clifford, the great castle builder and restorer.

On Nine Standards, on a fine day, on this northernmost summit of the Pennine Dales, you can see almost all of northern England, including the Lakes and the Howgills. Eastwards are the smoking chimneys of Middlesborough. Westwards, Wild Boar Fell (above Mallerstang) where the last wild boar in England is reputed to have been slaughtered by Sir Richard Musgrave, during the 15th century. When his tomb in Kirkby Stephen Church was opened during restoration of the side chapels in 1847, a boar's tusk was found therein, suggesting that the story is true. Standing alone among these giant cairns, surrounded by the bleating of sheep and lambs, hearing the cries of curlews, the laughing sound of the wind through the rushes, and the occasional gurgle of water, there is nothing of man to disturb the silence.

Incidentally, on the way up to Nine Standards, one passes Faraday Gill, named after Michael Faraday, the largely self-taught 'Father of Electricity'. His parents could only afford an elementary education for him, yet, as everyone knows, he made important contributions to physics, chemistry and electrolysis; no less than to the relationship between magnetism and electricity, which led to the invention of the dynamo. He and his wife remained devoted to the teachings of the Sandeman Sect, a fundamental Christian order who based their beliefs on a literal interpretation of the Bible. The Faraday family lived near Kirkby Stephen, moving to London in 1791. Michael was born there shortly afterwards but, one feels, there ought to be a museum, or some recognition of the man, or his achievements, hereabouts.

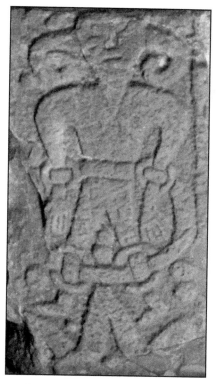

The Loki Stone, Kirby Stephens Church

Reaching Kirkby Stephen, one has completed the long ascent from the headwaters of the Swale, arriving in an area that pays homage to the Norse invaders who once worshipped here. The names change to sacred groves (lunds), and mounds (haughs), as opposed to temples. While one is largely ignorant of which gods they worshipped, in Kirkby Stephen Church, at its western end, there is a block of stone about a meter in height, named the Loki Stone, which is decorated with a carved figure with horns (see above). The object is thought to depict the Scandinavian God, Loki, who, in Scandinavian mythology, was a mischief-maker who caused the death of Odin's son. As a punishment, Odin had Loki chained up below ground.

Market Place, Kirkby Stephen

The ancient market town of Kirkby Stephen is positioned at the head of the Eden Valley and has, so far, escaped mass tourism. It sits on the doorstep of one of the few remaining wild and unspoiled landscapes of the region, with hundreds of quiet trails and paths emanating from it. The town has a pleasant appeal, and its market place remains at the heart of things. There are welcoming cafés as well as attractive buildings, clinging to the main road. With its setting on the bank of the River Eden, and almost completely surrounded by the mountains of the Pennine Range, it stands supreme. There are, in addition, many relics of Roman Occupation: old feudal castles and ancient monuments. The best estimate is that early man was living here from 7000-5000BC, according to the dating of the stone implements found in the district (for example, Celt stone axes, bound with sinew or fibre). Several ancient earth works and burial mounds in the locality date from the Bronze Age, 1800-1600BC. It is probably the first town or village of Norse origin, and the name, Kirkby, is derived from the Norse word *Kirke* and *bye,* meaning church town, though the origin of Stephen is obscure.

The Shambles, Kirkby Stephen

History records that in the year 1070, Cumberland and Westmorland became, by conquest, part of the Kingdom of Strathclyde under the King of Scotland. Years later, it again came under the King of England. This latter period was before the Doomsday Book was written, so there is little mention of the place anywhere. Lady Anne Clifford-Combes of Pembroke (1590-1676) was a great builder and restorer of castles in the area. In 1643, she at last inherited, after a legal struggle, her father's great estates of Appleby, Brougham, Brough and Pendragon (below). She resided for a while at the latter in October 1661, having repaired the castle the previous year, following an invasion by the Scots. Alas, her grandson (a Tufton), the Earl of Thanet, barbarously demolished parts of the castles of Pendragon, Brough and Appleby, selling their timber and materials, giving little thought to the inscription placed over the gate of Pendragon Castle by Lady Ann, during its restoration:

Pendragon Castle

'And they that shall be of thee shall build the old waste places; thou shalt raise up the foundations of many generations, and thou shalt be called the repairer of the breach, the restorer of paths to dwell in.'

Pendragon Castle was the one-time favourite of Lady Ann Clifford and stands on a small round hill above a bend in the River Eden, with a deep moat around it crossed by two causeways. The one on the north-west side is the original entrance to the castle and from here there are magnificent views of the Wild Boar and Mallerstang Fells. Pendragon was, probably, originally an isolated peel-tower, or keep, built in the 12th century. The place is a now shadow of its former self, its foundations undermined by 'prospectors' digging beneath its walls for the legendary Arthurian gold.

A mile from Pendragon Castle are the ruins of Lammerside Castle, built by the Wharton family of Wharton Hall (see below). The castle had fallen into disuse by the 15th century. Like Pendragon, Lammerside is associated with the Arthurian

Lammerside Castle

legend, appearing as 'Castle Dolorous', the home of Sir
Tarquin who, reputedly, ate children. Over the years, much
of the masonry of Pendragon has been carted off. Now, little
remains of either castle. Lammerside is little more than a barn,
a mile from Pendragon. Legend says the two castles are linked
by an underground tunnel. If true, no-one has found it.

As far as Arthur himself is concerned, he was held in great
affection by the populace. For example, in Bodmin, in 1113, a
denial that he was still alive produced a near riot. That said, he
seems to have been more of a folkloric or mythical figure. His
origins go back as far as the mid-6th century – possibly earlier
– which is right at the beginning of the historical horizon. He
was held up as a 'great warrior', a slayer of mythical beasts and
monsters. And it all adds up to the romance of the place.

Two miles south of Kirkby Stephen is the parish of
Wharton and, within its borders, apart from Pendragon and
Lamerside Castle, is Wharton Hall – thought to have been the
earliest known residence of the Whartons, or de Quertons, as
the name was written in earlier times.

Wharton Hall

The Whartons began to live at the hall, now a farm, in the 14th century. A large kitchen was added in 1540 by Thomas Lord Wharton. The gatehouse was added in 1559. At the main entrance, which is eight feet high and leads into a courtyard, are still traces of the shaft for the portcullis. Over the archway above is a tablet carved with the Wharton arms. The original building became ruinous, and was restored by the Earl of Lonsdale in about 1785. It is a fine example of a large medieval mansion.

The earliest record of the house of Wharton dates from 1292, when Gilbert de Querton proved to the justices of Appleby his right to the Manor of Querton. Gilbert married a daughter of the great family of Hastings. As a consequence, a 'maunch' – or lady's sleeve – was added to his coat of arms, the maunch being the ensign of the house of Hastings. Thomas Lord Wharton, as Captain of Carlisle Castle, with the aid of Sir William Musgrave, routed a vastly superior Scottish Army at Solway Moss in 1542. Three years later, with Lord Dacre, he sacked Dumfries. Thomas founded the grammar school at Kirkby Stephen in the year 1566, and the second Thomas Lord Wharton represented various constituencies in parliament, from 1545 to 1585. James the First visited his son, Philip, at Wharton Hall in 1617. Thomas, the fifth baron Wharton, being the eldest son of Philip (a strict Covenanter), was created first Marquis of Wharton in 1715, and, as a boy, was forced to suffer sermons lasting three hours. When he came of age, he avenged himself by plunging headlong into the gaieties of London. Estimates of his character, mainly uncomplimentary, vary considerably. An anonymous writer at the time described him in the following lines, commencing:

> 'Nor bribes nor threat'nings could his zeal abate,
> To serve his country and avert her fate,
> Firm to her laws and liberties he stood,
> Submitting private views to public good.'

But Dean Swift wrote of him as 'the most universal villain that I ever knew', and Macaulay, while acknowledging the Marquis's abilities, agreed.

Possessed of astonishing intelligence and a sponge-like memory, he was created Duke of Wharton; the single historical instance of a Dukedom being conferred on a minor. At his coming of age, his father having died, his income was an estimated £16,000 a year. Unfortunately, he lost £120,000 in the South Sea Bubble. In a further blunder, he espoused the cause of the Jacobites, leaving England to join the Old Pretender, in 1725. For this act of treason he was outlawed and subsequently deprived of all his titles and lands. He went to Spain, where he was cared for by the monks of a Cistercian Monastery in Catalonia, dying in 1731. Pope portrayed his character in the unflattering lines below:

> 'Wharton the scorn and wonder of our days,
> Whose ruling passion was the lust of praise,

Born with whate'er could win it from the wise,
Women or fools must like him, or he dies.'

So ended the life of the first, and last, Duke of Wharton. The great House of Wharton, after a long record of 500 years, ceased to exist, and it is hard to imagine a greater calamity. His demise benefited the Lowthers, whose successors were subsequently ennobled as the Earls of Lonsdale and purchased the hall.

Following an indifferent night at Kirkby town's YHA, I headed towards the medieval road that once ran through the vale from Kirkby Stephen to Orton, coming up quickly on Smardale Bridge which once carried the medieval road over Scudal Beck. Here we see the intriguingly named Giants' Graves, or pillow mounds which, mundanely, are not the resting places of large beings who once roamed the Earth, but ancient rabbit warrens established to feed the locals. Over to the right, we see Smardale Viaduct, which carried the former Tebay-to-Dartington railway. It almost seems the vale was built for communication, and Scudal Beck makes a good coffee stop. It is a deafeningly peaceful place, becoming the more so as we cross Crosby Garett Fell – the site of prehistoric field systems marking the terminus of field boundaries.

Smardale Bridge

Perhaps I had been too long on my own but, on taking up my sack again, I had the distinct impression that I was being watched. The feeling was so strong that I cast about me in expectation of seeing someone or something to justify the impression. I saw no-one at all. But I began to wonder if the prehistoric souls of those who had once inhabited the area were still at large, keeping watch over their crops and animals, scrutinising interlopers. Certainly the area is among the oldest inhabited parts of Westmorland, embracing Smardale and Crosby Ravensworth Fell, and the latter has been described as an 'Empty Quarter', enclosing the remains of prehistoric village settlements and tumuli. All around are ancient Celtic burial mounds. Some have been excavated and found to contain human remains, bronze ornaments, and tools. In Mallerstang Dale, mentioned above, is pre-historic Croglin Castle, an ancient hill fort constructed by the Brigantes, the Celtic tribe that dominated the area before the Romans came. Incidentally, in terms of the bird life, here are not only red grouse and curlew, but golden plover and redshank.

Smardale possesses an ancient hall, the residence of a family named de Smardale – comprising a square building with a round tower at each corner. It is built in the Scottish baronial style of architecture and is now used as a farmhouse. The quiet graves in the area must have been what Gray had in mind when he wrote his elegy:

> 'Beneath those rugged elms, that yew trees shade,
> Where heaves the turf in many a smouldering heap,
> Each in his narrow cell for ever laid
> The rude forefathers of the hamlet sleep.
> Far from the madding crowd's ignoble strife,
> their sober wishes never learned to stray;
> Along the cool sequester'd vale of life
> They kept the noiseless tenor of their way.'

As I drew closer to Great Yew Fell, still feeling somehwat admonished, I may have experienced some form of hallucination – or was it? For, lying on top of a rocky outcrop directly ahead of me, I was confronted by the largest sheep I have ever seen. Indeed, even before I came up to it I thought it was a cow lying down. Nearby, on a smaller rock, was a smaller sheep, though still of great size, about the size of a small horse. They were so intimidating that I took a wide detour. To this day I have been unable to make sense of the episode, though I noted the name Great Ewe fell on the map, and subsequently wondered if there was some substance to the 'illusion'. Has anyone else seen a sheep as big as a cow hereabouts?

Below this place, adjacent to Bent's Farm, are some striking rock formations, of rounded form, which look as if man has had a hand in their formation but, apparently, are straightforward geographical features. Below is the village of Newbiggin on Lune, another bewitching place, which can be easily reached by descending the track past Bent's Farm and Brownber Hall. Here lived the last (alleged) witch to be burnt at the stake at Tyburn. The lady's name was Elizabeth Gaunt, who lived at Tower House, still standing in the village. I must say, however, that far from being the black-hearted hag of fiction, she was a woman of generous disposition who, with what little she had, helped the poor and sick. Unwisely, however, she aided one James Burton, who had been implicated in the Rye House Plot (so called, because of a plan to assassinate King Charles II of England and his brother (and heir to the throne) James, Duke of York, hatched at the Hertfordshire manor of Rye House). How this poor, righteous woman must have suffered as the flames licked her body can only be imagined. I fancy her screams are still taken up by the breeding seabirds of Sunbiggin Tarn (below) [above] in the parish of Orton, whose presence is betrayed by them flying above the water long before the tarn itself comes into

Sunbiggin Tarn

view. On the day I passed, apart from a very large collection of black-headed gulls, there were numerous wild duck. I saw a lovely little teal duck, and also moorhen, coot, and common snipe, and a little jack snipe. A fisherman I met on its shores told me the tarn contained trout of three varieties, of which Loch Leven was the most common. I can't imagine a more pleasant place to spend a day with a rod, admiring the wildlife, though the fish caught must be rather small. Further along on the right, below the flash of Knott Hill, can be seen, over a wall, Gamelands Druidic Stone Circle – see below. All its stones are tumbled down now, and none exceed a height of one meter. It lies a few metres east of the track that runs northwards from Orton, where it joins the Raisbeck road, on private land, used as a meadow. With the exception of one limestone rock, the thirty-nine other stones in the circle are of Shap granite and form an elongated ring forty-four by thirty-nine metres. The stones present as sheep lying down in a well-disciplined circle, reminiscent of the Druids' Circle of Penmaenmawr, in Gwynedd, North Wales. It is the only complete example in

Gamelands Stone Circle

Cumbria of an embanked stone circle. Some may know of another Druid Circle at Haverigg, near Ulverston, overlooking Morecambe Bay. Locally, Gamelands is known as the Druidic Temple. The curious thing is that the stones, of Shap granite, ignore the local limestone. To the Druids, the granite stones must have held some special significance, else why would they have bothered to transport them to this particular location?

At one time, there was a sandstone slab within Gamelands circle, possibly the corner of a burial cist, but this has since disappeared. Decay does not detract from its mystery and atmosphere, or that of similar grand megaliths in the larger area, such as Castlerigg Stone Circle, near Keswick, and Long Meg and her daughters, near Penrith; or, a little further along the trail, Oddendale Stone Circle, which stands on the summit of a low hill adjacent to a limestone pavement east of Iron Hill. Here, a compact inner kerb of stones sits inside a near-thirty-yard-wide outer ring. The place makes a good vantage point to view the colourful Fells and sits at the heart of, no less than, eleven early British settlements of Neolithic and early Bronze Age field monuments.

The attractive village of Orton sits at the southern foot of Orton Scar, a lofty limestone plateau effectively dividing the

At Orton

waters of the Lune and Eden. The western sector consists of peaty moorland, given over more to sheep than dairy farming. It is cleft by the unfrequented Valley of Bretherdale, beyond which is a tangle of wild fell reaching to the M6 near Shap summit. Shap summit is something of a landmark, and over it blows the notorious Helm Wind – the only named wind in the whole of the country. The place was granted a charter to hold a weekly market in 1658 by Oliver Cromwell. The parish church, All Saints, which has watched over the hamlet for eight centuries, has a white dressing of lime on the tower, for protection, and is something of a landmark. The Helm Wind, incidentally, takes a regular toll on livestock – if not people. I spoke to a farmer's wife who told me that they'd lost almost half their flock after one bad blow.

The population of Orton is noted for its longevity. George Whitehead, the Moses of the Quaker Magna Carta of 1696,

A disused limekiln on Orton Scar

was born here. The parish takes in a slice of the Howgills, and the northern sector contains an attractive limestone plateau comprising Great Asby and Orton Scars and Beacon Hill. The highest point in the parish is The Calf, at 2,220 feet. The parish includes the previously mentioned Sunbiggin Tarn, as well as a limestone pavement formed from rock laid down 350 million years ago when the area was covered in a warm shallow sea. What remains today is the glacial debris left behind by meltwater during the last Ice Age.

By the way, on our journey to Oddendale, we pass the headwater of the Lynnet, where we find Black Dub monument, a mere stone's throw upstream. It marks the spot where King Charles II stopped to refresh his army on his march down from Scotland in 1651. As I approached there were skylarks overhead, and it seemed a very pleasant place to stay. The vicarage at Orton was my overnight stop. After the giant ewe, the giants' graves, and the prehistoric burial mounds, I felt in need of Christian symbolism. My hostelry didn't disappoint.

Orton Church, by the way, stands on high ground at the northern edge of the village, built of local limestone and sandstone. Its massive tower was built as a defence against

The Black Dub Monument

the Scots in the 16th century, and there is a coffin of a child in the belfry. An unusual feature of the floor of the knave is a great frame, holding three large bells, one being recast in 1637. The church includes a bracket, carved with a nail-head, and a piscina (at the south side). The two coffin lids in the porch are 13th century, and the pulpit was made from a three-decker. There is a medieval dug-out chest, six feet long, with a chamfered lid, hewn out of a single oak tree which was once one of the glories of Lowther Park. Lying in the churchyard is one William Farrar, a well known 18th century doctor, whom the locals believed practiced black magic in the hills.

Orton's most famous son, of course, was George Whitehead, a Quaker born in the village in 1636, who fell in his youth, under the irresistible influence of George Fox, the English Dissenter and founder of the Religious Society of Friends –

ceremoniously known as Quakers. His chosen religion much distressed his family for, in those perilous times, Quakers were the sport of Anglicans, Presbyterians and Baptists, who would bait and bludgeon Quakers. Poor George was hardly ever out of prison, and was regularly beaten. Enduring gaol fever, which nearly cost him his life, and further abuse, he was placed in the stocks at Saffron Walden and whipped and generally mistreated. If St Paul suffered a thorn in the flesh, George Whitehead suffered many. Just the same, nothing shook or deterred him from his cause, and he eventually found his way into the presence of King Charles who, at Whitehead's request, freed every captive Quaker, including the famous John Bunyan, who wrote *The Pilgrim's Progress*. Unfortunately, the wheel soon turned full circle again when a measure aimed at Papists also threw 1500 Quakers into gaol, pitilessly robbing them of their estates. With the accession of James II, the Quakers secured immunity from the king, who desired to free all creeds – including that of Roman Catholicism.

Whitehead stood, unabashed before several sovereigns and obtained concessions that were incorporated into the Quaker Magna Carta of 1696. He personally congratulated William, Anne and George I on their accession to the throne. He visited the future George II, to urge him to grant liberty of conscience to all, dying in 1723, aged eighty-six which, at that time, was a good span of years – perhaps the legacy of having been born in long-living Orton.

Moving along the dry valley to Crosby Ravenworth Fell, I encountered Robin Hood's Grave, whose namesake's bay we left in Yorkshire. I must say, for someone who no-one ever met, or claims to have met, he is the most famous outlaw of all time. Here again, it seems, legend is more powerful than reality.

He is believed to have lived at the turn of the 13th century, during the reign of Richard the Lionhearted. Thought to have been a Yorkshire man, or else a man from Nottinghamshire

A Poor Quaker

according to most accounts, he was born into the Yeoman class – neither rich nor poor. As was the case with an outlaw in those days, everyone had the right to kill him. Thus he lived in the Greenwood Forest and, like wolves, had a bounty on his head. Indeed, he was also known as 'Wolf's Head'. The forest during this time was full of desperate men with a bounty on their heads. His followers were known as the Merry Men. They were lawless folk living off the king's deer, which roamed the forest, at that time a legal jurisdiction rather than an extensive area of woodland. Established by William the Conqueror, the local population were forbidden to hunt deer or chop wood therein, and the consequences for such infringements were severe.

In Sherwood today, there still stands a preserved 1000-year old oak (called Major Oak) where Robin allegedly met his Merry Men. The archer was famous for his vigilante style of justice, which he visited upon those who were corrupt. Remarkably, against the odds, he defeated authority claiming a higher good by giving from the 'haves' to the 'have not's'. This nobility of purpose sustained his reputation down the centuries, aided by the medieval ballads of the 14th and 15th centuries. For example, a poem in the late 1370s, by Piers Plowman, gives our hero two lines, referring to him as a slaughterer of twelve of the Sheriff of Nottingham's men. A number of four-line couplets, written 200 years after his death, suggest that he could have been one Robert Hode, whose name is listed in the Yorkshire court roles, and who owed a large sum of money to a monastery in York. The latter might explain his legendary disdain for the clergy. On the other hand, it is speculated that the name 'Robin Hood' could be a generic name for an outlaw, as opposed to a specific individual. In this respect, there are similarities between Robin and King Arthur. But I like to think that he was a real person who lived a secluded, if not a restful life, in the forest with Maid Marion and his Merry Men. His idea of the redistribution of wealth, from rich to poor, has served as a beacon for social equality down through the centuries. He certainly ticks a lot of boxes as 'hero'.

Moving on from Robin's grave, on the way to Shap, Howdendale Nab and Howdendale Quarry are encountered. This belching monster is evidence of the granite works, and comes as an incongruous, shocking, intrusion into the landscape after the peaceful rural landscape. The Shap granite has a pinkish hue, and some of it was incorporated into St Paul's Cathedral. There is another similar quarry south of Shap, adjacent to the A6. Shortly afterwards, we encounter another fuming monster, the M6, which roars up and down between the Midlands and Carlisle. We approach it along a thin path through hawthorn scrub and boulders. Crossing over the footbridge, the monster roars at us ineffectually from below. Crossing fields we arrive at Shap itself, an uninspiring linear settlement forgotten by the motorway.

A little south of the town, we encounter a notable piece of prehistoric vandalism. When the West Coast main line was pushed through by Shap, during the middle of the 19th century, it destroyed the great terminating stone circle of Carl Lofts (or Kemp Howe, or the Shap Stones, or whatever you want to call them), discarding the ancient standing stones.

The remnants of these now lie, desecrated in a pasture field by the side of the A6, a mile and a half south of the village, six

Carl Lofts

boulders in all, the largest being ten feet in length. The above-pictured Carl Lofts was reputed to have been eighty feet wide at one point, forming an avenue which headed north-west towards Shap and Skellow Hill (on which latter is a tumulus). The width of the stone avenue was thought to have been eighty-eight feet as it passed by Shap village, but varied along the length of the avenue. Following demolition of the circle, further destruction was caused locally by the blasting of the stones to clear land. Removal of the stones for building, and further mutilation over the 18th and 19th centuries, including the land enclosures in the early 19th century, completed its destruction. Posterity has certainly been deprived of a significant and splendid prehistoric monument and, in the process, forfeited information about our ancient past. The monument would have been quite a draw were it still standing today, and was possibly a Druidic construction, rivalling that of Stonehenge, but the truth about it has now probably vanished forever.

Thankfully, some stones remain, including the easily visited Goggleby Stone, west of Shap village, a seven or eight feet high slab of Shap granite with a cup mark (a 'petroglyph') on its north-east angle. It has been suggested that it is of Neolithic

The Goggleby Stone

Age, as has been proposed for the Kenet Avenue of southwest England, linking the great circle-henge of Avebury with its Sanctuary, though it may be of earlier date. Further north we find the much larger Thunder Stone, located on private land, and not so easily visited – though I managed to do so and nearly got flattened by a belligerent bovine for my trouble. It may be, however, that the Thunder Stone was not part of the Shap Avenue, but merely a glacial erratic – a boulder left behind by the Ice Age. For the reason pictured below, it wasn't possible to examine the stone for cup marks!

If continuing in megalithic mood, one may travel fifteen miles further north to Penrith, where, striking north-east for six miles, one can see the stone circle of Long Meg and her Daughters. This is an impressive grouping. Long Meg is a column of Triassic sandstone 3.7 metres high, standing a short distance to the southwest of the stone circle formed by her daughters – reputably a coven of witches turned to stone by a magician as they celebrated their Sabbath. The legend claims, that if you count the stones and achieve the same total twice, the enchantment that holds the witches in their petrified

The Thunder Stone

The Belligerent Bovine

stance will be broken, at which point, no doubt there is a need to depart with alacrity. Wordsworth considered that the circle surpassed any other relic of the dark ages, in singularity and dignity, other than Stonehenge. The place inspired him to write the following sonnet:

'A weight of awe, not easy to be borne,
Fell suddenly upon my spirit – cast
From the dread bosom of the unknown past,
When first I saw that family forlorn.
Speak Thou, whose massive strength and stature scorn
The power of years – pre-eminent, and placed
Apart, to overlook the circle vast –
Speak, Giant-mother! Tell it to the Horn
While she dispels the cumberous shades of Night;
Let the moon hear, emerging from a cloud;
At whose behest uprose on British ground
That Sisterhood, in hieroglyphic round:
Forthsodoing, some have delved, the infinite
The invisible God that tames the proud.'

In 1715, when Dr Stukeley undertook his '*Iter Boreale*', there were many cairns, remnants of circles, and lines of stones scattered about the area. These have since disappeared. Long Meg and her Daughters, according to legend, had been brought together by the famous wizard, Michael Scott, who seems to have been everywhere in northern England. The giant Tarquin (mentioned earlier as residing at Lammerside Castle), was involved until slain by Sir Lancelot de Lake, in the King Arthur 'fable'. Legend says these knights met at King Arthur's Round Table, on the Westmorland side of Lamont Bridge (another curious relic).

A mile or so further south of the Shap Stones is the Abbotts Well Hotel, once a POW camp for German naval officers (mainly submariners) during the Second World War. You can still see the Nissen huts and watch towers in the grounds of the hotel. People once flocked to Abbotts Well for the alleged healing properties of its spring. The waters here are said to have similar healing qualities to that of Leamington Spa. Staying at the hotel is a reasonable alternative if you don't fancy any of the pubs in the village. There is an abundance of red squirrels in the grounds and, at feeding times, they race around the wooded stream faster than the eye can follow.

Shap itself, just off the M6 motorway, fifteen miles south of Penrith, is ten miles north of Kendal. Nearby is Shap Abbey which, like Grace Priory on the North Yorkshire Moors, described above, is a Premonstratensian monastery. Now a remnant of its former self, it lies quietly on the bare banks of the once forested River Lowther. Its ancient name is Heppe, and the monastery was founded by Thomas Gospatrick in about 1170, and dedicated to St Magdalen. Upon Dissolution of the monasteries by Henry, in 1536, the abbey and monastery were given to Thomas, Lord Wharton, mentioned above, for his support against the Scots when he was Governor of Carlisle. It was he, who, with a detachment of 1400 horses and foot routed an army of 15,000 Scots at Salom Moss, seizing the baggage of the army and several noblemen. The abbey and monastery and, as previously mentioned, Wharton Hall were later purchased by an ancestors of the Earl of Lonsdale, whose seat is Lowther Castle. Their estate forms part of the 600 acres on the east side of the wooded vale of this part of the Lowther.

As one heads towards the eastern shore of Haweswater, what remains of Naddle Forest feathers the slopes above the lake. The lake is one of the deepest in Lakeland, and like Thirlmere, has an igneous bottom. Elizabethan Haweswater Hall, my hostelry for the night, sits quietly at the head of the vale. One can see the craggy eminence of Wallow Crag, whose ponderous jaws (legend has it) imprisons the errant spirit of Jamie Lowther (the first Earl of Lonsdale), said to be a man of stern demeanour, and greatly disliked because of his despotic use of local power. His ghost was reported to roam about the vale, terrifying the local populace, until a priest, 'skilled in the management of refractory apparitions…' imprisoned him 'with the aid of diverse exorcisms,' in the centre of Wallow Crag. Some believe he still haunts the dale.

Further on lies Mardale Green, a village which was submerged in the late 1930s by Manchester Corporation, to provide water for that city. The place had a small church and a pub (The Dun Bull), which latter parts are exposed during times of drought or of low water. Ninety-seven sets of human remains

Mardale Green at Evening

were disinterred from the churchyard and transferred to the nearest hallowed ground at Shap. The Haweswater Hotel, still standing, was also moved to the other side of the lake, requiring a new access road to be built.

Alfred Wainwright, famous for his pictorial guides to the Lakes, protested vehemently about the proposal to drown Mardale, which he had enjoyably visited. But his protestations fell on deaf ears. Submerged in the waters of the dale is the hamlet of Measard, and a plaque on the trail, at this point, records where the water from two adjoining side valleys was diverted to the lake.

The mountains in view, looking down Haweswater are, from left to right, Wallow Gag, Bronstree, Harter Fell, Pyat Crag, High Street, Kidsty Pike and Lad Crag. Between the Whilter and Randale becks, towards the far end of the lake, is the Iron Age hill fort of Castle Crag, and excavation has revealed evidence of hearths and floors in the huts.

We are soon past Speaking Crag, climbing up towards

The Farmhouse at Measand

Kidsty Pike, Long Stile and High Street. Looking to our left, towards Riggindale, there is the hope of catching a glimpse of 'the only nesting golden eagle' in England. Presently, we reach High Street where, a couple of centuries ago, horse races and other sports were held at the Mardale shepherds' meet. It is quite something to imagine it taking place at such heights.

The Church at Mardale

Haweswater from Mardale Head

Also on High Street, at 2,700 feet, is the legendary Roman road which joined their fort at Brougham with the one at Ambleside.

Leaving High Street, we march across the skyline and descend towards Patterdale. Below, Haveswater, which supplied water to Penrith, can be seen on the way. In view at Angle Tarn can be seen Saint Sundy Crag, Striding Edge and Helvellyn. Just here, not long after leaving High Street, I was treated to an unexpected sighting of a deer and a glimpse of the male golden eagle soaring over the Knott before disappearing towards Haveswater. One may glimpse Ullswater. The descending path goes through the wooded glade of Goldmill Beck, crossing it to reach the YHA hostel – a modern, well-run place. Incidentally, Patterdale is named after St Patrick, and Patterdale is known as St Patrick's Dale.

The next day broke with torrential rain from a lowering cloud base. Forced to abandon a planned return visit to Striding Edge, I joined the substantial gaggle of folk heading up Grisedale Beck. After the isolated traverse of Kidsty Pike, on the previous

On the Outskirts of Patterdale

day, I almost resented their company, pushing on ahead to Dollywaggon and Grisedale Tarn. At the latter, I spared a rain-soaked sandwich for a man from Bolton, drenched and ill-prepared for mountain travel. There had clearly been some upset from whence he came, and his mind seemed more wretched than his clothing. He did not seem to be able to tell me, in any definite sense, where he was heading. Nevertheless, he trailed after me down Raise Beck until, finally, he fell behind and I lost him a few hundred yards or so from the road. But at least, I thought, he could not fail to get off the mountain.

Arriving in Grasmere, I headed, rain-soaked, for the Wordsworth Hotel, my hostelry for the night. I entered reception, looking rather like a drowned rat, and the expression on their faces was a pastiche of curiosity, disapproval and disbelief. I could almost hear them say, 'What is this strange, dripping, waterproofed creature that has swept in?' But I wish to point out that I hadn't chosen this establishment; the choice had been made for me. It was the 150th anniversary of the poet

Grasmere Church

William Wordsworth. The Wordsworth Hotel was the only place in which I could find a room for the night. Once inside, I divested myself of my waterproofs and, after a half-hearted swim in the pool, was glad to eat dinner and remain indoors, the rain hammering on the window with extraordinary velocity. A couple of pints later, I retired to my single room above the entrance hall and fell rapidly asleep, hoping that the lost soul I'd met at Raisebeck Tarn had also found food and shelter.

It was here in Grasmere, of course, that William Wordsworth, the poet lived. He was born at Cockermouth on 7th April 1770, the second of five children. He lived in Grasmere with his sister, Dorothy, to whom he was very close all his life, Dorothy being born the following year. She continued to live with William at Dove Cottage, following William's marriage to his childhood friend, Mary Hutchinson. With his poetic friend, Samuel Taylor Coleridge, Wordsworth helped to launch the Romantic Age of English Literature, notably through their joint publication, *Lyrical Ballads*. After attending a poor school in Cockermouth, he went to Hawkeshead Grammar School. His sister went to live with relatives in Yorkshire. His debut as a writer began in 1787 when he published a sonnet in *The European Magazine*, whilst attending St John's College, Cambridge.

In 1791 he visited Revolutionary France, falling in love with a French woman called Annette Vallon, with whom he had a child named Caroline. He returned to England the following year, when relations between France and England soured. In 1798, William and Dorothy travelled to Germany, and he began his famous work, *The Prelude*. In 1799 William and Dorothy returned to England and settled in Dove Cottage, Grasmere.

Mary and William had five children together, three of whom predeceased them. In 1813 they moved from Dove Cottage to Rydal Mount, above, where William remained until his death in 1850. He was poet laureate from 1843-1850.

Rydal Mount

In 1859, following Mrs Wordsworth's death, Rydal Mount was broken up and the furnishings sold at auction; a rather ignominious end to a home that, when the Wordsworths lived there, had drawn thousands of visitors. William was fortunate to receive endowments and legacies, giving him the ability to write free from worries about debt. He was a prolific poet, with an optimistic outlook on life, and the originals of his books of poems can be seen at the Wordsworth Trust, Grasmere. Scholars from all over the world come to examine his manuscripts.

From Grasmere village there are pleasant walks up to Easedale Tarn, where William used to fish, and where he took a last farewell of his brother, Captain John, whose ship, the *Earl of Abergavenny*, was wrecked off the south coast of England, John drowning. If staying over in Grasmere, for a day or so, Helm Crag is a good place for a scramble, though its bewildering summit deserves cautious exploration. Wordsworth compares the crag to a gigantic demolished building, and speaks of the 'Ancient Woman' seated upon it:

> *'The Astrologer, sage Sidrophel,*
> *Where at his desk and book he sits,*
> *Puzzling on high his curious wits;*
> *He whose domains is held in common*
> *With no-one but the Ancient Woman,*
> *Covering beside her rifted cell*
> *As if intent on magic spell.*
> *Dread pair, that spite of wind and weather,*
> *Still sit upon Helm Crag together!'*

The following morning, as I looked at the threatening sky, I stood outside the hotel trying to decide if I should go via the Langdale Pikes to Rosthwaite, where I was staying at the

Helm Crag

Royal Oak. Or via Greenup Edge – a much less exposed and, therefore, safer route into the Borrowdale Valley. As I looked at the snowy tops, I was reminded of a tragedy that occurred in March 1808, when two residents of Easdale; namely, George and Sarah Green, returning home from a furniture sale in Langdale, encountered a winter snowstorm. When they did not return, two of their six children raised the alarm. But it was three days before their bodies were discovered lying in the snow, not far from each other. Sarah's body was found near Miel Beck, above Langdale, not far from Dungeon Ghyll. Her husband's, his skull smashed, lay at the foot of a nearby precipice. We can conclude that, apart from the atrocious cold, visibility at the time would have been almost nil. Familiarity with the route in such conditions would have counted for very little, and the tragedy is a salutary reminder of the dangers of mountain travel. Even today, people do still simply walk off mountains in bad weather. I had previously experienced heavy snow in the Lakes, one April, and decided against such an exposed route. Only the foolhardy persist in traversing a route in inclement weather, especially if there is reduced visibility.

The Greens' home, incidentally, was one of the poorest in the valley. It was heavily mortgaged. Dorothy Wordsworth, William's sister, recorded that the Greens' cow had grown old, producing little milk, and that they could not afford another. The community rallied round. Out of sympathy for the orphans, a general appeal raised in excess of £500. Eventually it was closed up, on William Wordsworth's recommendation, on the grounds that if the fund were to amount to more it might unsettle the orphans by elevating them above their station. Is that an example of his professed egalitarianism and brotherhood with the working man?

Perhaps it's worth mentioning that, even in hot weather, the unwary can come unstuck. For example, one hot summer's day, some years back, a farmer who had been busy with sheep on the fells all day, descended to the Langstrath Beck or,

Black Pot

more precisely, to that fissure in the beck known as Black Pot, thinking to cool down. He jumped into the water fully clothed but became trapped beneath an underwater ledge. Visitors to the pot will see a tempting ledge that leads down into it and, no doubt, people still swim in it on a hot day. But the water is very deep and, given the farmer's death, I've always swum further down where the Langstrath kicks left towards Stonethwaite. Presumably the farmer's body was recovered, but it is another example of why Nature has to be treated with respect. Another casualty on the mountains, in summer, is heat exhaustion.

Consequently, I headed up Far Easedale Gill in my lederhosen, towards Greenup Edge where, Wainwright warns, we must be careful not to go right and end up down into Thirlmere. He refers to this as 'The Greenup Trap'. Coming up to it I expected an uneventful crossing. Then, as the clouds lifted, a pair of young women, seeing my lederhosen and exposed calves, had a fit of the giggles – one nearly choked on

A Pool in the Langstrath

her sandwich. The section of mirth, apparently, was the fleshy bit between the top of my socks and the hosen.

They detained me, and I must say with some interest, for half an hour recounting something they'd seen earlier in their journey. Without a hint of artifice, they told me they'd seen a black panther enter a small copse of trees between Seathwaite and Seatoller, and were quite excited by the event. Quite reasonably, I suggested that the creature might have been a large black cat glimpsed crossing the top of a rock. Yet they were adamant that what they'd seen *was* a panther. Their story reminded me of a report near Rosthwaite, some months earlier, of a large black cat, and I began to wonder if, like the alleged cat on Bodmin Moor, there was a Beast of Borrowdale. The latter tale, incidentally, is given greater credibility by the occasional reports of mutilated or killed livestock on Bodmin moor, allegedly set upon by the beast. As far as I know, however, no verifiable scientific evidence has ever been found to substantiate the presence of a 'big cat' anywhere in England,

The Lower Langstrath, showing Eagle Crag

and the conclusion is that livestock could just as easily have been mutilated by an indigenous species, wild or semi-wild, like a dog or fox, or an escaped zoo animal. This is, of course, all well and good, but the difficulty is in accounting for so many people's earnest beliefs at having sighted a big cat. It keeps alive the possibility that such creatures might still be abroad in wild country where there is easy prey – like sheep.

The account reminded me of the true story of the Wild Dog of Ennerdale, originally believed to be a gypsy's stray and, reportedly, a cross between a mastiff and a greyhound. The beast in question had streaked markings, similar to that of a tiger, and if someone saw the creature today they might have reported seeing a tiger on account of its stripes. This 'wild dog' would regularly kill half a dozen sheep, largely confining its activities to darkness and, cunningly, never attacked the same flock on consecutive nights. Though the creature was chased far and wide across the fells – in some cases as far as St Bees – with hounds, capturing it proved elusive. It refused poisoned meat and, though relentlessly pursued wherever it appeared, refused to leave the area. Finally, it was shot at Eskat Woods by a man named John Steel of Asby, and its carcass displayed at Hutton's Museum in Keswick – long since closed. It is said to have killed hundreds of sheep in Ennerdale in just a few months, and weighed eight stone.

It was, in fact, a Tasmanian tiger – known as a Thylacine – the largest known carnivorous marsupial that ever lived (except that, in northern Australia, they now think there lived a tree-dwelling, marsupial lion, weighing only a few pounds less than a modern lion). The creature gestated its young in a pouch, rather like a kangaroo, and it was a common sight to people living in Tasmania and Western Australia up until the time European settlers arrived. Engravings on rocks depicting the beast, go back at least 1000 years, and its population was believed to be at its height about 2000 years ago. As can be seen from the above

The 'Wild Dog' of Ennerdale

picture, it had, on average, of sixteen stripes and yellowish-brown fur. Sadly, the last of its kind died in captivity in 1936, in a zoo in Hobart, pushed to extinction by human settlement and an Australian government bounty on its head – for eating sheep. When frightened, it showed typical Antipodeans behaviour by rearing up on its hind legs. Imagine the incredulity at a reported sighting of such a creature today, Who would believe it? How the Thylacine ended up in Ennerdale is beyond speculation.

After my humorous and interesting interlude on Greenup Edge, I continued down Greenup Gill, past Eagle Crag, to Stonethwaite. The latter is a lovely hamlet, and particularly welcoming if you stay at Mrs Jackson's cottage, as I have done in the past.

Crossing the Langstrath Beck, I continued along to my hostel for the night, the Royal Oak Hotel at Rosthwaite, a very welcoming establishment. It is one of those places in which you can stay in on your own without feeling out of place. Neither do you have to wade through an extensive menu. At dinner time, when the gong sounds, you simply go into the dining room and eat what is put in front of you. The portions are always generous and, what's more, tasty and home cooked. Next door is the bar of the Scafell Hotel, always it seems packed with walkers of an evening. The Royal Oak Hotel is rather quiet but, if one is inclined to a wider social environment, or a greater choice of drinks, one can always pop next door.

If tarrying in Rosthwaite for a day, it is worth taking the very pleasant walk down the River Derwent – Wordsworth's favourite river – to ascend Castle Crag, which once boasted a Roman fortification, the remains of which have largely disappeared. A slate stone cairn on the summit is a memorial to those who gave their lives in the First World War. The view down the dale from the top of the rock, down Derwentwater, is magnificent.

Derwentwater itself is roughly oval in shape, about three miles long and one mile broad. The scenery doesn't have the softness of Windermere, but the surrounding fells – Skiddaw, Cat Bells and the dark gorge of Borrowdale – give it an almost

Rosthwaite in Borrowdale

sublime character. Their jagged peaks might almost be mistaken for an Alpine range. Its raw beauty is enhanced by the lake's many islands, such as Lord's Island and St Herbert's Island. The former, so-called, because it once had a mansion on it belonging to the Earls of Derwentwater. It was relinquished when the family took up their residence at Dilston, Northumberland. Jas Radcliffe, the unfortunate young Earl of Derwentwater, was beheaded at Tower Hill for supporting the Jacobite cause. His wife, fairly or not, was blamed for inciting his rebellion and was forced to escape up a ravine on to Walla Crag, after the locals heard of her husband's capture. The remarkable brilliance of the aurora borealis on the night of his execution (on 23rd February 1716), is still referred to locally, as 'Lord Derwentwater's Lights', on account of his popularity with the locals and their belief that heaven still mourns his passing.

St Herbert, of course, was the resident of the other island. Bede says that St Herbert left his cell on the island once a year, to visit St Cuthbert in Northumberland, and to receive from him 'the food of eternal life'. The site of his cell on the island, now only indicted by a shapeless mass of stones, means it is impossible to trace the foundation of any regular building. In the 14th century the place was still visited by pilgrims, and religious services are still held on the island. Curiously, it is thought that St Herbert and St Cuthbert died at exactly the same day and hour. They were very close, spiritually and personally. A sonnet by Wordsworth acknowledges the fact, which ends:

> *'Though here the hermit numbered his last day*
> *Far from St Cuthbert his beloved friend,*
> *The holy men both died in the same hour.'*

Walking up Borrowdale Valley, following the river – or otherwise – we come to Seatoller with its impressive yew trees,

Castle Rock in Borrowdale

and the site of a former black lead mine, the only one in the entire country. From Seatoller, it is best to ascend towards Honister by the old Toll Road, as it is preferable to the tarmac and gives spectacular views of the dale head.

Reaching Honister Pass, we are confronted by the sombre face of Honister Crag. The crag is riddled with tunnels and shafts dating from 1728, when green Westmorland slate was first extracted. According to a mine worker I spoke to, the deeper underground the slate, the better the quality of the material. On the mountain, which bears the scars of open cast quarrying, there are tracks where the miners used to trundle the slate down impossibly steep inclines on crude sledges (or hurdles) before the gravitational tramways were constructed. The strength and grit of these miners to undertake such arduous work must have been phenomenal. I can't envisage modern men being capable of such a task. Having reached the bottom of the incline, they then had to climb back up again (which took a laborious half hour) and start the process

Honister Pass

all over again. The empty sledges weighed 80lbs and, laden, brought down each time, approximately 640lbs.

Reaching the summit of Honister Pass, there is a choice of forward direction: either up Dale Head and along Robinson, towards Buttermere, or along the road which winds steeply down to the same destination. On the other hand, one can continue up the old drum line toward Grey Knotts and Green Gable, diverting right towards Loft Beck down to Black Sail, above which I discovered some stone axes. At the bottom of the beck, the walker may turn right to Black Sail Youth Hostel, cradled in the bosom of magnificent mountains. It was my custom, at the time, to visit Brian Wilkinson, the warden, and sleep on the Common Room floor. This was preferable to sleeping in the dormitories, which were often cold and damp. Brian, the finest and most hospitable of wardens, became a close friend of mine, and he often kept the hut open all day to provide a warm refuge for, not only YHA members, but passing walkers, sometimes even making them a cup of tea.

Together, often with others, we would go scrambling around the fells, or fishing up at Blackbeck Tarn. With those who knew him, to this we went later to scatter his ashes, following his death from a brain tumour in Santiago. It was fun damming the River Liza (in Icelandic, the River Lysa) to make a swimming pool, or go for an underwater swim in a cave in the forest. His legendary homebrew, too quickly consumed, often had members singing songs around the bonfire outside the hut. In the morning, we would find a few sheep sleeping in the dying embers of the fire.

Black Sail was a place of unsurpassed bliss in those days, nestled in the awesome shadow of the majestic mountains – the Gables, Kirk Fell, Pillar and Haystacks. One was made to feel infinitesimally small, and this somehow seemed to put everyday troubles into perspective. I remember saying goodbye

A Steep Incline in Honister Slate Mine

Brian Wilkinson, feeding Butter the Sheep

to Brian for the last time, just before he went travelling in South America. Even then, he reported suffering headaches and, tragically, unknown to himself, these were the warning signs of a brain tumour, from which he later died.

But the following morning, I set off down the gloomy fir-tree enveloped Ennerdale Valley, the River Liza hiding from me for the most part, among the trees. Pillar Rock, on one's left, presents as a most tremendous peak from the valley floor, and is a favourite spot for climbers – some of whom have 'come off' to their death.

Reaching the lake, two thirds of the way down the valley, is Anglers Crag (below Crag Fell), which juts out into the lake. It is the location of Robin Hood's Chair. I suppose, if he'd walked here all the way here from Robin Hood's Bay, he'd be entitled to a rest! Nearby once stood the Anglers Arms, out of whose windows one could fish the River Ellen, that runs out of the bottom of the lake, towards Ennerdale Bridge – where the

Wild Dog of Ennerdale was weighed. There is a chapel there. The scene inspired Wordsworth's poem '*The Brothers*'.

> *'I need neither epitaph nor monument,*
> *Tombstone nor name; only the turf we toed,*
> *And a few natural graves."*

The village sees relatively few tourists, but, beyond it, can be seen Kinniside Stone Circle, near where the path diverts to Calder Bridge. A few miles south, on the fell road from Ennerdale Bridge to Calder Bridge, can be viewed the quietly impressive circle known as Blakely Raise. The comparatively tall stones are free from the surrounding vegetation, and the eleven granite stones (originally thirteen) form a perfect circle. To the west are seen the factory chimneys of Whitehaven silhouetted against the sea. Blakely Raise merits an inspection, but little about it is known.

Onwards to Ennerdale Bridge, once described as 'filled

Ennerdale and its Lake

with roaring tipplers' it sees few visitors, but, in prehistoric times, iron ore was smelted and, later, haematite. Thence to Cleator, another (unattractive) village which, like many other mining villages nearby, lost what charm it possessed as a result of the industry.

Soon we approach the cliffs of St Bees, composed of red sandstone, desposed in horizontal layers of enormous thickness, intersected at irregular intervals by strata of light-coloured sandstone. The vast blocks are piled up as if by art, resembling, in many places, the buttresses of a castle. Many vertical fissures run through the rock, into which the sea boils and rushes at high water. It undermines the cliffs above and, consequently, masses of sandstone fall constantly on to the beach. It seems likely that the sea, at one time, flowed inland between St Bees and Whitehaven, as the soil is intermixed with sand and sea shells.

On towards the sandstone cliffs and the RSPB reserve, we see puffins, guillemots and kittiwakes. The spectacular cliffs and soaring seabirds keep us company all the way along the coast, past the white-painted St Bees Lighthouse. One stops to peer gingerly over the dangerous cliffs at the restless Irish Sea.

St Bees, incidentally, is said to derive its name from St Bega, the Irish virgin saint 'who lived here in the odour of sanctity', founding a monastery in the year 650. The legend has it that St Bega and her sisters were in a vessel wrecked and driven on to the cost of Whitehaven. Feeling sorry for them, Lady Egremont petitioned her husband, the Lord of Egremont, to grant them some land on which to found a monastery. He laughed and said that he would give them just as much land as snow should fall upon it on midsummer's day. Luckily for the saint, the following day snow covered the land from Egremont to the sea, a miraculous answer to prayer; whereupon, the Abbey of St Bega was built and endowed with all the land on which the snow had fallen, including the site of the present town of Whitehaven. What may still remain of the abbey structure is the Saxon

Sandstone Cliffs and St Bees Lighthouse

edifice of a tower, the rest being in the florid Gothic style, built of red freestone in a cruciform shape. It possesses fine carvings, lighted by the three lancet-shaped windows. Wordsworth, in his preface to his poem of 'St Bees' wrote:

> *'When Beza sort of yore the Cumbrian coast,*
> *Tempestness winds her holy passage crossed.*
> *She knelt in prayer – the waves their wrath appease*
> *And form her vow, well weighed in Heaven's*
> *Rose, where she founded the strand, the chantry of St Bees.'*

St Bees Bay

St Bees does seem to be a spiritual place. In 1981, in the south chancel of the priory church, they discovered, in a lead coffin, the bones of the knight, Sir Anthony de Lucy, who had been on the Northern Crusade. Wrapped in resin, his remains had lain there for seven centuries. Forensic examination indicated he had been killed abroad in a battle, and his remains shipped home. Blunt force trauma had fractured his jaw, and the ribs were also fractured, causing him to suffer a pneumothorax – a bleeding into the chest cavity. As his body had been returned home, it means he must have been a very wealthy knight as, otherwise he would have remained where he had fallen.

In those days, knights fought to bolster family honour and sought an opportunity to call themselves Crusaders – cashing in their credit to spend less time in Perjury, so they believed, when they died. The priory church at St Bees was one of the largest in England. Other medieval remains have also been excavated in the same location. The Church of St Mary and St Bega also boasts a number of Norman coffin slabs. In the transept is a beautifully incised effigy of Lady Johanna Lucy, who died in 1369, while, in the churchyard rest two mutilated knights – one knight bearing a shield with the arms of Ireby. More recently to be seen, in the churchyard, is a sentimental monument of a child asleep.

With the rain keeping off all the way to St Bees, I arrived in the town and think my walk was an achievement of sorts. It is probably the first long-distance walk in England I can remember; not so much for the places visited, but for the people I met, or revisited, along the way.

Norman Arch, St Bees Church

Boots at St Bees Bay

Many seeming coincidences and other events have not been recorded, in order to keep the travelogue to a reasonable length. On finishing the walk, I was reminded of the words of 'Lead Kindly Light', which I read in an article on the journey, and which greatly encouraged me:

'So long thy power hath blest me,
Sure it still
Will lead me on
O'er moor and fen, o'er crag
And torrent till
The night is gone
And with the morn those angel faced smiles
Which I have loved long since
And lost awhile.'

Dragons o ⎯⎯ ⎯⎯

Nigel Pennick

Dragons of the West

©1997 Nigel Pennick

ISBN 1 86163 0077

Cover illustration by Nigel Pennick
Cover design by Paul Mason

Illustrations credits:
Original drawings by Nigel Pennick: 1, 2, 4, 7, 8, 10, 12, 17, 18, 19, 24 25, 29, 30, 31, 45, 48, 50, 51, 59, 61, 66, 69, 71. Photographs by Nigel Pennick: 55, 62, 68. Original drawing by Helen Field: 37. Original drawing by Cali Silk: 73. Engraving of Frau Percht, 34: Deluciana. The Honourable Guild of Locators: 6, 46, 52.

Published by:

Capall Bann Publishing
Freshfields
Chieveley
Berks
RG20 8TF

Cunning, experience, practice, prudence, patience, grace, nature, reason, speculation and holy living.

The Ten Virtues of the Adepts.

Thanks and Credits

The author wishes to thank the following for various help and information:

Helen Field, John Frearson, Tim Holt-Wilson, David Jackson, Rosemarie Kirschmann, Keith Macdonald, David Lobb, Lindsey Pennick, Rupert Pennick, Cali Silk, Phil Underwood, Eva van Eeghen, Jennifer Westwood and the staffs of the Castle Museum, Dragon Hall and Bridewell Museum in Norwich, the Cambridgeshire Collection, the Cambridge University Library and the Museum of London.

Cybele

Contents

Introduction

Although the dragon is a wholly fantastic and fictional beast, nevertheless it has held the attention of people for centuries, and continues to do so to-day, as the existence of this book attests. The English word 'dragon' comes from the Latin word *draco*, which is a version of the ancient Greek *drakon*. In ancient Greece, the meaning of *drakon* seems less well defined than the modern English 'dragon'. It appears to refer to a large snake, but also to a flying creature nearer to the classical medieval version we know so well.

For more than three thousand years, fabulous serpents and dragons have been the stuff of myth and travellers' tales. Along with winged horses, giant cockerels and other legendary beasts, the chariots or cars of gods and heroes were said to be pulled by dragons. In Greek myth, when the enchantress Medea was deserted by Jason, she killed the children she had borne him and escaped to Athens by air in a vehicle drawn by flying dragons. The Roman poet Lucan wrote of the dragons he believed to live in the Africa of his time: "*You too, the dragons who shine with golden brilliance.....you move on high with wings, and, chasing huge herds, you tear apart massive bulls, constricting them in your coils. Even the elephant is not safe from you because of his size; you condemn every animal to death, and you have no need of venom to bring death*". Pliny the Elder also wrote that "*Ethiopia brings forth dragons, not so large as those from India, even so, twenty cubits long*". As late as 1589, Richard Hakluyt wrote of Robert Gainsh's visit to Africa, where he saw elephants in "*continuall warre against Dragons*".

1

Thus, from the earliest times, serpent and dragon have been interchangeable categories. Modern classification and taxonomy of the world only dates from the eighteenth century. Throughout history, some have asserted that ordinary snakes can grow and be transformed into winged, fiery, dragons. Such crowned and winged serpents appear in the wall-paintings of Pompeii, overwhelmed in the first century CE, and sacred serpents were kept in the *temenoi* and holy groves of trees sacred to the appropriate goddesses and gods. Dragons also guarded treasure, whether the Golden Fleece of Jason or the great hoard taken by Sigurd.

There is something of value present in the world of these archetypal reptiles, for the serpent or dragon can heal as well as kill, and it is necessary to understand with which kind of beast we are dealing if we are to live in harmony with existence. The image of the dragonslayer, which is described in this book, is often that of the brutal man who despoils the world of nature in order to glorify his persona or his religion. However, the way of the hero is a dangerous one, not just a risk-free display of skill, and so dragonslayers are often depicted amid the bones and armour of those men who came before and were slain. Dragons are dangerous, and he or she who overcomes one mindfully creates a transformation that is apparent internally as well as externally. Consequently, the dragon is more than a beast of tall stories, myth and fairy-tale, for it is a symbol of the awesome power of nature which appears in many variant forms, but which we can understand only in symbolic or allegorical form. Thus, it appears in religious symbolism, alchemy, medicine and geomancy as well as in the more literal tales of bards and storytellers. Ultimately, the dragon is a product of the human mind, for there are dragons of various kinds lurking deep within us all.

Nigel Pennick,
Bar Hill,
The Nones of May 1997 CE.

Chapter 1

Dragons: Definitions, Taxonomy and Ecology

Dragons, Wyverns, Lindwurms, Salamanders and Cockatrices

Among the multiplicity of Western mythological beasts, there are a number of related legendary creatures that include and are related to the dragon. Because they are not actual biological animals, their definitions tend to be indistinct, and, as in ancient Greece, they fade into one another. There are a number of main categories, however, which are broadly the dragon proper, the wyvern, the lindwurm, the salamander and the cockatrice. Over a long period of time, there has been a strong consensus on what a dragon looks like. The essential dragon is reptilian in form, being covered with scales like a lizard. It has four legs with scales and claws, bat-like wings, and a long tail, sometimes ending in a barb. The dragon's head has two eyes, two ears, and sometimes also horns. It breathes fire from its mouth and nostrils. A 1685 Yorkshire ballad about the '*Wantley Dragon*' is typical, describing the beastie as a formidable creature having "*two furious wings, a sting in his tail, long claws and four-and-forty teeth of iron*".

In his *The Faerie Queene*, published in London in 1596, Edmund Spenser gives a wonderful poetic description of the dragon fought by The Knight of the Red Crosse. It is given in full in Chapter 4. This dragon's tail was "*bespotted as with*

3

Several dragon-slaying legends involve spiked armour or other special spiky paraphernalia. This knight seems particularly cavalier in his pursuit of the serious matter of fighting potentially lethal monsters.

shields of red and blacke", and the appearance of roundels on
the body is a common element of dragon depictions. Often,
they resemble the 'eyes' of the peacock's plumage or on certain
butterflies. In art, there are many examples.

One of the most famous images of St George and the Dragon,
by Paolo Uccello (1396 - 1475), in the National Gallery in
London, actually shows a wyvern. On its wings are large
roundels. The upper side bears yellow roundels with green
centres, whilst the underside of the wings has red roundels
with green centres. The dragons on the astronomical clock in
Strasbourg Cathedral, made in 1842 to replace others designed
by Tobias Stimmer (1539 - 1584), have spots and roundels. The
chariot of Saturn is drawn by a black-and-gold dragon spotted
with red, gold and black roundels. The 'Obby Oss' (Hobby
Horse) paraded each May Day at Minehead in Somerset is
bedecked with similar roundels to this day.

The Wyvern is similar to the dragon proper, being depicted
conventionally with the head of a predatory animal, with ears.
This is conjoined with a reptilian body which has one pair of
forelegs. Its back bears wings, and its rear part is a prehensile,
snake-like body and tail. The Wyvern's legs are forelegs, and
the posterior portion of the beast is serpent-like. Medieval
representations of this symbolic beast are found all over
Europe, from manuscripts and carvings in both sacred and
secular contexts. An Icelandic representation of Jormungand,
the World Serpent which is said to lie at the bottom of the
ocean, encircling the world, is shown in just this form.

The wyvern is one of the dragon family used widely in
heraldry. In his book, *An Essay to a More Correct Blason*
(London, 1682), John Gibbon describes various coats of arms
including those of Slavonia and the King of Denmark. These
arms are identical, being a red shield bearing a crowned gold
dragon. *"This Dragon hath but two legs, and so is the same
with our Wiberne, which I took to be only an imaginary Beast,
till reading the Travels of Peter Van den Broeck a Dutch man, I*

The Wyvern

observe he acknowledges such an Animal in Angola as big as a Ram, wings as a Dragon, a long tail and snout, and having but two legs. I think to have said above, Draco Bipes, had not been amiss".

The salamander is a real biological amphibian noted for its striking yellow-and-black warning coloration, called Feuersalamander in German. However, in alchemy, it is depicted as an immortal spirit of fire, which links it to the fire-breathing dragon. As 'The Lizard in the Midst of Flames', it was used as the emblem of King Francis I of France (1515-1547). It has the motto, *Nutrisco et extinguo*, 'I nourish and extinguish'. This is a shortened version of the older Italian alchemical motto, *Nudrisco il buono e spengo il reo*, 'I nourish the good and extinguish the bad', as fire purifies the good metal and eliminates the dross. In France, the salamander is used in the arms of Fontainebleau and Le Havre. In heraldry, the salamander is often green, like the most favoured colour for dragon inn signs. The fibrous mineral asbestos was once called 'salamander's wool', for it is fireproof.

The lindwurm is a central European dragon-like beast, sometimes shown with a segmented, scorpion-like tail, as on the medieval fountain in the centre of Schwäbisch Hall in south Germany. Sometimes, the lindwurm is shown without wings, as in the municipal shield of Murnau in Bavaria, which is a wingless wyvern. Other depictions show it with four legs and wings, a classical dragon. The arms of Lindenhardt in Bavaria and the fine sculptural lindwurm fountain in Neuen Platz in Klagenfurt, Austria, depict the lindwurm in that way, so the lindwurm appears to be, for practical purposes, interchangeable with the dragon.

The cockatrice is a beast compounded from a wyvern and a cock, being essentially a wyvern with a cock's head, or a cock with a reptilian body. According to tradition, the look of the cockatrice causes instant death. In *Twelfth Night*, William Shakespeare writes: "*They will kill one another by the look, like*

7

The fiery salamander badge of King Francis I of France.

cockatrices". The cockatrice is sometimes referred to as a basilisk, from the crown-like crest upon its head. It is said to be hatched from a nine-year old cock's egg incubated by a toad on a dunghill. Sometimes basilisks are depicted with the tail terminating in a dragon's head. The arms of the Russian city of Kazan is a crowned basilisk.

Knights errant in medieval romance often encounter these beasts or hybrids of them. In the vast corpus of Arthuriana, Sir Perceval slays a number of serpents, some of which breathe fire or project poison. Sir Launcelot encounters '*sepent griffons*' casting forth fire, and there are other beasties that fall into the general category of which the dragon is the core. We will encounter many of their variations further on.

Wyrm, Wibber, House-snake and Dragon

When it is not seen as a symbol of evil, the serpent recalls a traditional 'old wives' tale' that snakes never die, but renew themselves periodically by shedding their skin. As an image of regeneration, if not immortality, the serpent appears as one of the emblems of the ancient Greek god of healing, Asklepios, whom the Romans called Aesculapius (see below). Sacred snakes were kept at the healing shrines of Asklepios, for both their venom and body-oil are the bases for certain remedies in European traditional medicine. The sigil of Asklepios, a staff around which a serpent coils, remains the emblem of the medical profession to this day, even if its practitioners no longer prescribe snake oil. Even in pre-Asklepian times, the serpent was venerated, as the famous Cretan snake-goddesses, richly dressed ladies who hold a snake in each hand, richly attest. Thus, in the Pagan tradition of Europe, although there are serpent- and dragon-killing legends, the snake is not always unwelcome, for it has its place as the temple- and house-snake.

*The fire salamander of alchemy, 'Emblema XXIX' from Michael Maier's
Secretioris Naturae Secretorum Scrutinium (Frankfurt, 1687).*

The best recalled house-snake traditions in northern Europe are those along the southern coasts of the Baltic Sea, where, unlike most other regions, they have continued to this day. This is because indigenous Paganism continued in its fullest form there well into the Renaissance period in the regions of Old Prussia, Latvia and Lithuania. In Pagan times, every homestead possessed its own guardian snake, the Zaltys, whilst in the temples, consecrated holy temple-serpents were fed milk by priestesses, and brought offerings by lay people. In contemporary Baltic Paganism, the Zaltys, which lives by the house stove, is venerated as sacred to the sun-goddess Saule, who is the guardian goddess of the fire.

Baltic Pagan traditions thereby maintain a more integrated solar-serpent tradition than pertains in those places where the Christian solar myth of St Michael has obliterated the lore of the elder faith. The custom of keeping house-snakes is not restricted to the Baltic countries. They are known in Norway as *husormen*, which were kept in remote farmsteads and villages long after the imposition of the Christian religion. The sixteenth-century commentator Olaus Magnus tells that in his time, nearly 400 years after the destruction of the last Pagan temples, Scandinavian house-snakes were venerated as gods. Their presence was necessary for the continued good luck of the household, and so they were welcomed into the house and treated well. In 1995, a German informant told me that when he was a boy in Bavaria, farmhouses in his neighbourhood kept house snakes which were the southern European species called the Aesculapian Adder.

In Wales, folk-tales tell of house-snakes that have been fed on woman's milk, and thereby transformed from mere common serpents into something more fearsome and sacred - the Wibber - a name related closely to the word for the empowering earth-serpent, Nwyvre. 'Wibber' is generally translated into English as 'Dragon'. In former times, each Wibber was held in dread by the common people, and held to be the beast of wise women or witches. Thus it may be that

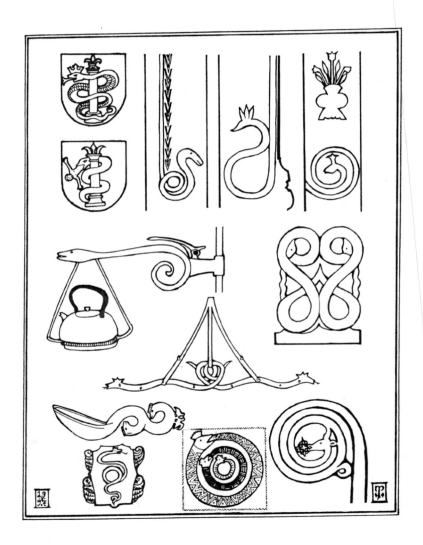

Welsh tales of dragon-slaying Christian monks and priests actually recall historic events where they killed sacred snakes that had become *geas* by feeding on human milk. Among people who held such snakes in reverence and awe, someone who could kill one without fear of divine retribution, and without receiving immediate supernatural punishment, must have been impressive. When a Christian monk or priest had the confidence to kill such a consecrated animal, he demonstrated an exceptional personal power which naturally he claimed for his god. Thus, I suggest, the killing of a sacred snake, accompanied, perhaps, by the destruction of other holy things of the elder faith, marked the end of an era, and the beginning of Christian worship there.

Medieval images of *Terra Mater* - Mother Earth - on Romanesque churches in mainland Europe frequently show a woman suckling serpents at her breasts. Notable examples exist on the portal of the cathedral of San Marco in Venice in Italy; a painting in the apse of St George's at Limburg-am-Lahn, Germany; a church font at Vester Egede, and another at Braby, both in Denmark. Viborg museum has a fragment of a Romanesque tympanum showing a woman suckling a dragon and a salamander. Architectural historians call this image of Mother Earth nurturing the symbolic beasts of the earth, "*la dame aux serpents*", the lady with the serpents, or snake-

---

Opposite: 7 Serpent emblems in European heraldry and symbolic folk-art. The shields show emblems of the Visconti family Milan, Italy, the ancient Ceitic central city of Mediolanum, the centre of the world. Top three pillars are door-surrounds from Germany, left, Heidendor f, Lippe, Wes t phali a; middle Hunnebruck, Kreis Herford; right, Reichenau, Kreis Höxter. Snake with kettle is from Deornum, East Frisia, Germany. The twin ser-pents are a traditional German chair-back. The long twin serpents are the Lauenbeger Herdschlange, for hanging utensils over the fire. The spoon in the lower left is from the Lötschental in Switzerland, The shield below it is a house-snake from Prague, Czech Republic. The Or-oboroses are on a Swiss biscuit-mould, whilst the serpent head in the spiral is the top of the ilth century bishop's crozier of St Godehard, from Hildesheim, Germany.

The Snake-Goddess of Crete, from Knossos (c. 1600 BCE).

woman. The nineteenth-century French expert on so-called 'Gothic' architecture, Emile Mále, asserted that the oldest examples were in the Languedoc in France, at Moissac and St Sernin's cathedral in Toulouse. Images of *Terra Mater* and the connection of the serpent with the Earth Mother in Baltic Paganism seem to be continuous with the Welsh Wibber tradition.

Another possible origin of dragon-slaying legends may come from a linguistic mix-up. Whilst the name *'Wyrm'* was given to dragons and serpents, the old German word *Gewurm* was used to refer to any kind of dangerous animal, such as the wolf. The English word vermin has the same origin. Hence, killing any sort of wild animal could be considered to be extirpating a 'worm'. It could be argued from this that many 'worm-killing' legends refer to the despatching of a beast far less exciting than a dragon, such as a ravenous wolf, bear, wolverine or even a wild boar.

Later misinterpretation of the meaning of "worm" as a wyrm in the dragonesque sense may have led in some cases to the formation of local dragon legends. The Pollard Worm of Bishop Auckland in County Durham in northern England is a good example, where the local legend gives an alternative version where it is a wild boar and not a dragon that has to be slain.

The word *wurm* or *wyrm* for a serpent or dragon is very old however, and in Old Norse, the word *ormbedr* (Wurmbett or Wyrm's Bed) is a poetic kenning for gold, for the guarding of treasure is one of the dragon's most favoured occupations. Thus the Norse Hvitorm lies with gold, which is called *Linnar Logi*. *Saemundr's Edda* tells how a god-bearing dragon appears as a house-spirit, bringing out its gold in sunny weather.

The dragon as the corpse-eating earth. From Michael Maier, Atalanta Fugiaens (Oppenheim, 1618).

The Lindworm

Another word commonly connected with the dragon is *lind*. The *Volsunga Saga* tells of the wyrms called Lyngvi or Lyngorm that go through the air by night. The Lindwurm of central Europe is connected with the Linden Tree. It is said to live in the earth for its first 90 years, in the linden tree for the next 90 and then in the desert for the final 90 years of its 270-year life. The linden tree is a holy goddess tree. In Latvia, it is sacred to the goddess Laima, who gives it its English name, Lime. In Roman Catholic parts of Germany, images of Our Lady treading on the lindwurm adorn holy lime trees.

The Pagan Alamanni in what is now south Germany buried their dead in coffins fashioned from tree-trunks, on the lids of which were carved serpent- or crocodile-like heads and spiky vertebrae. The lindwurm's presence in the earth is noted at many places in central Europe. In Munich is a street called Lindwurmstrasse; there are dragon mountains called Lintburg, such as the Limburg in south Germany, and the Wurmberg in the Harz mountains, places where the presence of the earth dragon can be felt strongly now. It cannot be a coincidence that Terra Mater is depicted with serpents in a church at a place called Limburg-am-Lahn. In Norway, the Lindorm is said to begin its life on the earth, then to live and grow in lakes, and finally migrate to the sea, where it becomes a sea-serpent in the mould of the World Serpent, Jormungand, which is described below. Sometimes, the lindorm is depicted with a horse-like head. There are a number of Germanic women's names including the 'lindwurm' element *linths* (Anglo-Saxon *Lith*), names such as Sigilint, Sigrlinn, Sieglinda, Lindsey, and Linda. Perhaps these names originated in the ceremonial name of a priestess or guardian of holy serpents in pre-Christian times.

In central Europe, the linden tree serves as the central point of traditional villages and towns, the Dorflinde. Traditionally, village lindens are trained to take the form which reflects the

17

The Cosmic Axis with the serpent of the underworld, Nidhoggr, snaking through the roots of Yggdrassil.

layered arrangement of the cosmic axis, with flat plates of vegetation stacked one above the other. Sadly, the tradition is rarer than in former times, and many fine trained lindens have been allowed to grow out. A fine example of *lindeboom*, planted in 1898, exists at Borger in Drenthe Province in the Netherlands. A far more recent example is growing in the village of Hausen, near Murrhardt in south Germany.

Sometimes, village lindens are explicit in their symbolism. The ancient linden that stands at the centre of Fraueninsel, one of the islands in the Chiemsee, the largest lake in Bavaria, has a painted image of Our Lady, standing on a lindwurm, attached to it. Another important linden tree connected with the dragon was the 'Murtenlinde' which stood at the centre of Fribourg in Switzerland. Planted as a commemoration of a military victory that freed the town from foreign threat, this fine linden tree grew in a triangular enclosure in the middle of the road near to St George's Fountain and the City Hall. It was hit by a car driven by a drunk driver in 1983, and was dead by 1985, and so was cut down. Cuttings had been taken before the venerable linden tree was killed, so a new tree, genetically identical with the medieval one was planted near to the medieval fountain with a sculpture of St George killing the dragon. The tradition lives on.

The World Serpent and the World Tree

Norse myth tells of the Midgardsorm (Serpent of Middle Earth) called Jormungand lying at the bottom of the ocean. Like many other Nordic monsters, Jormungand is the offspring of gods and giants. Along with the goddess of death, Hela and the demonic Fenris-Wolf, Jormungand is the progeny of the giantess Angrboda and the trickster-god Loki. At some point in its life, so it seems, every notable dragon or monster comes into conflict with the world of gods and humans. So Jormungand is unlucky enough to encounter the mighty thunder-god Thor. Accompanied by the giant Hymir, Thor goes

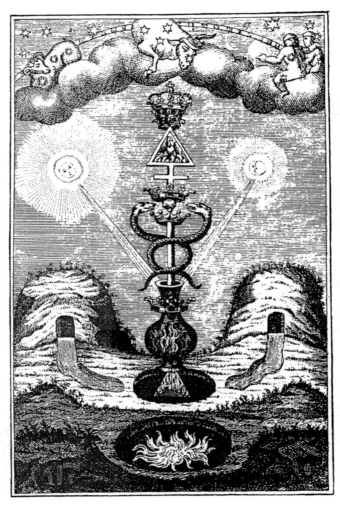

The Cosmic Axis as the serpent-twined caduceus of Mercury, linking the powers of the underworld and the earth with those of the heavens. From A.T de Limojon de Saint-Didier, Der Hermetische Triumph (Frankfurt, 1765).

fishing in the middle of the Atlantic Ocean for the Midgardsorm. This episode of the Norse Gods is depicted in a number of ancient illustrations, including a fragment of dual-faith stone cross at Gosforth in Cumbria. Thor uses as bait the head of a mighty black ox, Sky-Bellower. The head of Jormungand immediately rises from the main, having taken the ox-head bait. Thor then attempts to kill the World Serpent by raining down blow on its head with his mighty hammer, Mjöllnir.

But the giant Hymir, terrified by this earth-shattering conflict, cuts the fishing-line, and the blooded but living serpent falls back beneath the waves to the ocean bed. A Christian parallel of the Norse myth was recorded in the medieval manuscript from Alsace known as the *Hortus Deliciarum* (*The Garden of Delights*). An illustration from this shows God the Father fishing for the Leviathan, depicted as the World Serpent. Here, unlike Thor's ox-head, the crucified Christ is the bait used to hook the monster. A later folk-tale recounted in R. Kühnau's *Schlesische Sagen* (Leipzig, 1910-1913) tells how in the sixteenth century a knight of Trautenberg found a dragon's lair in a chasm. He baited a huge iron hook with a sheep, and fished for the beastie, which he caught. The skin of the dragon was hung up in his castle for many years. Norse legend tells how, at the end of this cycle of time, at Ragnarök, the World Serpent will arise from the depths and be killed by Thor's Hammer. Thor, however, although nine feet away from the serpent's mouth, will die as well, poisoned by the venomous breath of the monster:

> "Midgard's Veor (Thor) in his rage
> Will slay the wyrm.
> Nine feet will go
> Fjörgynn's son,
> Bowed by the serpent
> Who feared no foe".

Thor fishing for the World Serpent. Jormungand.

The Etruscan gods and goddesses are much less well known than the Greek, Roman, Germanic and Celtic. However, like all European deities, they have links with those of other pantheons. In the *Tomba dell' Orco* at Corneto in Italy, a tomb-wall painting shows the Etruscan god Charun. Like Thor, he holds a hammer in his hand, the left one in this instance. In his right hand, he holds a serpent, whose back end coils around his arm. Perhaps there is some ancient link between the mythos of Charun and that of the northern Thunder God.

The Celtic parallel of the Nordic water-monster is the Péiste, sometimes depicted as a water-horse. Whilst some legends may refer to the Whale-Horse (Walrus) or other ferocious marine mammals, at least some are presented in the classical form of monstrous serpent, lindwurm or dragon. An Irish legend recorded in *The Dean of Lismore's Book* tells how the Tree of the Gods grew on an island in a loch, and around its roots coiled a Péiste. Every month, the tree bore the sweetest fruit. One berry was sufficient to satisfy a man's hunger for a long time; one berry's juice prolonged human life for a whole year, and was the cure of many ills. The hero Fraoch went to the island and killed the Péiste, but the fruit of the magic tree was to no avail, and he died of his wounds.

Another version of this monster is the Addanc or Avanc. In the Mabinogion, the hero Peredur (Sir Perceval) kills a number of serpents, among them the cave-dwelling Avanc of the Lake. In a legend reminiscent of Thor's fishing-expedition, the Welsh hero-god Hu Gadarn catches another Avanc in a lake. He catches the beast with an unbreakable chain, then, using long-horned oxen, he pulls the dangerous Avanc from the lake. He then takes it to Glaslyn, a lake in Snowdonia, north Wales, where he sinks it in the bottomless depths. Hu Gadarn's disposal of the Addanc echoes two other legends, that of the Lambton Worm, told later, where the worm is caught in a river and tipped down a well; and the burial of two captured dragons nearby in Snowdonia by King Lludd.

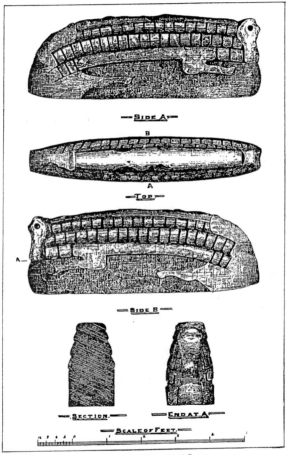

Recumbent Monument at Govan.

Carved 'hogsback' stone tomb-marker in the form of a reptile, in the manner of earlier Alamannic wooden coffins, dating from the time of Ragnar Lodbrok. Govan, Glasgow, Scotland.

According to the ancient Roman author Lucan, the Druidical groves of the Continental Celts contained oak trees around which dragons were entwined. In Northern Tradition mythology, among others, the serpent Nidhoggr (Corpse-Swallower) twines itself around the roots of the world tree Yggdrasil. *"There are more serpents under the Ash Yggdrassil than fools imagine"*, The *Prose Edda* tells us, " *Living-Deep-In-Earth, Moor-Dweller and the sons of Grave-Wolf, Grey-Back and Field-Burrower, Ofnir and Sváfnir. I think they will totally extirpate the Ash-tree's branches."* Here, the translated names of the serpents, are, in the original are Góin, Móin, Grafvitnir, Grábak and Grafvöllud. Unlike most of the gods, goddesses, giants and demons, Nidhoggr will survive the fateful Ragnarök.

The Druiòical Serpent's Egg

Druidic tradition, ancient and contemporary, tells of the mystic serpent's egg. Perhaps the oldest literary reference to this is in Pliny's *Natural History*, where he writes:

"There is also another kind of egg, of much renown in the Gallic provinces, but unknown by the Greeks. In the summer, countless snakes entwine themselves into a ball, held together by a secretion from their bodies and by their spittle. This is called anguinum. The Druids say that hissing snakes throw this up into the air, and that it must be caught in a cloak, and not permitted to touch the ground; and that one must take flight on horseback at once, as the serpents will give chase until a stream cuts them off. It may be tested, they say, by seeing if it floats against the current of a river, even though it be set in gold. But as it is the way of magicians to set up a cunning veil around their tricks, they pretend that these eggs can only be taken on a certain day of the moon, as though it rested with humans to make the moon and the snakes to coincide in the moment of the operation. I have seen one of these eggs myself,

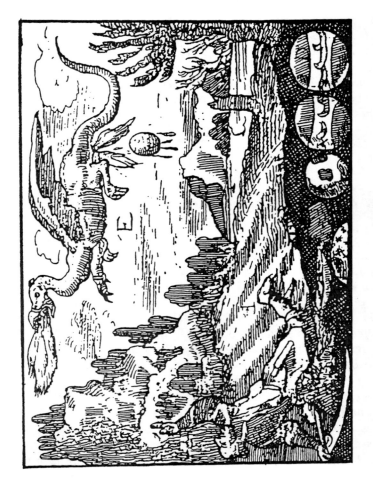

The dragon that flew over Luzern, Switzerland, dropping the drachenstein which is still preserved in the local museum. From L. Cysat, Bechreibung des berühmter Luzerner oder Vier-Waldstätte See (Luzern, 1611).

26

however; it was round, and about the size of a small apple; the
shell was cartilaginous, and pocked like the arms of a polypus.
The Druids esteem it highly. It is said to ensure success in law-
suits and favourable reception with noblemen; but this is
wrong, because a man of the Vocontii, who was also a Roman
knight, kept one of the eggs close to his chest during a trial, and
was still put to death by the Emperor Claudius, for that reason
alone, as far as I can see."

After two thousand years, there is still dispute as to the nature
of the Druidical serpents' eggs. One that reputedly fell from a
dragon that flew over the town of Luzern in Switzerland is
preserved in the museum there. It resembles a variegated
snooker ball. An illustration by Leopold Cysat (1611),
reproduced here, shows the *Drachenstein* falling from the
beast as if it were laying a fiery egg. Luzern is the location for
a number of other fantastic dragon sightings and visitations
over the years. The ancient glass beads favoured by the Celts
have been described as 'serpents' eggs' or 'snakestones' in
Cornwall, Wales and Scotland. Magical glass balls or stones
are kept in Ireland to this day by their hereditary keepers,
who use them in healing. Lewis Spence tells of the glass balls
covered with skin called in Welsh *Gleiniau Nadredd*. He
thought that the 'adders' that assembled to make the 'serpents'
eggs' were the Druids themselves, for the Welsh Druids were
known as *Naddred*.

The Dragon as Crocodile

It has been suggested that many dragon legends can be
explained as the result of uneducated rustics seeing the stuffed
crocodiles that once were common in apothecary's shops or
displayed by travelling showmen. It is possible, too, that
stuffed crocodiles were hung up in churches or civic buildings
(as in several dragon legends) to depict the victim of a local
dragonslaying story. In the nineteenth century, just such a
crocodile hung in a passageway leading to the Town Hall at

27

The cosmic dragon's egg is the epitome of planetary conjunction, from Heinrich Jamsthaler's Viatorum Spagyricum (Frankfurt, 1625).

28

Brünn (now Brno in the Czech Republic). It was said to be the body of a lindwurm, preserved "from a very remote period". Other similar stuffed reptiles once hung in the church of Santa Maria delle Grazie, near Mantua in Italy, and the cathedral of Abbeville in France. Churches at Marseilles, Lyon, Cimiers and Ragusa also formerly sported crocodiles-as-dragons. In 1898, a writer in the journal *Folk-Lore*, identified only by the initials A.H.S. reported that the skin of the dragon killed by St Bertrand hanging in the cathedral dedicated to him at Commingues in the Garonne region of France was actually that of a crocodile. At Mons in Belgium, the reputed head of the dragon slain by Gilles de Chin was identified in the nineteenth century as a crocodile's skull.

The Dragon as Peacock

The flying peacock resembles closely the accepted image of the wyvern, its trailing tail with the famous 'eyes' resembling the scales and roundels of the classical dragon. The head of the peacock, too, in flight, bears an uncanny resemblance to the classical dragon, and may be the ultimate origin of the image taken to be the mythic dragon. Perhaps some of the seventeenth century 'dragon' appearances, such as 'the flying serpent' of Henham in Essex of the 1660s, were actually peacocks that had escaped from the fashionable pleasure gardens of the aristocracy. A farm labourer in a remote village, who had never heard of a peacock, but had seen pictures of dragons, might assume the exotic bird to be a dragon.

The Dragon as Natural Phenomenon

In many parts of Europe, the dragon is associated with floods, perhaps the result of whirlwinds or Typhon in action. *The Chronicle of the Dominicans of Guebwiller* tells how after a flood in Alsace in 1304, a ferocious worm came out of the

29

waters near Isenheim, and wrought great havoc among people and livestock. In 1480, a great serpent with four feet emerged from the River Aare in Switzerland and wandered down the mountain from Zoffinger to Ryckern. It is a folk-idiom in German-speaking Switzerland that when there is a flood, "the dragon has taken flight".

Comets and the Aurora Borealis or Northern Lights have also been seen as dragons of an aerial nature. Just as in myth the appearance of a dragon was dreaded as the harbinger of destruction, so comets are considered portents of ill omen. There are many instances from history of the appearance of comets that were interpreted as fiery dragons threatening the land.

There are many instances where a comet was seen as a dragon, for instance in *The Anglo-Saxon Chronicle*. In the year 1177, many dragons were seen in England, perhaps a reference to a comet visible in the south as well as the north of the country. In 1274, on the Vigil of St Nicholas's Day, the people of Newcastle-upon-Tyne were thrown into terror at the appearance of a comet that they saw as a dragon. Elsewhere, there was an *"earthquake and thunder and lightning"* caused, it was believed, by the "fiery dragon".

Again in April 1395, *"there was seene a fierce dragon in manie places of England, which dreadful sight as it made many-a-one amazed, so it ministered occasion of mistrust to the minds of the marvellous, that some great mischeefe was imminent, whereof that burning apparition was a prognostication"*. It was only after the development of scientific astronomy and universal education that the terror subsided and a sense of awe and majesty was produced whenever a comet appeared.

Another manifestation of the dragon as a cosmic phenomenon is the Aurora Borealis. The Northern Lights circle around the north polar regions appearing as wisps of fiery light, composed of brilliantly-charged particles in the circumpolar magnetic field of the Earth. Satellite photographs show that sometimes, the dragon-like trails encircle the Earth like the World Serpent.

Traditionally, the dragon is also associated with the movements of the Moon through the sky. The tidal Moon Dial on the medieval church of St Margaret at King's Lynn in Norfolk has a green dragon for a pointer. In astrology, the dragon appears as the nodes of the Moon. Caput Draconis, the Head of the Dragon, refers to the Moon's north node, the point where the ascending orbit of the Moon intersects the Ecliptic. Sometimes, the 'dragon' part of the name is omitted, and the point is just called Caput. At the other end of the dragon is the tail, Cauda Draconis, which in astrology signifies the descending node of the Moon. This is the Moon's south node, at the point where the descending orbit intersects the Ecliptic.

In this 15th century woodcut, the female serpent snakes around the tree at the centre of the Garden of Eden, flanked by the archetypal first man and woman, Adam and Eve, who, in the Northern Tradition are themselves born of trees, Askr (Ash) and Embla (Elm).

Chapter 2

Dragons in Tradition Myth and Legend

European myths and legends have many episodes in which dragons or serpents play an important role. In most of them, gods and heroes fight and kill the awesome beasts, but this is not the whole story. All things have some use, dragons and serpents included, and in the tradition of Classical Paganism, the notable deities of healing as well as the Great God Pan, nurture and support the serpent. The following tells the stories of some of the more prominent figures in the European dragon mythos.

Zeus

The Greek father of the gods, Zeus, is ranked among dragonslayers as the god who overcame Typhon, the offspring of Gaea, the Earth-Mother, and Tartarus, the Underworld. Typhon appeared in the form of a whirlwind or typhoon, towering above the mountains and scraping his head against the sky. He had a hundred dragons' heads, many wings, and limbs that were serpents. When he appeared at Olympus, all the goddesses and gods fled to Egypt to escape destruction. All, that is, except Zeus, who stood his ground. He attacked Typhon with thunderbolts, and then cut him down with a sickle fashioned from Adamant. Typhon fled to Syria, where he took refuge on Mount Casius. There, he fought his last stand against Zeus, tearing great furrows in the earth, and entwining God the Father with his serpentine limbs. He tore the sickle from Zeus's grasp and used it against him to cut him through the sinews of the wrists and ankles.

Then Typhon held Zeus captive in a cave in Cilicia, under the guardianship of the dragoness, Delphyne. However, Zeus's sons entered unseen, magically restored his sinews, and released him. Mounting his chariot pulled by winged horses, Zeus renewed his attack and drove Typhon westwards to Sicily, where he thrust the demon through the Earth's crust and into the underworld. In order to prevent Typhon from escaping, Zeus threw up a vast mountain of rock over him, Mount Etna, where, to this day, bursts of Typhon's fire emerge to terrorise human beings. Similarly, the Greek hero Bellerophon, having poured molten lead down its throat, cast down the Chimaera into the earth, where it feeds a volcano. Commemorating the Allfather's victory, Jupiter Columns, erected first in Rome in 66 BCE and later all over Gaul, are topped by a sculpture of the thunderbolt-wielding Jupiter, the Roman version of Zeus, riding down a serpent-legged giant that is Typhon.

Apollo

Serpents are integral parts of the myths of creation and birth. In Greek legend, when Apollo was very young, he killed the serpent that Hera had sent to persecute his mother, Leto. He came to Delphi in his mother's arms. Although a small child, he held his bow and arrows in his hand. He was met by a dragoness called Delphyne, meaning 'womb', who lived there with her consort, Delphynes. Apollo shot the Python, whose body was dissolved by the solar power of Apollo. The place where this happened is called Pytho, and Apollo received the name Pythias. The Python was the guardian of the holy place of Gaea or Themis there, the *omphalos* of Delphi, the middle of the world.

According to tradition, the power of Delphi was discovered by some shepherds whose flocks were pastured in the vicinity of a chasm in the earth. Whenever a sheep approached the chasm, it was seized with convulsions. People, too, suffered the same attacks, but received the power of prophecy, which caused them to venerate the *anima loci* and raise a magnificent temple at the place. In commemoration of Apollo's defeat of the serpent at the place, the temple was dedicated to the solar god. This was a great oracular shrine, at which the priestess called the Pythia would give pronouncements of things to come.

The oracle was conducted with strict ritual. In Classical times, the Pythia was led into the temple by three priests, and placed by them on a tripod stool that was set up over a hole in the earth, from which issued subtle chthonic influences. The power of the earth, symbolised by the transfixed Python, empowered the entranced priestess to utter prophetic revelations. At first, oracles were only given on one day a year, the 7th of the month of Bysius, but, as demand for oracles grew, the performances became monthly. Oracles continued to be pronounced monthly for many centuries, until Delphi was finally suppressed by the Christian church in the fifth century CE, the temples looted of their treasure (which became church property) and the buildings demolished for stone to be re-used elsewhere. The *omphalos*, however, was not destroyed, and is still in existence.

Herakles

Herakles (Hercules to the Romans) is the epitome of masculine strength and physical ability. Like many human heroes, he was the mortal son of divine beings, fathered by Zeus and born of Alcmena. When he was a baby, Zeus's jealous consort, Hera, sent two serpents to the cradle to strangle Herakles. But he raised his head and "*made the first trial of combat, gripping both serpents by their throats*" and killed them. As a boy, he was taught the martial arts. His uncontrollable temper was notable. He stopped playing the lyre after he killed his teacher.

Herakles, the epitome of male power- in the Greek tradition, wearing his lion-skin.

He terrorised all around him, and killed the lion of Mount Cithaeron, after which he made love to King Thespius's fifty daughters on fifty successive nights. But when he grew up, he was compelled to undertake twelve labours in expiation of his mad crime of killing his own children in a berserk rage.

As the epitome of the violent man, most of Herakles's labours involved killing members of the animal kingdom. First, he killed another lion, which lived in a cave at Nemea. Afterwards, he wore its skin as an example of his bravery. Next, he slew the Hydra of Lerna, a seven-headed wyrm which grew two new heads whenever one was cut off. Herakles was failing to destroy the beast until assisted by his nephew Iolaus, who burnt the necks whenever a head was severed. Thereafter Herakles used the Hydra's blood as poison for his arrows. The other beasts killed by Herakles were the Erymanthian Boar, the Ceryneian Hind, the Stymphalian birds and the Cretan Bull. As the archetypal hero, Herakles remains the image of human bravery and ingenuity allied to destructiveness, a dangerous combination of abilities that, unchecked by spirituality, threatens the stability of earthly existence.

Caòmus anò Jason

The Greek hero Cadmus is famed as a founder, both of city of Thebes, and of the Greek alphabet. He founded the city as the result of his quest to save his sister, Europa, from Zeus. Cadmus consulted the Oracle of Delphi before setting out on his quest, and was sent to a holy well sacred to Ares, god of war. The waters were guarded by one of Ares's sons, a dragon, which proceeded to kill some of Cadmus's men before the hero finally despatched it. Athena appeared to Cadmus and told him to pull out the dragon's teeth and sow half of them in the earth. He did so, and from them sprang up a squad of fully-armed men who threatened to kill him. However, Cadmus threw stones at them, and the warriors, blaming each other, fought among themselves. All but five died in the free-for-all,

The chalice and the serpent, traditionally the symbol of Aesculapius and Hygeia, respectively the god and goddess of medicine and health. A version of this emblem is used to-day in Germany to denote pharmacies.

and these became the founders of the nobility of the city of Thebes that Cadmus founded there. The other half of the teeth were taken away by Athena, who gave them to Jason, who sowed them similarly, and dealt with the troublesome warriors in the same manner as Cadmus. Jason, too, had to despatch a dragon to gain the famed Golden Fleece.

Asklepíos

Although much European mythology tells of the extirpation of serpents and dragons, the snake is also the symbol of healing. To this day, a representation of the staff of Asklepios, round which a serpent twines, is the emblem of medicine. Asklepios was the son of Apollo and Koronis, a king's daughter. From the fifth century BCE, the Greek cultus of Asklepios was centred at Epidaurus, where an enormous healing shrine complex was built. The cultus was taken to Athens around 420 BCE during an epidemic, and a shrine built at the Acropolis. From Athens, his veneration spread all over the Greek-influenced world. One of his most impressive shrines was at Pergamon, reconstructed by the Roman Emperor Hadrian around 125 CE. A stone relief in the Pergamon museum in Berlin shows a doctor as the personification of Asklepios. Nearby is a tree on which a serpent climbs.

The worship of Asklepios (as Aesculapius) was taken to Rome in 292 BCE. During a plague, the oracular *Sybilline Books* were consulted by the Augurs, who were told to bring Aesculapius to Rome. A ship was sent to Greece, and the god appeared in the form of a serpent, which was taken on board. When the ship reached Rome, the serpent slithered overboard into the River Tiber and swam ashore on an island. This omen located where the shrine of Aesculapius was built.

To this day, the southern point of the Tiber island has the carved stone replica of the prow of a ship, bearing in relief the head of Aesculapius and his serpent stave. Bronze medallions

39

of Antoninus Pius depict the arrival of the holy serpent of Aesculapius at Rome.

Roman shrines of Aesculapius followed the Greek pattern. Healing came about through sleep, and holy serpents were kept in abundance. Holy images of Aesculapius are often accompanied by his daughter, Hygeia, the personification of health. They are shown together flanked by giant serpents which donate their venom into bowls held by the god and goddess. These images of Aesculapius and Hygeia and the serpents are very close in appearance to later Christian representations of Adam and Eve and the Serpent. Thus, the Pagan chthonic health-bringing serpent is transformed by a different ethos into the personification of deception. Once the cultus of Aesculapius and Hygeia was accepted by Rome, it spread to southern parts of the Empire in the present countries of France, Germany and Switzerland. Important relics of Aesculapius have been found at Bonn, Mainz and Godesberg in Germany; Vichy in France and Basel in Switzerland.

Daniel

The Jewish prophet, Daniel is best remembered for his sojourn amid the lions. He is also the archetypal religious dragonslayer who sees others' gods as evil dragons. According to the *Book of Bel and the Dragon*, the king of Babylon worshipped a great dragon, which Daniel believed was a brass image. "*And the king said unto Daniel, 'Wilt thou say that this is of brass? Lo, he liveth, and eateth and drinketh; thou canst not say that he is no living god: therefor, worship him!' Then said Daniel, 'I will worship the Lord my God. For he is a living god. But give me these, O king, and I shall slay this dragon without sword or staff'. The king said, 'I give thee these'. Then Daniel took pitch, and fat, and hair and did seethe them together, and made lumps thereof: this he put in the dragon's mouth, so the dragon did eat and burst in sunder: and Daniel said 'Lo! These are the gods ye worship'*". Like Herakles, Daniel deals with both lion and dragon, the two alchemical-geomantic opposites developed in later European medieval esoteric symbolism.

Sigurð Fafnirsbane

Dragonslaying stories exist in northern Europe, too. According to the *Volsunga Saga*, Fafnir was the son of Hreidmar, who, in years of gloating over his share of Loki's treasure had gradually been transformed into a dragon. His abode was Gnitaheid, the Glittering Heath. In order to extirpate the dragon Fafnir, the hero Sigurd asked Regin to forge him a powerful sword. Having done so, Regin gave the sword to Sigurd, who immediately broke it on the anvil. A second sword was forged, which also shattered on the anvil. Finally, Sigurd obtained the broken remains of his father Sigmund's sword from his mother, Hiordis. From this, an even better sword was made. It was strong enough for Sigurd to cut the anvil in two, but also so sharp that it cut a skein of wool that floated on a nearby stream. This was a weapon worthy of being called dragonslayer.

After some adventures on the way to fight Fafnir, where Odin in the guise of Feng assured favourable winds, after riding over the mountains, Sigurd came to a desert plain which was the domain of Fafnir. There, he encountered a one-eyed stranger who advised him to dig a trench in the middle of the track used by Fafnir to reach the nearby river. He was to lie in wait there until the dragon passed over him, and then to stab it in the heart from below. This he did, and the dragon was slain.

Sigurd's companion, Regin, then came up, and asked him to roast the dragon's heart for him, so that he could eat it. He cut out the heart and roasted the heart over a fire. When Sigurd tested the meat with his fingers to see whether it was cooked, he was burnt. Immediately placing his thumb in his mouth to

41

cool the burns, he tasted the dragon's blood. Immediately, he gained the power of understanding the song of the carrion-eating birds that had been attracted by the carcass of the dragon.

One bird told him that Regin now planned to kill him and have the dragon's treasure for himself. He should, he was told, kill the old man at once and eat the dragon's heart himself and drink some of its blood. So Sigurd killed Regin with the same sword that slew Fafnir, drank some blood and ate the heart. In the hoard of dragon's treasure he found the *Aegishjalmur*, the 'Helm of Awe', the magic ring Andvaranaut and the Haberk of Gold. The *Aegishjalmur* gained by Sigurd from the dragon's hoard remains one of the most powerful magical sigils in the Northern Tradition, bringing the wearer irresistible powers.

In medieval heraldry the Helm of Awe was known as the Escarbuncle. One of the oldest representations of this heraldic Helm of Awe in English heraldry can be seen in St George's Chapel at Windsor Castle. It is the oldest metal-and-enamel heraldic plate among many others that commemorate past Knights of the Most Noble Order of the Garter. This one is the coat of arms of Ralph, Lord Bassett, which was put in the chapel around the year 1390. It has a shield surmounted by a gilt helm with black mantling with a boar's head crest. Next to the boar's head is a separate roundel of an escarbuncle with a bleeding heart at its centre, which appears to be an allusion to the dragon's heart. As the Escarbuncle, the Helm of Awe was also the badge of the Earl of Sussex, Sir John de Warenne around the same period. These, and other, heraldic emblems demonstrate the continuity of the dragon traditions of earlier ages into medieval times and hence into the present day..

Ragnar Lodbrok

The historic Viking leader, Ragnar Lodbrok, features in a dragonslaying tale, recorded in the *Ragnar Lodbrok Saga*.

Ragnar, son of Sigurd Ring by his first wife, Alfid, acceded to the throne of the Danes when he was only fifteen. When he fought in battle, he was protected by a magic shirt, woven and "nowhere sewn" which prevented injury:

"Wounds will not bleed,
Nor edges bite thee
In the holy garment.
It was consecrated to the gods."

On a Viking expedition to Norway, Ragnar met a seer who possessed a magic mirror in which the warrior saw the image of a beautiful woman. She was Thora, daughter of Earl Herrand of Ostergotland. He asked the wizard who the woman was, and was informed that the lady had suffered a great misfortune. Her father had given her an egg, which she incubated beneath a swan. When it hatched, out came a dragon, which grew rapidly until it coiled itself around the house where Thora lived. Here, she was kept prisoner, for the dragon only permitted a servant to pass, bringing food for Thora and a daily ox for the dragon to eat. To liberate her from her imprisonment, Earl Herrand had offered a reward of a huge amount of gold, and Thora's hand in marriage, to any knight with enough bravery and skill to kill the dragon. None had succeeded, having succumbed to its breath of fire and noxious gases.

Ragnar swore to the wizard that he would be the one who liberated Thora from the coils of the wyrm. Ragnar travelled to Ostergotland, and clothed himself in a special coat of leather and wool, covered all over with pitch. And, as he later sung when he was dying (*Ragnar Lodbrok's Death Song*):

"In arms I reached the Gothic shore,
To work the loathly serpent's death,
I slew the reptile of the heath".....
I pierced the monster's scaly side
With steel, the soldier's wealth and pride".

Pagan tombstone of the Danish period discovered in the churchyard ot St Paul's Cathedral, London. It depicts a version of the battle between the lion and the lindworm.

In memory of the protective clothing he wore on the day he killed the dragon, Ragnar was known by the surname or epithet, Lodbrok, 'Leather Breeches' (or 'Hairy Breeches').

Years later, when Thora was dead, having borne him two sons, Ragnar made a viking expedition to England, where he was defeated in Northumbria, and taken prisoner. King Aella ordered that the Viking should be executed, so Ragnar Lodbrok was thrown into a pit full of venomous snakes. But he remained unharmed, because of his magic dragon-proof clothing. Noticing this, Aella had Ragnar pulled from the pit, and stripped of his clothing before being thrown back in again. Realising now that this was the end, Ragnar uttered his famous death-song, which was memorised by Aella's bard as he sang.

"Grim stings the adder's forked dart;
The vipers nestle in my heart.
But soon, I know, shall Vidar's wand
Fixed in Aella's bosom stand.
My youthful sons with rage will swell,
Hearing how their father fell....
Cease, my strain! I hear a voice
From realms where martial souls rejoice;
I hear the maids of slaughter call,
Who bids me hence to Odin's hall.
High seated in their blest abodes
I soon shall drink the mead of gods.
The hours of life have glided by;
I fall, but laughing shall I die!"

Ragnar, whose fame and love came through dragonslaying, fell by serpents. Soon, his death was avenged by his sons.

Sir Perceval

Sir Perceval, otherwise Percivale or Peredur, is one of the most prolific serpent-slayers of Arthurian legend. For a work of medieval chivalry, Sir Thomas Malory's *Le Morte D'Arthur* is surprisingly short on dragons. In Book XIV, Chapter VI, Sir Perceval encounters a lion attacked by a great serpent. So he goes to the assistance of the lion, which is having the worst of the fight:

"And Sir Percivale thought to help the lion for he was the more natural beast of the two; and therewith he drew a sword, and set his shield afore him, and there he gave the serpent such a buffet that he had a deadly wound".

This not particularly heroic deed is noteworthy because Malory records the belief that the serpent is somehow a less 'natural' animal than a lion, and therefore deserves to be exterminated - an example where 'vermin' and wyrm coincide. However, symbolically, the battle of the lion and the dragon represents the confrontation of opposites in both Western alchemy and locational geomancy, and as such, it is not insignificant.

In *Peredur the Son of Evrawc*, in the *Mabinogion*, Peredur (Perceval) kills a serpent in a desert, the traditional dwelling-place of old lindwurms. Before the feat, Peredur's sword was broken and reunited. Like that of Sigmund that Sigurd used to kill the gold-guarding dragon, Fafnir. Peredur *"heard that there was a serpent that lay upon a gold ring, and suffered none to inhabit the country for seven miles around"*. Peredur came to the place, and *"angrily, furiously, and desperately fought he with the serpent; and at last, he killed it, and took away the ring"*.

Later, Peredur encounters a black man called the Black Oppressor. He fights and defeats him, then finds that he has only one eye, which he lost in combat with the Black Serpent of the cairn on the Mound of Mourning. In this cairn lives the serpent, which has a magic stone on its tail. Whichever man can hold the stone in his hand may have as much gold as he wishes for. Travelling to the place, Peredur comes to the Palace of the Sons of the King of Tortures, where, every day, one of the inhabitants is slain by the Addanc of the Lake that lives in a cave nearby.

Peredur offers to help the inhabitants in their quest to slay the Addanc. He meets a fair lady seated on a mound, who tells him that "*He has a cave, and at the entrance of the cave is a stone pillar, and he sees everyone that enters, and none see him; and from behind the pillar he slays every one with a poisonous dart*". The lady offers him a stone of invisibility if he should love her above all women. "*I will, by my troth*" swears Peredur. After some other adventures, Peredur reaches the Addanc's cave, taking the magic stone in his left hand, and his lance in the right. Invisible, he impales the Addanc on his lance, cuts off its head and gives it to three young men who had arrived.

Later, Peredur reaches the Mound of Mourning where the Black Serpent of the Carn dwells. An army of three hundred men surrounds the serpent's lair, keeping it in until it dies of natural causes. Peredur defeats two hundred warriors in two days, and the other hundred surrender to him and do homage. Peredur goes alone to fight the serpent, and kills it without the assistance of the hundred men-at-arms. He pays off the men with the serpent's treasure.

In another great Arthurian text, *The High History of the Holy Grail*, Perceval encounters "*a serpent, great and evil-favoured that had issued from a hole in a mountain*". Later, he kills another serpent that had terrified a damsel. This one is nearer to the classical dragon, for it comes towards Perceval with "*jaws yawning*" and "*casteth forth fire and flame in great plenty*". He employs the same technique with which he overcame the fire-wielding Knight of the Dragon who had killed Alein of Escavalon on the Island of Elephants. Sir Perceval rams his sword directly down its gullet. When he cuts

Illustrations from Olaus Magnus's 16th century works showing the struggles between kings and dragons or serpents.

48

open this dragon, he finds a chain and key, red-hot from the flames within the beast.

Kíng Lluðð ab Belí

The Story of Llys and Llyvelys in the *Mabinogion* tells of three plagues that befall Britain. The first was the arrival of hostile immigrants, a race called the Coranians, perhaps the Celtic Coritani tribe, whose "*coin was fairy money*". The second was a shriek which came on every May Eve, over every hearth in the Island of Great Britain. This went through the people's hearts, and terrified everyone so much that the men lost their vigour, pregnant women miscarried, young men and women went insane, and the animals, trees, land and waters, were rendered barren. The third plague affected the king's household. However much food was stored, even if a year's provisions, then after the first meal, there was none left.

The effect of these three plagues was to bring ruin upon the British nation. King Lludd took counsel with his brother, Llevelys, King of France. Llevelys gave Lludd some insects to breed, so that he might use biological warfare against the Coranians. He was to call all the Coranians together with the Britons for a conference, then exterminate them with an insect poison that would not kill Britons, but was lethal to Coranians. The second plague, Lelvelys told him, was caused by a dragon, with which another dragon of a foreign race was fighting, and attempting to overcome, "*And therefore does your dragon make a fearful outcry*". The third plague was caused by a thieving giant, whom Lludd could overcome in single combat if he could keep awake until he entered the royal hall.

To end the second plague, King Levelys advised King Lludd to: "*cause the Island to be measured in its length and breadth, and in the place where thou dost find the exact central point, there cause a pit to be dug, and cause a cauldron full of the best mead that can be made to be put in the pit, with a covering of*

49

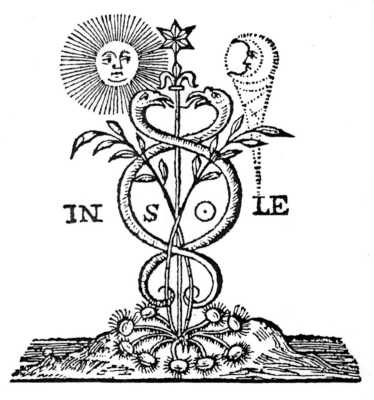

The opposing serpents of the caduceus linking the earthly with the celestial. Sixteenth-century engraving.

satin over the face of the cauldron. And then, in thine own person do thou remain there watching, and thou wilt see the dragons fighting in the form of terrific animals. And at length they will take the form of dragons in the air. And, last of all, after wearying themselves with fierce and furious fighting, they will fall in the form of two pigs upon the covering, they will sink in, and the covering with them, and they will draw it down to the very bottom of the cauldron. And they will drink up the whole of the mead; and after that they will sleep."

Lludd returned home across the Channel, and the royal surveyors were sent out to measure the island and determine the 'central point', the *omphalos* of Great Britain. They found it was at Rhydychen, where the foursquare city of Oxford now stands. There, they dug the pit at the point which is now the middle of the Carfax crossroads at the centre of Oxford. In the pit, they set up a cauldron and filled it with the best mead that could be made, and over it the satin sheet prescribed by Llevelys. Lludd ab Beli sat watching on May Eve, and the dragons came to fight. When they were weary, they fell down into the cauldron, drank the mead and slept.

Lludd folded the satin cover around the beasts, and his men transported them to "*a kistvaen, in the strongest place*" of Britain, called Dinas Ffaraon, afterwards called Dinas Emreis (modernly, Dinas Emrys). Dinas Emrys is a natural wooded hill overlooking Llyn Dinas in Snowdonia between Beddgelert and Capel Curig. An Iron Age hillfort used continuously until the Middle Ages, Dinas Emrys still has the remains of the castle mound and some walls of a twelfth-century keep.

At Dinas Emrys, the continuing battles underground of the trapped dragons, centuries later, led to the discovery of Merlin, recounted in the writings of, among others, Nennius and Geoffrey of Monmouth. "*At the head of the Snowdon Mountains*", writes Giraldus Cambrensis, "*not far from the source of the Conwy, which flows from this region towards the north, stands Dinas Emrys; that is, the promontory of*

51

Ambrosius, where Merlin, sitting on a rock, prophesied to Vortigern". Nennius tells us that King Vortigern, having been defeated, retreated into Snowdonia, and chose Dinas Emrys as a place to build a castle. However, the building could not be made to stand, falling down each night. His wizards advised him that the tower would not stand unless a fatherless child was used as a foundation-sacrifice. Vortigern's men sought such a child, and found some boys taunting another that he was a fatherless bastard. They brought the boy to Vortigern, so that he could be sacrificed. He was Merlin, who, having local knowledge, told them that he knew why the tower was overthrown each night. He was spared, and Vortigern's military engineers dug deep beneath the foundations, where they discovered the dragons buried there by Lludd ab Beli centuries earlier.

When the engineers dug up the dragons, one red and one white, they awoke and began to fight. The white at first was winning, but finally, the red one prevailed and expelled his opponent. Merlin then gave his famous rambling *Prophecy*, that the white dragon represented the Anglo-Saxons, and the red, the Britons. Vortigern then built the fortress, and when he left finally, took the soothsaying youth with him as his advisor. Later, of course, Merlin was instrumental in obtaining the conception of Arthur, and the subsequent elevation of Arthur to the throne of Britain. Vortigern re-named Dinas Ffareon as Dinas Emrys, after the Welsh name of Merlinus Ambrosius, Merddyn Emrys. Thus the dragon is central in the primary concerns of the Matter of Britain.

Chapter 3

Dragons in Folk Tales and Oral History

Some European Local Dragonslayers

Local traditions all over Europe tell of heroes who rid their localities of pestilential dragons. There are hundreds of different stories, many of which have common elements. Below are some of the more complete or striking secular serpent- and dragonslaying tales, mostly from England. Religious dragonslayers are dealt with in a later chapter.

John Lambton

The story of the Lambton Worm is localised by the River Wear in north-eastern England. At an indeterminate time in the Middle Ages, John Lambton, the young heir of the Northumbrian Lambton family was fishing in the River Wear near Washington (the original one in northern England). It was a Sunday, perhaps even Easter Sunday, upon which in the medieval Christian tradition it was forbidden to work. Having caught nothing, the young lord swore loudly at passers-by on their way to church. Finally, though, he made a catch, and appeared to have caught something large. After a great struggle, he pulled not a fine salmon but an insignificant but weird-looking worm from the river. Angered that he had not caught a fish worth eating, he was enraged, and tossed the

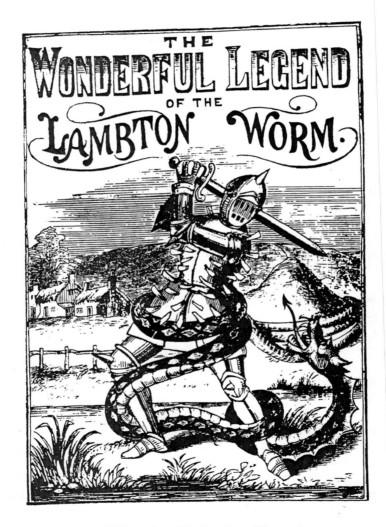

An 1875 version of the Lambton Worm story.

54

worm down a well nearby. He went back to the river, and tried again. Another passer-by stopped and asked him whether he had caught anything. Lambon replied, "Truly, I think I've caught the Devil", and showed the passer-by the worm in the well. He looked at it and thought it was a newt or salamander, except that it had nine holes on either side of its mouth. Whatever it was, he said, no good would come of it.

Soon afterwards, John Lambton decided to join the Knights of St John of Jerusalem and go to defend the Christian island of Rhodes against the Turks. While he was away fighting against militant Islam, the worm remained in the well, growing so large that it left its trap and returned to the River Wear. There it lay, coiled around a rock during daytime. At night, it came out and slept coiled nine or ten times around a small artificial knoll called Worm Hill in the parish of North Biddick on the north bank of the River Wear. To feed, it rampaged around the district, eating lambs and suckling on cows. Having wiped out the livestock to the north of the river, the worm came south and entered Lord Lambton's estate. Lambton consulted his staff, and they decided to make a stone trough to feed the worm. Each day at a certain time, they filled the trough with milk from nine cows, and the worm came to drink it. If the portion were not exactly nine cows' worth, then the worm would coil around trees and tear them from the earth in rage. Clearly, this was an unsatisfactory state of affairs, and many knights errant attempted to kill the monster, but without success, and many lost their lives in the attempt. The worm continued to grow in size, and appeared invincible because it had the power to reassemble itself when it was cut in two.

After seven years, John Lambton came home from the Mediterranean. Instead of the prosperous estate he had left, he found a wasteland, ravaged by the monstrous and invincible worm. His father told him what had happened, and John felt remorse for his disastrous mistake. Vowing to undo the disaster, he went to consult a local wise woman for the means to defeat the beast. She advised him to have a new suit of armour made, which should be studded all over with sharp blades. Then he should go to the island when the worm was away, and await it there. Before it arrived, he should swear that if he were successful in killing the worm, he would sacrifice the first living thing that he met afterwards in thanksgiving.

Lambton had his armourer make the special armour, and did as the wise woman advised. Before leaving to fight the worm, he warned his father that when he sounded three calls on his horn, his father should let loose his favourite hound. He would then kill the dog as the thanksgiving sacrifice. John Lambton went to the rock, and swore the oath. The worm appeared, and coiled itself around the gallant knight. The blades cut into its body, and it fell, wounded. With his sword, Lambton cut the worm into pieces, and they were swept away by the river's current. Returning home successful, he blew three blasts on his horn, but his father, overjoyed that his son was safe and well, ran to greet him without first loosing the hound. Of course, no-one would kill his own father as a sacrifice, but for breaking his solemn vow, John Lambton brought a curse upon the family that for nine generations no Lord of Lambton would die in his bed.

Worm Well, where the Lambton Worm spent its early life, is close to Worm Hill, on the south bank of the Wear. In former times, it was a wishing well resorted to by local people on Midsummer Eve. In an attempt to generate tourism in the 1970s, another well was made by Washington Development Corporation because the original well was thought to be too close to the river-bank and therefore a hazard. So engineers located the underground stream that fed the original well and diverted it to make a new one.

The Lambton Worm is celebrated in a number of folksongs. The song mentioned above was popularised in a pantomime performed at the Old Tyne Theatre in Newcastle in 1867.

"One Sunday morning Lambton went a-fishing in the Wear:
And catched a fish upon his hook he thought lenk't very queer.
But whatt'n a kind of fish it was young Lambton couldn't tell -
He wanted fish to carry home, so he hoyed it in a well.

Whisht' lads, hold your gobs, and I'll tell you all an awful story,
Whisht' lads, hold your gobs, and I'll tell you all about the worm.

Now Lambton felt inclined to gan, and fight in foreign wars,
He joined a troop of knights that cared for neither wounds nor scars,
And off he went to Palestine where queer things him befell,
And very soon forgot about the queer worm in the well.

Whisht' lads, hold your gobs, and I'll tell you all an awful story,
Whisht' lads, hold your gobs, and I'll tell you all about the worm.

But the worm got fat and growed and growed, and growed an
*   awful size,*
With great big teeth and great big gob, and great big googly eyes.
And when at nights he crawled about to pick up bits o' news,
If he felt dry upon the road, he milked a dozen cows.

Whisht' lads, hold your gobs, and I'll tell you all an awful story,
Whisht' lads, hold your gobs, and I'll tell you all about the worm.

This fearful worm would often feed on calves and lambs and sheep,
And swallow little bairns alive when they laid down to sleep.
And when he'd eaten all the cud and he had had his fill,
He crawled away and lapped his tail ten times round Pensher Hill.

Whisht' lads, hold your gobs, and I'll tell you all an awful story,
Whisht' lads, hold your gobs, and I'll tell you all about the worm.

The news of this most awful worm and his queer gannins on,
Soon crossed the seas and got to the ears of brave and bold Sir John.
So home he came and catched the beast and cut him in two halves,
And that soon stopped his eating bairns and sheep and lambs and
*   calves.*

Whisht' lads, hold your gobs, and I'll tell you all an awful story,
Whisht' lads, hold your gobs, and I'll tell you all about the worm.

Mars fighting the dragon. From the emblems of Lambsprinck, Tractatus de lapide Phiosoforum (written in German in the 15th century, Published 17th century).

58

So now you know how all the folks on both sides of the Wear
Lost lots of sheep and lots of sleep and lived in mortal fear.
So let's have one to brave Sir John that kept the bairns frae harm,
Saved cows and calves by making halves of the famous Lambton
    Worm.

Now, lads, I'll hold my gob, that's all as knows about the story
Of Sir John's clever job with the awful Lambton Worm."

Peter Loschy

A similar tale is told at Nunnington. In the parish of
Stonegrave, the Nunnington Dragon was slain by Peter
Loschy, who wore a suit of armour studded with blades.
Accompanied by his dog, Loschy went to fight the dragon,
which coiled around him. But this constrictor was soon cut in
pieces by the blades and Loschy's sword.

Like the Lambton Worm, this dragon had the power of
regeneration, for, as soon as it was cut asunder, it reconnected
itself and was whole again. But then Peter Loschy's dog
carried off part of the dragon, and took it to a hill about a mile
away. As Loschy cut up the dragon, so the dog carried off the
pieces to the hill. Finally, only the head was left. But then the
dog went too close, the dragon-venom fell on it, and it was
poisoned.

Sir John Conyers

Another northern English dragon tale concerns the local hero
Sir John Conyers who killed the Sockburn Worm. According to
Bowes's Manuscript in the British Library, the beast was
"monstrous and poisonous vermin, wyvern, ask or werme,
which had 0overthrown and devoured many people in fight: for
that the scent of the poison was so strong that no person might
abide it. And by the providence of the Almighty God, the said

59

John Conyers, Knight, overthrew the said monster and slew it....That place where this great serpent lay was called Graystone, and this John lyeth buried in Sockburne church....".

According to some traditions, Sir John Conyers wore a suit of armour studded with razor-sharp blades, like those of Sir John Lambton and Peter Loschy. The magic weapon Conyers used was a falchion, a type of sword with a broad blade about 75 cm in length. It is still in existence, and can be dated as 13th century work. The cross of the sword bears dragons with foliated tails. This weapon was the title deed of the manor, and had to be used when the Lord of the Manor met each new Bishop of Durham at his entry into the diocese in the middle of Neasham Ford or on Croft Bridge.

The ceremony, which, after having lapsed, has been restored, includes the address by the Lord of the Manor:

> *"My Lord Bishop, I here present you with the falchion wherewith the champion Conyers slew the worm, dragon or fiery flying serpent, which destroyed man, woman and child; in memory of which, the King then reigning gave him the manor of Sockburn, to hold by this tenure, that upon the first entrance every bishop into the county this falchion should be presented".*

The new bishop takes the offered sword, then returns it to the Lord of the Manor, with a speech that wishes health and prosperity to him and the manor.

The falchion is kept in the cathedral treasury at Durham. It is one of the few dragon-slaying weapons still preserved for public view.

Guy, Earl of Warwick

Best known for killing the terrible Dun Cow of Dunsmore Heath, Guy of Warwick also slew the dragon at Longwitton in Northumberland. The *Legend of Sir Guy* in Thomas Percy's *Reliques* tell us:

> *"A dragon in Northumberland*
> *I also did in fight destroye,*
> *Which did both beast and man opresse,*
> *And all the countrye sore annoye".*

Edmund Spenser, in his *Faerie Queene* also recounts the legend. Three wells near Longwitton Hall are the location for Earl Guy's exploit. The dragon was usually invisible, but Guy ordered it to appear and remain visible. It did, and they fought, but each time it was wounded, it would put its tail down a well, and thereby renew its vigour. Finally, Guy man-ouvered himself between the dragon and the wells, and was able to pierce it through the heart and finish it off.

Like the well of the Lambton Worm, the Longwitton Dragon Wells are holy wells with curative properties, being resorted to at Midsummer for festive games, eating gingerbread and drinking the empowering waters.

Piers Shonks

Piers Shonks, a twenty-three feet tall giant, lived under an oak tree on an island in Shonks's Moat in Peppsall Field at Brent Pelham in Hertfordshire. He was a benevolent figure, having rid the area of demons. One day, whilst out hunting with his three winged hounds, Piers Shonks encountered a terrible dragon, which, according to the Reverend W. Wigram, was *"kennelled under a yew tree which stood between two fields....and the stile of the pathway which crossed them was set up in the stemm of this tree when it was split open, as such*

61

PIERS SHONKES SLAYS THE PELHAM DRAGON.

*Piers Shonks slays the Pelham Dragon, from Nigel Pennick's
unpublished (and lost) work, The Secret Arrow: Archery and Geomancy
in the Western Tradition, 1975.*

trees do, with old age." Shonks shot the dragon with an arrow, and it died. Upon hearing of this outrage, the Devil swore that he would possess the soul of Piers Shonks when he died, whether he were buried inside or outside the church.

Years later, when he was on his death-bed, Piers shot a last arrow to determine the site of his grave. This form of divination is also ascribed to other English rustic heroes like Robin Hood and Jack O'Legs. Piers's arrow was directed towards the church of St Mary the Virgin of Brent Pelham. It passed through a window on the south side and embedded itself in the north wall. The hero was buried in that wall, neither inside nor outside the church, thereby outwitting the Devil.

Like grave-divination by arrow, tales of burial in a wall to thwart the Devil are told elsewhere, at places including Tolleshunt D'Arcy and Tolleshunt Knights in Essex, and Tremeirchion in north Wales, where, respectively a watchman, a knight and a wizard were saved from damnation by the ploy.

The tomb-slab of Piers Shonks was noted by John Weever in his *Funeral Monuments of Great Britain* (London, 1631): *"In the North Wall of this Church lyeth an antient Monument of Stone, wherein a Man is figur'd, and about him an Eagle, a Lyon and a Bull, all having wings...under the Feet of the Man is the Cross Fleurie, and under the Cross a Serpent."* The 'serpent' described by Weever is not a snake but a Wyvern whose fiery breath attacks a floreated equal-armed cross. Painted over the tomb is the epitaph, said to have been composed by the Reverend Raphael Keen who died in 1614:

"O Piers Shonks,
Who Died, Anno 1086.
Nothing of Cadmus nor St George, those names
Of great renown, survives them but their fames;
Time was so sharp set as to make no bones
Of theirs, nor of their monumental stones.

The tomb-slab of Piers Shonks in Brent Palham church, Hertfordshire, England.

64

But Shonke one serpent kills, t'other defies
And in this wall as in a fortress lies."

There is also an alternative epitaph of Piers Shonks recorded by W. B Gerish at the beginning of the twentieth century:

"Cadmus his fame, St George his fame alone,
Their tombs and ashes all are gone:
But Shonks who valiantly the serpent wounded
In spite of Satan, here he lies entombed."

More of More Hall

The Wantley Dragon of Wharncliffe Chase, to the north of Sheffield, is told of in a 1685 ballad recorded in Percy's *Reliques*:

"Old stories tell how Hercules
A dragon slew at Lerna,
With seven heads and fourteen eyes,
To see and well discern-a.
But he had a club, this dragon to drub,
Or he had ne'er done it, I warrant ye:
But More of More-Hall, with nothing at all,
He slew the Dragon of Wantley."

The dragon of Wantley is among those local dragon-slaying stories that are short on facts. It has been suggested that the ballad actually recounts an attack by brigands upon the area in 1591, who killed animals and committed other acts of violence. When the original incidents are forgotten, satirical or symbolic accounts can be taken literally, and hence another dragon legend came into being. But perhaps the dragonslaying association of the More family is older than 1591, as the More coat-of-arms bears a green dragon.

The Wantley Dragon, from a 17th century Yorkshire broadsheet.

66

Central and Southern European Dragonslayers

Herzog Karast

Klagenfurt in Austria has its local hero, Herzog Karast, who killed a lindwurm that infested a fen near the place where the city now stands. The local people lived in the hills around, and ventured there only when their livestock strayed into the area. Then, when they went looking for their beasts, they, too, fell prey to the voracious lindwurm. To eliminate the lindwurm, the duke built a strong tower close to the fen, and recruited men-at-arms to defend it. They chained up a fat bullock as bait to lure the lindwurm from its lair, using a chain covered with spikes. The lindwurm was impaled and done to death by the duke and his men-at-arms with spiked clubs. A magnificent fountain, the *Lindwurmbrunnen* in the Neuen Platz, commemorates the dragonslaying. It was made in 1590, its head being based on a lindwurm's skull found at Klagenfurt in 1335, and preserved in the city museum. According to modern paleontology, the lindwurm skull is that of an extinct woolly rhinoceros.

St Beatus

A British missionary of the Celtic Church is remembered at a cave overlooking the Lake of Thun near Interlaken in Switzerland. Although his name means 'Blessed' in Latin, Beatus was a real man. He is best remembered, however, for driving out a dragon. Sent to preach Christianity, and accompanied by his companion, Justus, Beatus travelled through what is now Switzerland. One day, they met some shepherds near the settlement of Sundlauenen on the Wendel Lake (now the Lake of Thun). They were told that everyone there lived in constant fear of a terrible dragon, which lived in

*St Beatus, his assistant and attendant ravens chase away the dragon
from St Beatushöle by the Lake of Thun near interlaken, Switzerland.
Engraving by Urs Graf from Daniel Agricola's Das Leben des heiligen
Bychtigers und Einsiedlers Sant Batten, (Solothurn, 1511).*

68

a cave. The missionaries decided to attack the dragon, and went immediately to the cave. There, they saw the dragon, which breathed fire at Beatus. He immediately raised his cross towards the beast, and invoked the Holy Trinity. The dragon was overcome by the magical formula, and fell down the cliffside into the lake, which boiled where the dragon sank. Beatus and Justus then occupied the cave, which became the centre for their missionary activities in the region. Many years later, the oral legends and the other activities of Beatus were collected together by Daniel Agricola, a Franciscan monk from Basel. They were published in his book, *Das Leben des heiligen Bychtigers und Einsidlers Sant Batten* (1511), illustrated by Urs Graf, the famed engraver from Solothurn, whose work is reproduced here.

The Lindwurm of Brno

In former times, a stuffed 'lindwurm' hung in an arched passage that led to the Town Hall in Brinn (now Brno, Czech Republic). According to legend, this lindwurm once plagued the region, devouring livestock and children. The knight who slew it employed a calf's skin which he filled with quicklime and left as bait at the entrance to the lindwurm's cave. Having swallowed the calf whole, as the result of the quicklime the lindwurm became so thirsty that it drank so much that it burst open and died.

The Knights of Rhodes

In 1342, the Knights of St John on the island of Rhodes, in the Mediterranean, of whom Sir John Lambton was said to have been a member, were forbidden by their Grand Master to attempt to kill a huge reptile, said to be a crocodile, that lived in a marsh. Several knights had tried to kill it, but had themselves been slain. Then, having trained two bulldogs to attack the underbelly of a dummy, the knight Dieudonné de

69

Gozon set about the beast and killed it. The head of the 'dragon' was preserved, and even after the island fell to Turkish troops in 1623, it remained there.

Esoteric Dragonalia

Dragon Numerology

The number nine appears specifically in several northern British dragon legends. The Lambton Worm coiled around its hill nine times; it had nine spiracles or gill-like holes in each side of its head, and it demanded the milk of nine cows at each mealtime. Similarly, the Hutton Rudby dragon coiled nine times around the hill called Sexhowe, and demanded the milk of nine cows. In Scotland, the Strathmartin dragon had more substantial fare, for it ate nine maidens.

The Anglo-Saxon *Nigon Wyrta Galdor* ('Nine Herbs Charm') is a magical medical formula that invokes the power of Woden for healing infected wounds. The physician prepares a remedy consisting of nine 'herbs' that are macerated and made into an ointment by addition of water, beaten egg, apple juice and ashes. As each 'herb' is added in turn, it is praised and encouraged in its duty by formulae. After the addition of six herbs, the spirit of the infection is envisaged as a wyrm sneaking towards the patient:

> *"A wyrm came crawling, it ripped a man's flesh. Then Woden took nine glory-twigs; he hit the adder, so it flew apart into nine".*

Here, Woden is seen as a magical wyrm-slayer who heals by destroying the agent of illness. This motif appeared later in the medieval dragon-pageants, where St George was seen as the destroyer of pestilence in the form of the dragon. Similarly, St

1921 Soviet propaganda poster depicting the communist leader Leon Trotsky as St George slayig the top-hatted serpent of 'Counter-Revolution'.

71

Michael, as healing saint and dragon-slayer, partook of some of the essence of Woden.

Dragons and Serpents in Political Propaganda

The immediately-recognisable image of St George and the Dragon has been used in everything from advertising to political propaganda. A Russian revolutionary poster from around 1920 shows the Communist leader, Leon Trotsky as St George. Mounted on a white charger, defended by a shield with a red star containing the hammer-and sickle emblem, Trotsky spears the top-hatted serpent-dragon of Counter-Revolution. On the other side, the Russian fascists, too, employed the serpent-slayer as a symbol of the destruction of their enemies. The May 1937 cover of the Russian national socialist journal, *Natsiya*, published in exile in China, shows a Russian worker, hammer in hand like Thor, about to smash the head of a serpent labelled 'Judocommunism'.

Chapter 4

The Military Dragon

Ancient European Military Insignia

From early times, the dragon has had a military connection. Greek mythology tells how Cadmus, founder of Thebes, killed a dragon and sowed its teeth into the ground like seeds. From each tooth grew a fully-armed man, each a son of the dragon. Some of the earliest references to dragons as human artifacts are to military flags or banners in the form of dragons. Flags appear to have originated in the Pagan tradition as guardian images of the goddesses and gods flown above ships, buildings or armies. In Classical times, Greek ships had consecrated figureheads and flags that protected those who voyaged within them. The ships of Boeotia had Cadmus as their spiritual protector, represented with a dragon in his hand as founder of the city of Thebes. Shields bearing apotropaic devices were also carried by Greek warriors. In his *Seven Against Thebes*, the playwright Aeschylus described the shields of the seven generals of the army of Adrastus that fought against Thebes. The fourth, Hippomedon, had a shield bearing

> "A *Typhaeus* huge,
> Disgorging from his foul enfoundered jaws,
> In fierce effusion wreaths of dusky smoke,
> Signal of kindling flames; its bending verge
> With folds of twisted serpents bordered round..."

Shields in the National Museum of Crete in Iraklion, stolen from the Dictaean Cave on the edge of the Lassithi Plateau, the birthplace and most holy shrine of Zeus, bear animal and eagles' heads that protrude threateningly from the boss. The Celts, too, carried battle-horns with dragon-like jaws with them into combat to terrify the enemy by their sound and fearsome appearance.

The flying dragon in western Europe seems to have been spread by the Roman Empire, for wind-socks or kites in the form of dragons were used as military standards by units of the Roman Army. It seems that this dragon battle-standard was not of Roman origin, however, as they had adopted it from Parthian, Scythian and Dacian custom. In the Parthian army, a dragon banner flew over each batallion of one thousand men. The dragon was encountered by the Roman military in their wars against the Scythians and Dacians. An early representation of this is on the triumphal column of Trajan at Rome, set up in the year 113 CE to commemorate that Emperor's victories over the enemies of Rome. Among the carvings on the column are scenes showing the Dacian army with dragon standards borne before or flying above it. Around the year 175 CE, the Roman army itself adopted the dragon as a standard, which by the third century denoted a cohort. In the late Western Roman Empire, the standard-bearer of a cohort was called a *draconarius* (dragon-man). According to the writer Vegetius (late 4th century CE), "*The primary sign of the whole legion is an eagle, carried by the aquilifer (eagle-carrier). Dragons, however, are carried into the fray by the draconarii of each cohort*".

The Genesis of the Welsh Dragon

When the Roman Empire split into two parts, the Emperors of the East, ruling from Constantinople, adopted the dragon banner called the draconteion as their emblem. When the eastern Emperor, Constantius II, arrived at Rome, Ammianus

Marcellinus tells us, he was surrounded by dragons, woven from purple thread and flying on the bejewelled golden tips of spears. The dragons were in the form of windsocks, having wide mouths that caught the breezes and hissed as if aroused to anger. In the year 458 CE, Sidonius wrote a panegyric to the Emperor Majorianus, who had recently fought Vandal forces. He tells how the embroidered dragon flashes amid the armies, its throat swelling with the zephyrs as the wind makes the fabric ripple. To this day, kites are called the words for 'dragon' in various languages, including Scottish, where a kite is a Dragon. In the eastern Empire, the *draconteion* was used until the tenth century as a military banner.

When Britain was collapsing in the early fifth century, the dragon of the cohorts must have been a welcome sight to beleaguered Romano-British citizens. When the legions were withdrawn, most of the local units left would have been of cohort strength or less, making the dragon the symbol of what was left of the old order. Thus, in the modern Welsh language, words connected with the dragon appear to originate in Roman military usage, Christian symbolism and descriptions of celestial phenomena. Thus, *draig* is Welsh for 'dragon', but also 'warrior', 'leader', 'chieftain' and 'prince'. It can also mean lightning that flashes without thunder, sheet lightning and a meteorite. Another meaning of *dragon* is the Christian Devil. In Welsh, *dragon* can mean 'warrior', 'leader', 'chieftain', 'prince' or 'military power'. *Dragonwys* means 'brave', 'ferocious' and also 'commanders' or 'heroes'.

In early Welsh literature, we can find many references to 'dragons'. The Bard Aneirin, in his *Gododdin*, which has been dated to the late 6th century CE, refers to his patron, Mynyddog Mwynfawr with the compliment, 'dragon'. Describing the Battle of Catraeth, Aneirin calls Gwernabwy mab Gwën a 'dragon'. Taliesin, the 'Primary Bard of Britain' also uses the epithet 'dragon' to describe military leaders. In his poem about Gwallawc, Taliesin recalls how the warriors lamented the death of their 'dragon'. Also, Taliesin describes

Owain ap Urien as *Owain ben draic,* 'Owen, the Chief Dragon', clearly a title which we recognise from Arthurian legend in the name of King Arthur's father, Uther Pendragon. An eleventh century text in the Welsh *Red book of Hergest* refers to Gruffudd ap Llywelyn, a successor of Maglocunus on Anglesey, as "draic o wyned", 'Dragon of Gwynedd'. The Bard Cynddelw Brydydd Mawr (The Great Poet), who flourished between the years 1155 and 1200, wrote a praise-poem for Owain Gwynedd, the 'fearless shepherd of Britain', which begins, "*I praise a patron, high-hearted in battle*", goes on to tell of "*Dragons encountered, rulers of Rome in combat with the Dragon of the East, Far Western Dragon, the best was his....*"

Although the dragon appears first as the emblem or epithet of the Britons' military leader, in recent times it has become the symbol of the Welsh nation. But in early literature it is clear that the idea of ethnic nations or peoples was different from that which underlies modern nationalism, being focussed in the feudal manner upon personal loyalty to a king or lord. The story of the discovery and prophecies of Merlin, which were recorded in *Historia Brittonum*, ascribed to the scholar Nennius, but dating from around the year 800 CE, are often quoted now as referring to the Welsh nation. By the time *Historia Brittonum* was compiled, the red dragon had come to stand for the British (Welsh) leader and the white dragon for the Anglo-Saxon (English) leader. It was to the king or lord, the 'dragon', that loyalty was due, not to the modern concept of the nation symbolised by a flag or emblem.

The medieval writer, Robert of Gloucester, stated that King Arthur rode into battle "*With helm of gold on his head......The form of a dragon hereon was ycast*". Perhaps this was a memory of the old Roman parade armour, often worn in battle by barbarian noblemen. The most significant promoter of the Welsh dragon was Geoffrey of Monmouth, whose mythologised history of the kings of Britain was the best-seller of his time. Although he has been dismissed as a charlatan who invented everything, he claimed that his work was based upon old

76

Welsh books. As these no longer exist, if they ever did, it is impossible to determine the historical accuracy of what he records.

Significant to the Welsh dragon story is the passage where a comet appears at the accession of Uther Pendragon to the British throne, a star of great magnitude and brilliance, with a beam shining from it. Uther Pendragon asks the wizard Merlin what this portent means, and then decides to make two golden dragons in the likeness of the comet. One of them he gives to the cathedral of Winchester, and keeps the second as a personal battle-standard. Jeremy Harte argues that Geoffrey of Monmouth's mention of Winchester is a memory not of the old Roman city in southern Britain before the Saxon conquest, but of the standard of Wessex at the erstwhile capital of England.

Medieval Military Dragons

The dragon was recognised widely in early medieval Europe as a military emblem, and in England it was considered to be an English symbol. The medieval chronicler Henry of Huntingdon records how in the year 752 CE, a battle was fought at Burford between the forces of Wessex and Mercia. The Wessex forces were headed by the alderman Edelhun, "*who bore the king's ensign in a golden dragon*".

Medieval standard-bearers were the best fighters in the army, and Edelhun distinguished himself by killing the Mercian standard-bearer. Later, in 1016, in the wars between the English under King Edmund Ironside and the Danes under King Canute, Henry of Huntingdon tells us that "*the valour of King Edmund was conspicuous, who, seeing the Danes fighting with more than usual vigour, left his royal station....between the Dragon and the Standard, and hastened to the front line*". From the eighth century at the latest, the dragon was an English royal sign.

During the tenth century, the Saxons of mainland Europe also carried dragon standards into battle. Early in the eleventh century, the *Saga of St Olav* tells us how the Christian King Olav of Norway *"had a white standard, and on it was a dragon"*. The Bayeux Tapestry, made by English women embroiderers around 1077, tells the story of the Norman victory at the Battle of Hastings in 1066. It shows two dragon standards, one fallen on the ground, and the other held aloft by a spear through its jaws.

More generally, the dragon was a universal symbol of kingship that was projected back upon the past. A ninth-century manuscript at St Gall in Switzerland ostensibly depicting the Jewish hero King David riding into battle, shows a dragon standard. Held aloft on a pole, the dragon breathes fire, an early record of the use of pitch and tar to add to the terrifying aspect of the military dragon. Of course, the ancient Israelites never used the dragon, but the idea of historical accuracy was unknown or unimportant to early medieval monks.

Despite the widespread use of the dragon standard by northern European forces, in the twelfth century it was still remembered that the dragon was a Roman sign. The French romance of *Athis et Prophilias* tells how the dragon was still a formidable symbol: *"The Romans used to carry this; it makes us very much to be feared"*.

Continuing Anglo-Saxon tradition, several English kings used the dragon. King Richard I Lionheart and King John both had dragon wind-socks in the Roman manner as their standards. Richard I set up his golden-headed dragon at Messina in 1190 and took it with him to the Holy Land on his crusade against Islam. Following the Northern Tradition, Richard's ship bore a dragon's head. His brother, King John, used the dragon against the French king. When the forces of King Louis VIII invaded in 1216, John, who was at Winchester, *"laid down his dragon and fled"*.

At the same time in mainland Europe, the Holy Roman Emperor, Otto IV, used an 'inflatable' dragon at the Battle of Bouvines in 1214. The English King Henry III adopted the red dragon in 1244, ordering that "*a dragon in the form of a standard*" be made, "*of red silk, sparkling all over with gold, the tongue...made to resemble burning fire, and appear to be moving continually, and the eyes of sapphires or other suitable stones*". It was set up first in Westminster Abbey. In 1245 and again in 1257, the royal dragon was used by the English army fighting against the Welsh, when the king "*unfurled his royal standard, which was the dragon, who knows not how to pardon, and so he threatened the total destruction of Wales*". In 1264, King Henry III used the dragon as his battle-flag at the Battle of Lewes during the Barons' War against the rebel forces of Simon de Montfort. Peter of Langtoffe, in *The Chronicle of Robert of Brunne*, tells how at the Battle of Lewes, "*The king schewed forth his schild his Dragon full austere*". Matthew of Westminster notes that "*the king's place was between the dragon and the standard*", so the dragon was not the standard itself, but the king's personal emblem in Roman style.

English heralry in this period used the wyvern or dragon. Roger de Quincey, Earl of Winchester, had a wyvern crest to his helm, as did Thomas, Earl of Lancaster in 1301. At the Battle of Crécy in 1346, the English king, Edward III, displayed a standard "*with a dragon of red silk adorned and beaten with very broad and fair lilies of gold*". When in 1401, the Welsh prince Owain Glyndwr claimed to be the rightful ruler of the British, he assumed the dragon standard ascribed to King Arthur, and raised it at Caernarfon in rebellion against English rule.

The first Tudor king, Henry VII, despite his Welshness, used a standard of St George in his battles for the English throne. Once he had won the crown, his coat-of-arms as king had a dragon and greyhound as the supporters. King Henry Tudor's dragon of Cadwallader' was popularised by Henry VII, and

The coat-of-arms of Oliver Cromwell, with opposed lion and dragon as supporters of his escutcheon.

appeared widely in heraldry, tournaments and pageants. His son, Henry VIII, had a lion and a dragon as supporters for the royal arms, as did Edward VI. Queen Mary I dropped the dragon, but it returned under Queen Elizabeth I, finally to disappear from English royal arms when the United Kingdom came into being under the Scottish king James I/VI. During his republic, Oliver Cromwell used the lion and dragon to support his escutcheon, but since the Restoration, the supporters of the royal arms have been the lion and unicorn.

Dragon Ships

The earliest dating of dragon-headed ships is uncertain. Bronze-age rock-carvings in Scandinavia can be interpreted as ships with serpent-head or dragon-head prows, but this identification is only one possible interpretation of the carvings. Later Norwegian rock-carvings of the 1st and 2nd centuries CE show more plausible dragon-prowed vessels. A dragon-headed ship carrying fully-armed men is shown on a memorial stone at Lärbro St Hammers on the Baltic island of Gotland, and it was during the Viking era that the dragon-headed ship came into its own. A Viking-age ship prow in the form of a beastie's head now on show in the British Museum in London, was found in the mud at the bottom of the River Scheldt in the Low Countries. It is a removable dragon-head.

A number of ancient ships have survived into the present day, having been buried in funeral rites and then dug up by archaeologists, the most famous of which are those excavated at Gokstad and Oseberg in Norway. The Oseberg ship was the burial-place of a noblewoman of the first half of the ninth century CE. She may have been the Norwegian queen, Asa. The tail of the Oseberg ship was destroyed by the grave-robbers who dug their way in before the archaeologists. It has been restored as a spiral. The fore end has a serpent's head at the centre of the spiral. Of the artefacts buried at Oseberg are furniture posts terminating in dragons' heads.

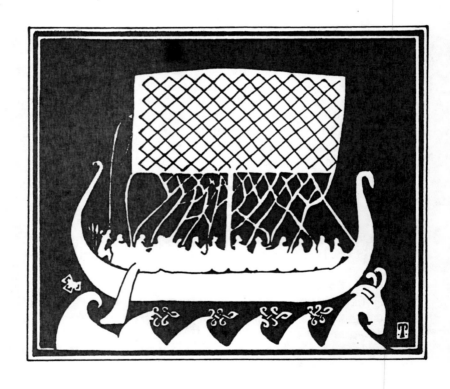

Carving of a dragon-headed ship from a memorial stone on the Baltic island of Gotland, Sweden, 7th-8th century CE. The sea beneath the ship is itself in the form of the World Serpent, Iormungand.

The Norwegian King Olaf Tryggvason owned a ship built in the winter of the year 998 called Ormrinn *Langi*, 'The Long Wyrm', usually translated into English as *Long Serpent*, and called by the kenning Ling Fish by the Bard Sigvat the Skald. It was a famous ship, whose dragon head was its identifying feature.

In *The Saga of Olaf Tryggvason*, Snorri Sturluson tells us how the allies, King of Denmark, Swein Forkbeard and Erik the Jarl, were attempting to identify the ship just before a sea-battle at Svölder in the Baltic in 1000 CE. Swein saw a ship without a dragon's head that he thought was *Ormrinn Langi*: "Olaf Tryggvason is afraid now", he said, "*he dares not sail with the dragon head on his ship*". Eric the Jarl corrected Swein, saying "*that is not the king's ship. It has a striped sail, it is owned by Erling Skjalson*". Dragons' heads were removable from Nordic ships, as this quotation from the *Saga of Olav Tryggvason* shows. Once the real *Long Serpent* had sailed into view, the battle commenced, ending when that ship was lashed together with two other ships, the *Short Serpent*, skippered by Thorkel Nevja, and the *Crane*, captained by Thorkell Dydrill. This impromptu floating fighting-platform was stormed and overwhelmed by Olav's enemies, and the king jumped into the sea, never to be seen again. The *Long Serpent* was captured by Eric the Jarl, and sailed by him thereafter.

Other kings named their ships after wyrms. In the three-way wars between the Norwegians, Danes and English in the early eleventh century, King Canute of Denmark sailed in his flagship, the *Dragon*. According to Snorri Sturluson in *The Saga of St Olav*, the Dragon had "*tall bulwarks like a castle, and a large crew, well armed and valiant*". Canute's *Dragon* had "*gold-decked heads*". Hakon the Jarl also had another *Dragon* of sixty rowing-benches. Both ships had red-and-green striped sails, and were painted above the waterline.

In the winter of 1061, the Norwegian King Harald Hardrada had a ship called the *Great Dragon* built at Ore, near Nidaros (Trondheim) so that he could attack the Danes. It was a copy of the famous Long Serpent owned first by Olaf Tryggvason and then Eric the Jarl: on its prow was a dragon's head, and at the stern, a dragon's tail. Both sides of the dragon's neck were overlain with gold. When Harald launched the ship, and it glided into the River Nid, Harald had the dragon's head set upon the prow. Then Tjodolv the Skald sung a praise-song about the *Great Dragon*:

> *"Fair maiden! The fine ship was*
> *Carried forth from the river to the sea,*
> *Note where the long body of the dragon*
> *Lies offshore.*
> *The gold-green mane of the dragon*
> *Shone above the deck; the neck*
> *Bore burnished gold. Then*
> *It slid from its moorings".*

Icelandic records tell us how in Pagan times respect for the *Landvaettir* (land-wights or earth sprites) meant that the dragons' heads of ships had to be removed when in sight of land or when beached, for fear of driving away the spirits and making the land *alfreka*. This infers that the dragon heads of ships were magically empowered to drive away spirits, good or bad. Presumably, at sea, the dragon-heads served to ward off the Midgardsorm, or World Serpent.

The Bayeux Tapestry shows how dragons' heads were put on and taken off of ships by the Normans, who were descendents of the Vikings. One of the earliest sections shows Harold Godwinson (later King Harold II of England), arriving in Normandy on a ship with a dragon's head. Later, another English ship comes to Normandy, also with a dragon's head. Then, in 1066, William of Normandy builds his invasion fleet. Ships shown under construction on the Bayeux Tapestry do not have dragons' heads, but those being launched do. Then, the Norman invasion fleet is shown at sea, and most ships have dragons' heads. When the ships are beached on the English shore, none have dragons' heads, but are shown with square holes in the prow post where the heads have been removed.

From these examples, it should not be inferred that all Scandinavian, Norman and English ships of this period bore dragon-heads. In the era of the Norse *Sagas*, there were other names and other figureheads. Although he used a dragon as his standard, Olav Haraldson (St Olav) called the ship he used at the Battle of Viken (Oslofjord) the *Carlhead* ('Man's Head'), which had a carving of a king's head as the figurehead. A later ship used by Olav was called *Visund*, 'Bison'. In the sea battle at Svolder, near the holy island of Rigen in the Baltic, in which Olaf Tryggvason perished, one of the key ships in the final struggle was the Crane. Dragon-headed ships continued to be made for several centuries after the eleventh. Dragon-headed ships and ships with vanes on the prow are depicted on an incised stick of the early thirteenth-century found at Bergen in Norway. Putting figure-heads on ships was a tradition that only ended with the demise of sail in the nineteenth century

The Dragon and Firearms

In Branch XVIII of *The High History of the Holy Grail*, we are told that Sir Perceval had to fight the Knight of the Dragon on the Island of Elephants. Unlike the usual opponents of the Knights of the Round Table, the Knight of the Dragon is not armed with a sword, battleaxe, mace or lance. He has a flamethrower. *The High History of the Holy Grail* describes the Knight of the Dragon as riding on horseback, carrying a shield and a red-hot sword. At his neck is a black shield, in the centre of which is a dragon's head. From this *"fire and flame in great plenty"* is projected, *"so foul and hideous that the field stank thereof"*.

85

When Sir Perceval arrives on the field of combat, there he sees the bodies of a knight and his horse, whom the Knight of the Dragon has just slain in a fight. At once Sir Perceval attacks the dragon knight with his lance, but is beaten back by a burst of flame that issues from the mouth of the dragon on his opponent's shield. Perceval is saved by his own shield, which is protected magically by having a phial of Christ's blood and a piece of his holy garment sealed in its boss. The flame is thus deflected and redirected back towards Perceval's adversary. On seeing this, the Knight of the Dragon burns up the bodies of the dead knight and his horse as a demonstration of the power of his weapon.

Sir Perceval then uses his sword to strike at the dragon-shield, which is damaged. Flamethrower fuel leaks onto Perceval's sword, and catches fire, appearing to burn the sword. Undeterred by this, Perceval next strikes the enemy knight a number of blows which culminate in him severing the dragon-knight's sword arm. Then Perceval's sword penetrates the gullet of the dragon-head, going in up to the hilt, and "*the dragon's head turneth towards his lord in great wrath, and scorcheth him and burneth him to dust*". By ramming his sword-blade through the muzzle of the flamethrower, Perceval severs the fuel line or penetrates the fuel-container, causing the knight to be burnt by the Greek Fire or whatever inflammable substance he used.

This account, written around 1220, is of great interest because it is an authentic medieval account of a dragon-weapon. In the early medieval period, flamethrowers were used by both the armies of the Eastern Roman Empire and Islam. The essential fuel of the early flamethrower, Greek Fire, was a secret composition reputed to consist of nitre, sulphur and naphtha. It was fired at the enemy through a tube, and, because of its unwieldy nature, was used principally in naval warfare. According to tradition, the flamethrower was invented by the engineer Callinicos of Heliopolis in Syria in the year 668 CE, and first used in combat by the Imperial Admiral Constantine

Pogonotus to destroy Saracen ships. Although it was a military secret, the Empire's opponents also discovered how to make Greek Fire, and it became part of the Islamic arsenal. By the 840s, the Muslim naval forces of Abdul Rahman, Emir of Seville in Spain, were equipped with flamethrowers that used naphtha as a fuel, which they used to good effect against Viking invaders.

Early flamethowers were unreliable and dangerous to their users, and it seems that experiments to find a safer, dry, fuel, led to the invention of gunpowder. When guns were invented, perhaps a direct development of the flamethrower, they, too, were recognised as dragon weapons, and made sometimes in the form of dragons. Among the finest of these is a remarkable early swivel-gun called *Der Drache*, ('The Dragon') made by Georg Guntheim von Spire at Strasbourg in 1514. Now preserved in the Historisches Muesum at Basel in Switzerland, this firearm has a decorated barrel that emerges from the mouth of a splendid Late Gothic dragon. As firearms improved over the years, the name dragon stuck, and guns continued to be made with dragons' heads. According to military lore, cavalrymen belonging to units armed with the short matchlock muskets called 'dragons' came to be called Dragoons, for, "*mounted on horseback with lighted match, he seemed like a fiery dragon*".

Between 1766 and 1783, an order of Freemasonry, called the Knights of the Dragon, operated at Strasbourg, Lyon and Bordeaux as a branch of the Knight Templar masonic order. They were not a military order, however, and never fought in battle with firearms or any other weapons. Their name was purely symbolic.

St George, patron of England.

Chapter 5

The Dragon Saints

St George

History and Legend

St George, the Patron of England has many faces, as befits an important legendary figure. According to Christian mythology, St George was the first Christian to die for his beliefs during the persecution instituted by the Emperor Diocletian at the end of the third century CE. However, this St George was not a dragonslayer. A legend formerly held to be creditable, but later discredited by Jesuit researchers was that the original St George of Cappadocia was the Arian Christian Bishop of Alexandria in Egypt who was done to death by the mob in the year 360 CE.

According to E.C. Brewer in his *Dictionary of Phrase and Fable* (London, 1894), St George was born in Armorica, the present-day Brittany, and beheaded as a Christian by order of Datianus under the Emperor Diocletian, on April 23, 303 CE. Later, St George was commemorated in prayers and services, for instance in the *Sacramentary* of St Gregory the Great (540-604 CE), who wrote a *Preface for St George's Day*. The Breton legend and others exemplify a persistent legend that St George was a Briton, or an Englishman. A medieval ballad recorded by Thomas Percy in his *Reliques* tells how St George was born in England at Coventry, the son of Lord Albert. But, contrary to the northern European connection, St George is also associated with the city of Beirut in the Lebannon, where a shrine is revered by Christian and Muslim alike.

The connection of someone called St George with a dragon appears to be an eleventh century literary construct from the Eastern Roman Empire, modelled on earlier Pagan and Christian dragonslayer legends. Earlier Greek hagiography tells of the Christian heroes Constantine, Demetrios and Theodore all killing dragons. These and other dragonslaying legends circulated within the Byzantine realms, and it was only when the story was connected with St George that it spread to the west. By the twelfth century, the story of St George and the dragon was in central Europe. German frescoes depicting St George fighting the dragon appear in the thirteenth century, and soon local legends grew up localising the fight between St George and the dragon. In places as diverse as Wurmlingen near Tübingen, Langenzenn in Franconia, Paulinzelle in Thuringia, all in modern Germany, and Uffington in Berkshire, England, the place where St George killed the dragon is still pointed out.

The ballad of St George mentioned above is as good as any account of the dragonslaying legend. St George was a good Englishman, the son of lord Albert, born at Coventry. The baby was special, for he had three birth-marks: on the chest, a dragon; on one arm, a blood-red cross; and around one leg, a garter. His mother died giving him birth, and the baby George was stolen by the Weird Lady of the Woods, who brought him up and taught him the martial arts. When he became a man, he went on a crusade against the Saracens. In Libya, he visited the city of Sylene, near which was a swamp inhabited by a fearsome dragon, which had slain *"many a city"* with its poisonous breath. It was thought to be invincible, having scales which *"no spear nor sword could pierce"*. Every day, the local people of Sylene gave a virgin woman to the dragon to appease its voracious appetite. Finally, there were no more virgins left except the king's daughter, Sabra.

90

The king's daughter was taken and tied to a stake as the other unfortunate women before her had been. But George had arrived by then, and he vowed to extirpate the monster once and for all. Mounted on horseback, George assaulted the dragon with his lance, and speared it to the ground, killing it. On his return to the city, the king was unwilling to marry his daughter to a Christian, and deported George to Syria, where he planned to have him murdered. However, George escaped his prison, took Sabra with him, and returned to England, where they married and lived in Coventry together for many years. There is a Cornish legend associated with Padstow that St George once visited the town. His horse 'made a mark' with one of its hooves and brought forth a spring from the earth there. This is now St George's Well. The *Padstow Day Song*, sung on May Day each year, has an explicit reference to St George:

"Awake, St George, our English knight, O!
For summer is a-come, and winter is a-go,
And every day God give us his grace,
By day and by night, O!
Where is St George, where is he, O?
He is out in his long boat, all on the salt sea, O!
And in every land O! The land that ere we go."

Ballads, both sung and printed, were an important means by which St George's fame was spread far and wide. Of course, they were popular entertainment, and had to compete with other themes, concerns and fashions of the day. In his play, *Bartholomew Fair*, acted first in London in 1614, the Jacobean playwright Ben Jonson has a ballad-seller, Nightingale, call out his wares:

"Ballads! Ballads! Fine new ballads!
Hear for your love, and buy for your money!
A delicate ballad o' 'The Ferret and the Coney';
'A Preservative again the Punk's Evil';
Another of 'Goose-green Starch and the Devil';

'A Dozen of Divine Points' and 'The Godly Garters';
'The Fairing of Good Counsel', of an ell and three
quarters.
What is't you buy?
'The Windmill blown down by the Witch's Fart!',
Or 'Saint George, that O! did break the dragon's heart!'".

St George as Patron and Protector

As his fame spread, St George became the patron saint of knights, *landsknechte*, weapon-smiths and box-makers. In Macedonia, he is patron saint of robbers. He also has a fertility element, as Green George, where he is invoked as the giver of children to childless women. The Pagan god of vegetation and fertility of the old Prussians, Balts and Estonians is honoured on the same day as St George, and is clearly his forerunner in these regions. According to German folk-tradition, St George fought against the Huns as well as the dragon. Soldiers carried coins bearing the image of the saint into battle with them, to protect them against harm. These apotropaic St George coins were particularly favoured in Bavaria, where they went under the name of Georgsthaler (St George's Dollar). The obverse of these coins was stamped with an image of the saint with the name Jörg, Jurgen or Irch. The last name, Irch, was the Pagan war-god of the Bajuwaren, the ancestral tribe of the Bavarians.

The obverse of Georgthalers show a ship with St Peter on board in a storm, with the Latin inscription *In tempestate Securitas*, 'Safety in the storm'. In addition to being protectors in battle, Georgsthaler were valued as apotropaic talismans against all forms of illness and danger to life. Another German tradition tells that if one kills a snake with a stick, calling upon St George during the action, then the stick is magically empowered, becoming an invincible weapon with which to overcome one's enemies. A serpent's head, cut off on St George's Day (April 23), is a magical remedy for fever. Certain places dedicated to St George have their own magical traditions. At Llan San Sior, near Abergele in Denbighshire in north Wales, the holy well of St George was resorted to for the cure of sick horses. Water from the well was sprinkled over their backs, and the prayer, *"Rhad Duw a Sant Sior arnat"* recited. On occasion, horses were sacrificed to St George at this well, the remains becoming the property of the parish priest.

St GeoRge in Olò Englanò

St George is known as the Patron Saint of England, a function he took over from earlier figures like the royal saints Edmund and Edward the Confessor. The traditional English battle-cry is "St George!", as recalled in William Shakespeare's play *King Henry V* (c. 1599): "The game's afoot: Follow your spirit, and upon this charge cry *'God for Harry, England, and Saint George!'"*. In medieval times, performances of Mummers' plays depicting St George's combat with the dragon were considered a means of combatting the plague. The annual appearance of the dragon called Le Lumecon in Mons commemorates just such a successful performance. St George appears in many of the traditional English Mummers' plays, performed at Pace Egging Time (Easter), St Stephen's Day (December 26), the twelve days of Yule, and Plough Monday (the first Monday after Twelfth Night). One Yorkshire version gives the following lines to St George, who is presented as the bringer of right orderliness to the world:

> *"In comes I, Saint George, from Old England did spring.*
> *My famous name throughout the world does ring.*
> *Many a goodly sight and kingdom I have known,*
> *And made false tyrants tremble on their throne.*
> *Once I followed a maiden to the dragon's gate,*
> *Where, confined in dungeon deep, she did await her fate."*

The Red Cross Knight kills the dragon. From Edmund Spenser's The Faerie Queene (London, 1596).

Further on in the play, where another 'ragged hero', Bold Slasher, is slain by St George, and resurrected by the Doctor, St George enters the action again, with the words:

"In comes I again, Saint George, the famous champion bold,
And with my trusty broadsword, I won ten thousand pounds in gold.
'Twas I who fought the fiery dragon, and brought him to great slaughter,
And by these wondrous deeds, I won the King of Egypt's daughter".

There are numerous versions of English Mummers' plays of the 'Hero-Combat' type, and these lines, or variants of them, can appear in other parts of the play. However, the basic elements of St George as the English knight who killed the dragon and saved the king's daughter are commonplace. The relationship between St George, mumming and sword dancing is tenuous, but enough to make it worth noting that one of the earliest illustrations of longsword dancing is an etching by Peter Bruegel the Elder, dating from around 1600, titled *The Fair of St George's Day*.

In his *The Faerie Queene*, Edmund Spenser wrote of the *Legend of the Knight of the Red Crosse*, who is St George. In Canto XI, "*The knight with that old Dragon fights two dayes incessantly; The third him overthrowes, and gayns most glorious victory*". Spenser's description of the dragon is among the most evocative of any in the English language:

"By this the dreadfull Beast drew night to hand,
Halfe flying, and halfe footing his hast,
That with largenesse measured much land,
And made wide shadow under his huge wast;
As mountaine doth the valley overcast.
Approaching nigh, he reared high afore
His body monstrous, horrible and vast,

95

Which to increase his wondrous greatnesse more,
Was swolne with wrath, and poyson, and with bloudy gore.

And over, all with brasen scales was armd,
Like plated coat of steele, so couched neare,
That nought mote pierce, ne might the corse be harmd
With dint of sword, nor push of pointed speare;
Which as an Eagle, seeing pray appeare,
His aery plumes doth rouze, full rudely dight,
So shaked he, that horrour was to heare,
For as the clashing of an Armour bright,
Such noyse his rouzed scales did send unto the knight.

His flaggy wings when forth he did display,
Were like two sayles, in which the hollow wind
Is gathered full and worketh speedy way:
And eke the pennes, that did his pineons bynd,
Were like mayne-yards, with flying canvas lynd,
With which whenas him list the ayre to beat,
And there by force unwonted passage find,
The cloudes before him fled for terrour great,
And all the heavens stood still amazed with his threat.

His huge long tayle wound up in hundred foldes,
Does outspred his long bras-scaly backe,
Whose wreathed boughts when ever he unfoldes,
And thick entangled knots adown does slacke,
Bespotted as with shields of red and blacke,
It sweepeth all the land behind him farre,
And of three furlongs does but little lacke;
And at the point two stings in-fixed arre,
Both deadly sharpe, that sharpest steele exceeden farre.

But stings and sharpest steele did far exceed
The sharpnesse of his cruel rending clawes;
Dead was it sure, as sure as death in deed,
Whatever thing does touch his ravenous pawes,
Or what woithin his reach he ever drawes.

But his most hideous head my toung to tell
Does tremble: for his deep devouring jawes
Wide gaped, like the griesly mount of hell,
Through which into his dark abisse all ravin fell.

And that more wondrous was, in either jaw
Three ranckes of yron teeth enraunged were,
In which yet trickling bloud and gobbets raw
Of late devoured bodies did appeare,
That sight thereof bred cold congealed feare:
Which to oincrease, and all at once to kill
A cloud of smoothering smoke and sulphur seare
Out of his stinking gorge forth steemed still,
That all the ayre about with smoke and stench did fill.

His blazing eyes, like two bright shining shields,
Did burne with wrath, and sparkled living fyre;
As two broad Beacons, set in open fields,
Send forth their flames farre off to every shyre,
And warning give, that enemies conspyre,
With fire and sword the region to invade;
So flam'd his eyne with rage and rancorouse yre:
But farre within, as in a hollow glade,
Those glaring lampes were set, that made a dreadfull shade.

So dreadfully he towards him did pas,
Forelifting up aloft his speckled brest,
And often bounding on the brused gras,
As for great joyance of his newcome guest.
Eftsoones he gan advance his haughtie crest,
As chauffed Bore his bristles doth upreare,
And shoke his scales to battell readie drest;
That made the Redcrosse knight nigh quake for feare
As bidding bold defiance to his foeman neare."

Norman-period Romanesque carving of St Michael in combat with a
wyvern, Ipswich, Suffolk, England.

St Michael

Unlike St George, who in legend was a human being of exceptional courage and power, the other major male dragonslayer,
St Michael, is wholly a supernatural being. He is mentioned
first in the Biblical *Book of Daniel*, where he is described as
the protective angel of the Jews. According to Jewish tradition,
the angel Michael is the High Priest of Heaven. In later
Christian interpretations, he appears as St Michael, leader of
the Heavenly Host. The Christian cultus of St Michael arose in
Phrygia, where it took over the roles of Aesculapius and
Serapis, respectively the Graeco-Roman and Hellennic gods of
healing. Significantly, both gods were depicted with snakes,
the healing animal. According to orthodox Christian medical
theory, all illness is caused by demons possessing the body, and
St Michael was invoked to cast them out and restore God's
order in the body. Later, St Michael's role altered, his healing
qualities were played down, and a new role, as commander of
the angels, in combat with the Devil, appeared.

A significant event may have accelerated this change. The
continental Saxons used a banner of St Michael in the war
they fought from the year 933 CE until 955 against the
invading Hungarians. Their successful defence of western
Europe against Pagan invaders appeared miraculous, thereby
greatly enhancing St Michael's status as defender of right
orderliness. Later medieval traditions, such as those recorded
in the *Lausitzer Saga*, depicted St Michael fighting giants and
dragons at the end of time, as slayer of the Antichrist.

St Michael's connection with the dragon is complex, for, in
orthodox Christian cosmology, he is the body of the Sun. This
belief tells us that when we see the Sun, we are seeing St
Michael. It is a part of Christian belief which, like the static
flat earth orthodoxy once enforced by torture and the stake,
has long since been discarded as the result of scientific
astronomy. Because of his connection with the sun, Pagan
solar holy mountains like the St Michael's Mounts in Cornwall

and Normandy were re-named in his honour. Often, St Michael is depicted clad in golden armour, overcoming the devil or a dragon representing him. St Michael holds his sword behind his head in the position for beheading a fallen opponent. Some images show him like St George, lance in hand. The powerful medieval image of St Michael guarding the entrance beneath the tower of St Michael's church in Schwäbisch Hall in south Germany, closely resembles unmounted versions of St George.

Because St Michael, is the Sun, esoterically, he represents time. Thus, in Christian mythology, he casts out Satan from Heaven, which marks the end of God's unchallenged power, and the beginning of the dualism that opposes evil against good. This mythos tells us that until the Last Judgement, when God destroys evil, and time ends, there is constant combat between the legions of Heaven led by Michael on behalf of God, and the armies of Hell, led by the Devil. Once the Heavenly Host has defeated the Fallen Angels and their supporters, the Last Judgement takes place with St Michael wielding the scales of Justice, weighing souls to determine whether they should go to Heaven or be cast into the Lake of Fire and destroyed. As scales-bearer, St Michael took over the role of the Egyptian god Anubis, depicted with a jackal's head.

In northern Christianity, Scandinavian memorial runestones call upon St Michael to protect the dead, for he is the psychopomp who conducts souls to the Otherworld. According to medieval German lore, on the first night after death, the soul is conducted by St Gertrude, who may be a version of the old Wendish god, Gerovit, whose shrine was at Wolgast in Pomerania. After the first night, St Michael takes over to guide the soul's journey. In Hungary, the bier on which the corpse is carried is called St Michael's Horse. Michael's festal day, Michaelmas, falls in the sign of the Scales, Libra, on September 29, very close to the day on which the Pagan Saxons celebrated their festival of the dead, October 1.

St Margaret

After St George and St Michael, St Margaret appears as the most widespread dragon saint. According to Christian mythology, Margaret was the daughter of a Pagan priest at Antioch, who changed her religion, and became a Christian. Like St George, she was killed in the persecution of Christians in the reign of the Emperor Diocletian in the year 300 CE. Perhaps because of this contemporaneousness, St Margaret often appears as the female counterpart of St George. Her most forceful icon shows her holding a dragon captive on a lead or chain. Sometimes, as at King's College Chapel in Cambridge, she tramples a dragon underfoot, an image also used in icons of Our Lady and the Lindwurm on Linden trees in Bavaria. In the 1450s, a woman personating St Margaret was added to the St George parade at Norwich. St Margaret's feast day is celebrated on July 20th, and it is the custom in central Europe that no snakes should be killed between July 13th and July 20th because in this week, the serpent is the holy beast of St Margaret. The main church at King's Lynn in Norfolk is dedicated to St Margaret, and the town's coat of arms bears three dragons' heads in commemoration.

Like St George and St Michael, St Margaret is a complex being with links to non-Judaeo-Christian traditions that run in parallel with her veneration by the Church. In Lower Saxony and the Netherlands, Margaret appears in a destructive form known variously as Schwarze Gret, Swatte Griet, Dulle Griet or Booze Margriet (Black Maggie, otherwise Evil or Mad Meg). In Schleswig-Holstein, she is seen as possessing two aspects, one of which is beneficial, and the other harmful. The good one appears in the form of St Margaret and the bad one as Mad Meg.

In his painting, *Dulle Griet*, dating from 1562, Peter Breugel depicts Mad Meg as a middle-aged woman, holding a sword and wearing a steel helmet, breastplate and gauntlet. She carries all of the various kinds of containers of the time:

Frau Percht, the Germanic goddess associated with the wintertime, has some of the attributes attributed to St Margaret and Greth Schell.

baskets, bags, a plate, dish, cup and frying-pan. The latter utensil is part of the 'regalia' of demonic or threatening characters like Beelzebub and Old Hub in English Mummers' plays. Breugel's Dulle Griet strides forcefully through an apocalyptic scene of demonic happenings that include the Maw of Hell crammed with demons, scenes of torture, death and destruction, the invasion of an infernal army and a dance of goblins and humans on a Linden tree trained in the form of the Cosmic Axis.

In her destructive aspect, Margaret appears as the ghostly Wild Huntress of Westphalia and as a weather-goddess. Breugel's image is one of the most forceful images of the destructive side of St Margaret. Mad Meg appears in the *Fastnacht* (Shrovetide) procession at Zug in Switzerland as the figure called Greth Schell, a woman carrying a man on her back in a basket. Although there are several stories accounting for her name, including an historical woman with a similar name, the figure of the ritual basket-carrier is an ancient one for a central European goddess, and is clearly archetypal in quality.

St Martha

Martha is another female saint with dragon connections. According to the Biblical books of St Luke and St John, Martha was the sister of Lazarus and Mary in Bethany, and so she is not a Christian saint like George, and Margaret, but a Jewish personage from the Bible. She is associated in the *Book of Matthew* with the 'woman with a discharge of blood'. This is an intriguing connection between menstrual blood and the fertilising blood spilt on the ground when the dragon is slain. Iconically, St Martha is shown sitting over a vanquished dragon, and at Tarascon in France, a girl or woman personating Martha appears leading the tamed Tarasque through the town. Certain other places associated with St Martha have dragon legends.

*St Martha overcoming the Tarasque, a French Roman Catholic
devotional print, c. 1825.*

Other Catholic Saints

Pope Sylvester I was called in to kill a dragon that lived in a moat and devoured three hundred people daily. He went up to the beastie, called out Christ's name, and bound its jaws together with a rope, which he then fixed permanently with the sign of the cross. St Sylvester is often depicted leading a dragon on a chain. St Donatus is remembered in Italy for killing a dragon that lived in a noxious spring near Arezzo. As he was praying by the waters, the dragon emerged and attacked the holy man. Donatus spat into the dragon's mouth, and it died from his spittle. Then the poisonous waters of the well miraculously became drinkable. In Croatia, St Hilarion destroyed a dragon by bidding the people to make a fire, into which he commanded the dragon to go. It did so, and was cremated.

Celtic Dragon-Slaying Saints

The legends of the Celtic saints read like a comprehensive account of magic, myth and miracles, so it is to be expected that dragons figure amongst their exploits. Many of them are rollicking tall stories befitting the entertaining spirit of Celtic Bardism. We have already met the British missionary St Beatus, expelling the dragon from a cave near Interlaken. St Samson is one of the more celebrated Celtic saints, having modified many standing stones into crosses, and having set up stones where there were none before.

According to legend, St Samson slew both a serpent and a dragon. In Wales, at Ynys Pyr, Samson and his assistants Amwn and Ubrafael came across some burnt ground on which lay a serpent. Samson went up to it, and, repelled by the saint's smell, it consumed itself, Oroboros-style, beginning with its tail. At Lewannick in Cornwall, there was a dragon that had devastated two *pagos* of land, and killed any human beings that dared to enter them. Samson went to its cave,

Dragon-slaying knight. Engraving by Lukas Cranach (1472-1553).

dragged out the dragon, using his linen belt, and threw the monster into the nearest river.

The virgin recluse, called variously St Cain, Keyne or Ceinwen, migrated from Brecknock in Wales to Keynsham in Somersetshire, where she used Christian magic to turn serpents into stone. Like St Hilda of Whitby, who also petrified the local snakes, her legend seems to have come into being to account for the fossil ammonites that abound in their respective districts. These woman saints were emulating their better-known male counterparts from Ireland. According to tradition, St Patrick banished all serpents from the island of Ireland, and the Isle of Man, too. Later, St Columba emulated the founder of Irish Christianity by expelling the serpents of the holy island of Iona. Whilst earlier writers were liable just to report these legends, or interpret them literally, Sabine Baring-Gould and John Fisher, who wrote the definitive work on the Celtic saints, *Lives of the British Saints* (London, 1907-1913) refused to take the dragon legends at face value, "*In some cases the dragon is a symbol*", they assert, "*When Meven and Samson overcome dragons, this is a figurative way of saying that they obtained the overthrow and destruction of Conmore, Regent of Domnonia* (Devon and Cornwall - N.P.). *In other cases it may have had a different origin. It may possibly refer to the saint having abolished a pagan human sacrifice by burning victims in wicker-work figures representing monsters. In the legend of Saints Derien and Neventer, we read that the holy men found a man drowning himself because the lot had fallen on his only son to be offered to a dragon. He was pulled out of the water, the boy was rescued, and the dragon abolished.*"

Baring-Gould and Fisher assume that one of the legends of St Samson refers to the overthrow of the Dumnonian princeling because he is referred to by the chronicler Gildas as "Insularis Draco", 'The Dragon of the Island", referring to military rank in the Roman manner. In Gaul, there were Pagan images of beasts now called dragons, such as the famous Tarasque du

The female power of the dragon, with her guardianness. Drawing by Helen Field, 1996.

Noves, which is a monster holding two severed human heads. If humans were sacrificed before such images, Baring-Gould's and Fisher's idea is plausible, at least in some cases. If we take this line of thinking, then the exploits of St Patrick and St Columba are symbolic of the extirpation of Pagan worship in Ireland, Man and Iona. For reasons of climatic history, Ireland never had snakes anyway. Also, whatever the reason, despite the dragon exploits of Welsh and Breton monks and priests, there is a relative paucity of dragon legends in Scotland and Ireland.

Meдíeval Dragon-Slayers

Among the numerous saints of the Christian Church are those who symbolise human strength overcoming the animal powers, or alternatively, the Christian religion superseding the elder faiths. All over Europe are local and minor saints and heroes who are remembered as snake-expellers, reptile-fighters and dragon-killers. Some of them are wholly historical figures, often missionaries or early bishops. Among these can be numbered Narcissus of Gerona (d. 306 CE); Adelphus, Bishop of Metz (c. 400 CE); Lupus, Bishop of Sens (d. 623 CE) and St Magnus, the Apostle of the Allgau in south Germany (8th century CE). All of them are said to have eliminated dragons to set up their respective episcopal sees.

One of the acts of St Patrick, the Apostle of Ireland, was to drive out all the serpents from the Emerald Isle as well as the Isle of Man. Less well located in time are the Alpine dragon-fighters, who include the British Celtic monk St Beatus. He drove out a dragon from what may have been a Druidical cave in the cliffs bordering the Lake of Thun in present-day Switzerland. St Mangold is another Alpine saint, who slew a road-blocking dragon in the Tyrol. Elsewhere in German and French-speaking lands, saints Armel, Clemens, Nikolaus, Procopius, Romain, Servan and Urgin, among others, carried on the Christian program of eliminating dragons and serpents from the land. Local heroes, too, not sanctified by benefit of clergy, assisted in the work of extinction of dragons, serpents and other allied monsters. Some are well known throughout Europe, but most, like the saints, are purely local. Like the saints, they include figures both wholly mythological and historic, such as Beowulf, Siegfried, Cu Chullain, Ragnar Lothbrok, Wolfdietrich, Guy of Warwick, Gilles de Chin, Frohto, Fridler, Dietrich von Bern, Tristan, Sir John Conyers, Perceval, Piers Shonkes, Osulf, Wigalois and John Lambton.

Chapter 6

The Dragon in the Western Esoteric Arts

Some Interpretations of the Dragon

The dragon plays an important part in the esoteric arts of the West, in alchemy, astrology, herbalism and in both forms of geomancy. The dragon is often seen as a symbol of chaos, pinned down and brought under control by the dragonslaying hero. When it appears as Orouboros, the alchemical serpent biting its own tail, it represents cosmic circulation, the antithesis of the destructive dragon. The dragon is a beast that has legs to walk on the earth; it can swim in water; it has wings to fly; and it breathes fire. Thus it is the quintessence of the four elements, that which encompasses all according to the Old English motto "*In On Is Al*", 'In one is all'.

The Alchemical Dragon

The dragon app;ears throughout alchemical literature, and in allegorical alchemical illustrations. As well as the circular worm Orouboros, it appears in typical form, both four- and two-legged. As the twentieth century alchemist Fulcanelli showed, alchemical symbolism and the symbolic arrangements within churches are one and the same. The green dragon appears in many medieval churches on the south side and the red or white lion on the north. The conflict between the lion

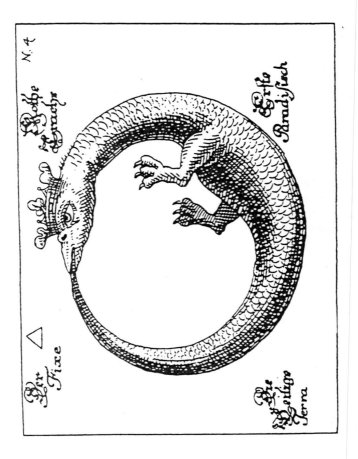

The Worm Orobouros as dragon. From Donum Uei by Abraham Eieazar (Erfurt, 1735).

and the serpent or dragon which is an episode in the acts of Sir Perceval is an emblem of the dynamic balance between the two complementary but opposing forces.

The symbolic battle of the lion and the dragon is shown on the lower left-hand panel of an engraving that shows the noted French alchemists Nicolas and Perrenelle Flamel in *Le Livre des figures Hiéroglyphiques* (Paris, 1612). This book contains representations of paintings that Nicolas Flamel (1330-1418) did in the Cemetery of the Innocents in Paris. A fine renaissance tapestry made for Wawel Castle in Cracow, Poland (which has a dragonslaying legend), depicts many dragons, including one getting the better of a lion in combat. The green dragon and the red lion represent both material substances in alchemy and archetypal qualities. They appear as symbols of opposites that must merge with one another in order that final unity may be achieved.

Another important alchemical text, *Practica una cum Duodecim* Clavibus (*Twelve Keys of Occult Philosophy*), ascribed to the German Benedictine abbot Basil Valentine (1394-14??), presents a series of allegorical illustrations of the alchemical process. The alchemical dragon or serpent appears thrice. The third *key* shows the dragon in the earthly sphere; the ninth shows three serpents emerging from human hearts, whilst the twelfth and final key depicts the alchemical lion consuming the serpent in the consummation of unity.

According to the alchemist-monk George (or Gregory) Ripley, who was sponsored by the Order of St John of Jerusalem, and from 1471 to 1490 had a laboratory in the monastery at Bridlington in Yorkshire, the Green Dragon is *Aqua Fortis*, a potent mixture of acids that will dissolve every known metal, including gold. The *Ripley Scrowles* in the British Library have many dragon illustrations. One manuscript illustration shows a double-headed wyvern whose blood flows in three streams to make the Red Stone, the White Stone and the Elixir. Another depicts the emblems of the Sun and Moon entwined with two

113

The union of the aerial dragon with the earthly wyrm. From Abraham Eleazar's Uraltes chymisches Werk (Leipzig, 1760).

The dragon is attacked within its earthly fire whilst its complementary opposite, the lion, looks on. 17th century symbolic engraving.

Sol and Luna (Sun and Moon) slay the dragon with their respective clubs. From Michael Maier's Atalanta Fugiens (Oppenheim, 1618).

wyverns, each biting the other's tail, within a circle of the signs of the zodiac.

A related motif that recurs in alchemical symbolism is the slaying of the dragon by Sol and Luna, the Sun God and Moon Goddess, who wield clubs. Sol slaying the dragon is a version of the myth of Apollo killing the Python, which is not balanced by his female counterpart doing the same in the Greek legend. Alchemically, as the dragon is emblematical of synthesis, the three principles must come together. In his *Atalanta Fugiens* (Frankfurt, 1617), Michael Maier states: "*The dragon dieth not save with its brother and sister, that is, with Sol and Luna*". In *Artis Auriferae Quam Chemiam Vocant...* (Basel, 1610), the dragon tells its assailants, "*Unless ye slay me, ye cannot be called sages*". The dragonslayer must be both philosopher and knight, in the tradition of the European martial arts, where the knight was a poet and musician, game-player and lover, as well as an efficient professional killer.

To gain an understanding of the inner symbolism of alchemy is a process in itself. It is not for everyone, and it is easy for those who cannot or will not come to terms with its complex language and symbolism to dismiss it as worthless. Present-day dismissals are usually based upon a simplistic under-standing of the nature of science. In former times, alchemy, like medicine, astrology and the priesthood, was seen by some as a kind of charlatanry, primarily concerned with making money for its practitioners.

In the seventeenth century, the complex symbolism and terminology of alchemy was satirised by the playwright Ben Jonson. In his play, *The Alchemist*, first performed in London in 1610, Surly, the Gamester, claims that "*alchemy is a pretty kind of game, somewhat like tricks o' the cards, to cheat a man with charming*". He goes on to criticise alchemical terms:

> *"Whereon no one o' your writers 'grees with other?*
> *Of your elixir, your lac Virginis,*

The dragon appears in stages of the alchemical Great Work, from
Johann Conrad Barchusen's Elementa Chemiae (Leiden, 1718), copied
from a manuscript in a Benedictine monastery in Swabia.

118

Your stone, your med'cine, and your chrysosperm,
Your sal, your sulphur and your mercury,
Your oil of height, your tree of life, your blood,
Your marcasite, your tutty, your magnesis,
Your toad, your crow, your dragon and your panther,
Your sun, your moon, your firmement, your adrop,
Your lato, azoch, zernich, chibrit, heutarit,
And then, your red man, your menstrues, and materials,
Of piss, and egg-shells, women's terms, man's blood,
Hair o' the head, burnt clouts, chalk, merds, and clay,
Powder of bones, scalings of iron, glass,
And worlds of other strange ingredients, Would burst
man to name?"

Subtle, the Alchemist, replies:

"All of these nam'd,
Intending to be but one thing: which art our writers
Us'd to obscure their art".

The Dragon in Astrology

The dragon is represented in the heavens by two distinct
figures: the constellation of Draco, and the Path of the Moon.
Astronomically, the constellation Draco circles around the
north pole like the World Serpent circling the Cosmic Axis. In
Classical mythology, it has a number of explanations.
According to one interpretation, Draco represents the guardian
dragon of the golden apples in the Garden of the Hesperides.
Another is that it is the Python slain by Apollo, or the dragon
used by the Titans in their war against the Gods. Between
circa 4500 BCE and 2700 BCE, the north celestial pole was
within the constellation of Draco, which at present circles the
pole from 63 degrees to 81 degrees from the equator.

Draco is also known by the alternative names of Serpens,
Anguis and Python. To the ancient Egyptians, it was the

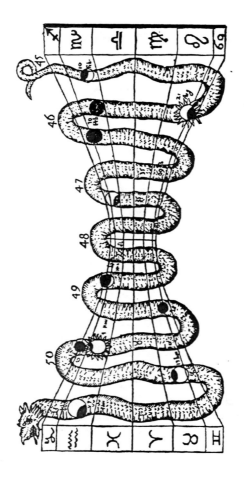

The celestial dragon-path of the Moon through the year. From Athanaius Kircher's Ars Maffna Lucis (Rome, 1665).

120

constellation of the Hippopotamus. Claudius Ptolemy likened the bright stars of Draco to Mars and Saturn. In traditional Western astronomy, the binary star designated as Beta Draconis is called Rastaban, a corruption of the Arabic *Al Ras Al Thuban*, 'The Dragon's Head'. It is the eye of the dragon, and has a stellar magnitude of three. The constellation in astrology brings craft, ingenuity and valour. It brings an emotional, artistic quality to those under its influence. But this is tempered with sombreness. Subjects of Draco have a penetrating, analytical mind, they travel widely and have many friends, but are in constant danger of being robbed or poisoned accidentally. Qabalistically, the constellation of the dragon is associated with the 13th card of the Major Arcana of the Tarot, 'Death'.

The body of the dragon symbolises the whole path of the Moon as viewed from the Earth, anciently 'The Sphere of the Moon'. The dragon is visualised as being coiled around the Earth, like the World Serpent. The head and tail of the dragon mark the extreme points, the nodes of the Moon. The lunar north node is the Dragon's Head, Caut Draconis. It marks the point at which the ascending orbit of the Moon intersects the Ecliptic. The dragon's back end, Cauda Draconis, marks the descending node of the Moon. Cauda Draconis is the point of the south node of the Moon, where Luna is in descent across the Ecliptic. The period of the Moon's motion between the same nodes (27.212 days) is called the Draconitic Period. Solar eclipses were once explained in terms of this lunar sphere dragon as its periodic swallowing and regurgitation of the Sun.

The Dragon in Herbalism

The substance called Dragon's Blood or *Draconis resina* is the most powerful representative of the dragon in herbalism. It is not one substance, various kinds of Dragon's Blood coming from different plants. The most widely recognised comes from Sumatra, from the Dragon's Blood Palm, *Daemomorops draco*

The epitome of the ancient philosopher, whose sphere of activities linhs the hermetic arts of alchemv and symbolism with astronomy anfd herbalism. 18th century engraving of the great Pagan teacher Apollonius of Tyana (1-90 CE).

Blume, the berries of which are covered with a resin which is Dragon's Blood. The resin is dark red. It was used formerly as a treatment for diarrhoea and syphilis, but it is never used internally to-day. It is sometimes burnt as an incense, when the breath of the dragon is produced by means of fire. Other 'Dragon's Bloods' come from related species that grow in Borneo and Malaysia.

On the Canary Islands, the Dragon Tree, *Dracaena draco*, which is believed by the inhabitants to be the most long-lived of all trees, was holy to the native Guanches. The Dragon's Blood was used in the Canaries for embalming the dead. Chinese Dragon's Blood, from *Dracaena terminalis*, is used in China as a red varnish, whilst from *Pterocarpus draco*, which grows in South America and the East Indies, comes Guadaloupe Dragon's Blood. Mexican Dragon's Blood, *Sangre del Drago*, from *Croton draco*, is used in Mexican herbalism as an astringent. In the European magical tradition, Dragon's Blood is used in a women's spell to regain the love of one who has forsaken her for another. "Two pennyworth" of Dragon's Blood (in nineteenth century monetary values) should be thrown on a fire to the following incantation:

> *"'Tis not this blood I wish to burn,*
> *But (name)'s heart I wish to turn.*
> *May he neither sleep nor rest*
> *'Till he has granted my request".*

The European plant known as Toadflax which also has the alternative names of Snapdragon and Dragon-Bushes (*Linaria vulgaris* Mill.) has a herbal use. In his *Herbal*, Gerard writes:

> *"The floures be yellow with a spurre hanging at the same like unto a Larksspurre, having a mouth like unto a frog's mouth, even such as is to be seene in the common Snapdragon".*

124

For medicinal purposes, Dragon-Bushes contains an acrid oil, allegedly poisonous, used in ancient European herbal medicine. It was used in veterinary medicine against the flowing of gall in cattle. Generally, the effects of Dragon-Bushes are astringent and detergent. It can be used as a purgative and a diuretic, used in cases of jaundice, scrofula, liver- and skin diseases.

Dragon Flower (*Iris pseudacorus Linn.*) is the native British Iris, or Yellow Flag, growing in the margins of bodies of water all over Europe and North Africa. It is the Flower de Luce, or Fleur-de-Lys, the heraldic emblem of the kings of France. In former times, Dragon Flower root was used in herbal medicine as a powerful cathartic, for the treatment of coughs, convulsions, dropsies, 'the evil spleen' and as a remedy against snake-bite. Gerard tells us that Dragon Flower Oil, "*is used to rub in the sinews and joints to strengthen them, and is good for cramp*". The American Blue Flag, (*Iris versicolor Linn.*) is also known as Dragon Flower or Snake Lily. The active part of this plant is also the root, used for the extract of Iridin, which has a powerful action on the liver.

Opposite: Miscellaneous Dragonalia. Top line, left to right, 1 - 4: sigils of Caput Draconis, the ascending node of the Moon; 5, 6: geomantic figures of Caput Draconis. Second line, 1 - 4: Sigils of Cauda Draconis, the descending node of the Moon; 5, 6: geomantic figures of Cauda Draconis. Third line: 1, the Northumbrian rune for, the World Serpent; 2, Nydrune, whose corresponding herb is Snakeroot; 3, Dragon's Eye sigil; 4, herbal sigil for Dragon's Blood; 5, the Aegishjalmur (Helm of Awe), sigil of irresistable power, taken by Sigurd from the dragon Fafnir. Fourth line: 1, heraldic Wyvern; 2, heraldic Dragon; 3, heraldic Cockatrice; 4, dragon from a manuscript in Wells Cathedral, Somerset, England. Fifth line: 1, mounted standard-bearer of the Israelites, from the 9th century Psalterium Aureum from St Gallen, Switzerland, depicting in reality ninth-century central European military practice; 2, dragon weathervane on the church of St Mary le Bow, London; 3, lindwurm fountain in Klagenfurt, Austria.

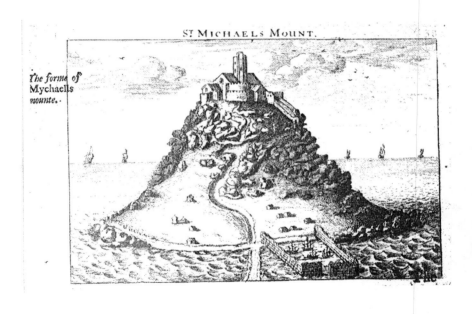

St Michael's Mount, Cornwail, England. 16th century engraving from Dugdale's Monasticon Analicanum.

126

American Wake Robin (*Arum triphyllum Linn.*), which is indigenous over most of North America, is known as Dragon Root. The root is usable in powdered form against croup, whooping-cough, asthma, bronchitis, laryngitis and flatulence. However, its dragon nature means that it must be used only when in a semi-dried state. It is inactive when dry, and ineffective when tea or other stimulants are taken. But when fresh, it irritates the mucous membranes violently; if chewed, it burns the mouth and throat; whilst if fresh root is taken internally, it causes gastro-enteritis which may end in death.

Another North American dragon plant used in herbal medicine is Dragon's Claw (*Corallorhiza odontorhiza* Nutt.). It is a parasitic plant that grows in rich woods on the roots of trees. Like Dragon Root, Dragon's Claw root is used in powdered form. Dragon's Claw is among the most powerful and effective diaphoretics, promoting perspiration without other effects. It is used in typhus, pleurisy and other inflammatory diseases. It also has a sedative effect.

It is not recommended that the reader unskilled in herbalism should attempt to use any of these remedies without first consulting a competent qualified herbalist who can identify wild plants with certainty.

The Dragon in Geomancy

In divinatory geomancy, or 'Terrestrial Astrology', the head and the tail of the dragon are two of the sixteen geomantic figures. Caput Draconis is associated with the element Earth and the zodiac sign Capricorn, whilst Cauda Draconis is ruled by Fire and linked with Scorpio. Caput Draconis represents *Limen Intrans*, the Interior Threshold, a place of entry, a doorway to the upperworld. It is a good figure, ruled by the planets Venus and Jupiter. Its fortunate days are Thursday and Friday, and it rules the left foot of the human body. The exact inversion of Caput Draconis, Cauda Draconis represents *Limen Exiens*, the

127

Beneath the world of Sol and Luna and human concerns lurk the
dragons deep within the earth. Engraving from Anatomia Auri by J.D.
Mylius (Frankfurt, 1628)

exterior threshold, the way out. It signifies possible problems, and is a bad figure. Ruled by the planets Mars and Saturn, its most potent weekday is Tuesday. Cauda Draconis rules the right foot of the human body. According to John Heydon, in his Rosicrucian work, *Theomagia* (London, 1664), the geomantic figure of Caput Draconis is linked with the spirits Kedemel and Hismael, whilst Cauda Draconis is connected with Zazel and Bartzabel. In Islamic tradition, the figures of geomancy are connected with prophets and saints. Thus, Caput Draconis is linked with Madi the Messenger, whilst Cauda Draconis refers to Lassima al Houssein. Full details of geomantic divination may be found in the author's book, *The Oracle of Geomancy* (Capall Bann, 1995).

In the locational geomancy of the West, the dragon plays an important role. Dragons are connected with the *omphalos*, the centre of the land and the Navel of the World. The Greek legend of Apollo tells how he slays the Python that guarded the omphalos at Delphi, and Cadmus founds Thebes after he slays the dragon at the holy well of Ares. Similarly, the Welsh story of *Llys and Llevelys* recounted above tells of how two dragons fought at Oxford, the centre of Britain, a place which was determined by the royal surveyors by measuring the land.

In many parts of Europe are dragon hills and mountains, with evocative names like Wormwood Hill or Wurmberg. In legend, they are the locations where dragons slept. They have provided much material for speculation. After William Stukeley in the eighteenth century, many antiquaries saw such earth mounds as relics of ancient serpent worship. He believed that the great megalithic circles and earthworks at Avebury in Wiltshire were an ancient British serpent-temple. Avebury had two 'avenues' of standing stones that appeared to intersect the major earthwork and stone circle like a serpent crossing an egg. Late nineteenth and early twentieth century archaeologists in Scotland like John S. Phene (*Serpent Worship in the West*) and Ludovic MacLellan Mann (*A Druid Temple Near Glasgow*), put forward ideas that earth mounds and other

Symbolic drawing of the eternal combat between the green dragon and the red lion.

structures that they excavated were in the form of serpents or saurians. This, they saw, as evidence for druidical ophiolatry.

Such esoteric serpent and dragon ideas from folklore and antiquarian speculation were brought together with anthropological reports from as far away as China and Mexico, and fused together in the 1970s to make a new subject called Earth Mysteries. The earth serpent was transformed thereby from being viewed as the last remaining relic of ancient British serpent-worship into the 'serpent-power', more fitting for a technological age. Soon, these new ideas were attached to theosophical speculations of the 1900s about 'Etheric Currents' travelling across the globe, and Alfred Watkins's idea from the 1920s of *The Old Straight Track*. Watkins claimed that there are what he called leys, straight alignments of ancient 'sites' of various kinds that run across the land oblivious to the terrain. From this syncretic brew of alternative speculation arose the further thought that the land might conceal a hidden network of 'dragon lines' that run dead straight for hundreds of kilometres across the landscape. Proponents of this school of thought claim that they are powered by an 'energy' which can be found by techniques once associated only with water-divining.

Whatever the reality of 'dragon lines' may be, the symbolic motif of the green dragon versus the red lion appears in many medieval churches. Here, the lion and the dragon are not usually depicted together in mortal struggle, but face one another across the chancel from north to south. In Tudor times, this alchemical-geomantic motif appeared overtly as the supporters of the royal coat of arms. The regicide Oliver Cromwell also had the lion and dragon as supporters for his escutcheon. The symbolic subtle fifth element personified by the dragon was recognised by pre-scientific, pre-industrial philosophies. It is an important element of European esoteric teaching.

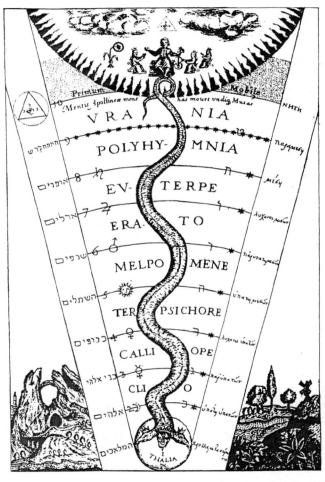

The three-headed cosmic serpent that binds together the planetary spheres and the activities of the nine Muses under the guardianship of Athansius Kircher, Rome 1665. Apollo. From Ars Magna Lucis

The ancient Greeks talked of the *pneuma*, which the medieval European alchemists identified with the Quintessence, the fifth element after Earth, Water, Fire and Air. In more recent times, independent researchers of subtle forces have called it Odyle, Vril and Orgone. Modern exponents of this 'force', especially those who talk of 'dragon lines' and the like, often view it literalistically as a physical force like gravity or magnetism rather than a symbolic view of the world. Historically, it appears in the Northern Tradition. In Scandinavia, it was called önd, and in Celtic lands, 'Nwyvre' (sometimes rendered 'Nwyfre' or the Breton-French 'Vouivre'). In modern Welsh, *nwyf* means energy, *nwyfriant*, vigour and vivacity, whilst nwyfre means the sky or 'firmament'. This modern meaning is the reason why the spelling *Nwyvre* is used to distinguish it in modern writings. The word is cognate with the English 'Wyvern'.

The nature of *Nwyvre* is explained in *Barddas* (Llandovery, 1866), the collection of Welsh Bardic texts of various ages that explain the elements of Bardism. One Bardic text describes the classical European five elements, thus: "'*Calas*'; fluidity; breath; *uvel* and *nwyvre*. From *calas* is every corporeity, namely, the earth and every thing hard; from 'fluidity' are moisture and flux; from 'breath' are every wind, breeze, respiration and air; from *uvel* are all heat; fire and light; and from *nwyvre* every life and motion, every spirit, every soul of man, and from its union with the other elements, other living beings".

In keeping with the magical-poetic world view of the ancients, *Nwyvre* was visualised in terms of non-human yet sentient beings. These took many different forms, each discrete form being but a specialised manifestation of the greater whole. Often, places at which this force can be felt by people sensitive to such things, have been venerated as holy. The *Nwyvre* as a semi-abstract power is depicted in the form of the mythological dragon-like being which can be found widely in medieval European art. Linguistically, the word '*Nwyvre*' appears to be related to the Indo-European root *wed*, which means water. The cognate Gallic word *Vobero* means underground water, which links it to the spiral patterns of underground water often found by water diviners of the British school. Modern water diviners have interpreted the legendary *Nwyvre* in terms of the effects of underground water.

According to late twentieth century geomantic ideas, the dragon, wyrm or serpent symbolises the unseen flows that move freely beneath ground level in the soil and the underlying rock formations. In former times, it was one of the functions of wizards and wise women to determine places where these serpentine flows were at their most potent, and the nature of the quality that they brought to a place, whether for good or ill. After long and meticulous scrutiny of a place, the *locator* would decide upon the best location to build. According to the principles of electional astrology, there is an instant in time when the conditions prevailing in the cosmos are optimal for foundation. At that instant, the locator would drive a pointed object into the earth, marking the place and time with what is called the Geomantic Act. Piercing the ground in this way is believed to fix the flows that water diviners can detect with the rod permanently in an accessible place. Equally, it is possible that such an act may create the effect that water diviners seek.

Whether or not this modern theory is objectively true, dragonslaying myths depict the outcome of the act as the triumph of order over chaos. It is the imposition of human order upon random and dangerous nature. Sometimes, as in the Northumbrian Lambton Worm legend, the disruption that must be dealt with has been caused initially by human interference with the natural world in an unnatural way. More generally, dragons seem to arise spontaneously, necessitating an appropriate remedy. Many depictions of dragonslayers show the hero transfixing the dragon with a stave, sword or spear, which frequently pins the beast to the ground below. In Greek myth, the foundation of both Delphi and Thebes comes about through the extirpation of a serpent or dragon, and it is not unreasonable to interpret some dragonslaying tales at least as symbolic of the geomantic manipulation of the earth.

The dragon or earth serpent also has an oblique connection with field labyrinths. In Norse myth, the roots of the World Tree Yggdrassil are encompassed by the serpent Nithogg, which coils around the axis in a manner similar to that of a labyrinth about a central marker. There are various legends, of which the Lambton Worm is one of the best-developed, where the dragon is said to coil itself around a rock or hillock. Coils around a central marker are the hallmark of many labyrinths cut in the turf. It is known that a number of European turf labyrinths had trees or stones at their centres. The *Rad* labyrinth at the Eilenriede Forest at Hannover in Germany still has a linden tree. An ash tree once stood at the centre of the maze on the common at Saffron Walden in Essex. It was destroyed by fire on Guy Fawkes' Night, 1823, and plans to plant a new one in the 1980s did not come to fruition. The now-obliterated turf labyrinth at Horncastle in Lincolnshire had a stone cross at its centre, and the existing 'maze' at Hilton has at its centre a monument erected to the memory of William Sparrow, who cut it to commemorate the restoration of King Charles II and Merrie England in 1660 after years of Cromwell's tyranny.

The legendary motif from Ragnar Lodbrok's life of the lady liberated from her house in the middle of the dragon's coils in East Gotland, a centre of stone labyrinths, is very reminiscent of other tales where a maiden is liberated from a labyrinth. Whilst many Renaissance engravings of labyrinths depict a woman, a man or the beastly Cretan Minotaur, occasionally a tree or spiral mountain is shown instead.

The serpent-like pathway of turf labyrinths was recognised in German-speaking countries, where the name *Schlangenweg* ('Serpent-Way') is used, for example the former labyrinth at Wunderburg, near Calbe on the River Saale. The church near

The labyrinth as serpent-path. Original labyrinth design by Nigel Pennick, 1994.

one of the surviving ancient turf labyrinths in Germany, at Steigra, has a dragon connection, for it is dedicated to St George. The dance called *Schlangenziehen* traditionally held at Naumburg in Germany is labyrinthine in form, and serpentine dances round village lindens and Maypoles are performed throughout Europe, such as the German *Plantanz* and *Rundumerdum*. At Salzsied at Schwäbisch Hall in south Germany, a festival was held every three years in which people danced around a linden tree where musicians played, and "*the dance remained the same all the time, except that it occasionally changes into a snake-like line*". The line of dancing people weaving in and out around the centre resembles the legendary dragon or wyrm coiling about the World Tree.

At the beginning of the fifteenth century, the children of the German city of Magdeburg were forbidden by the authorities there to play the Dragon Game, called *Wurme Spiel* in the previous century. What this was precisely is uncertain, it is equally likely to have been a snake-dance or a Mummers' Play, if not a combination of the two. It is traditional in England for sword-dancers to perform Mummers' Plays, sometimes, as recorded at Brighouse in Yorkshire in 1887, "the old drama of St George". Among others, the Coventry Mummers and the Handsworth Traditional Sword Dancers in Sheffield do both sword-dance and mumming at the same performances to-day. The performance of a St George and the Dragon play accompanied by dancing is therefore not an unlikely occurrence. One of the earliest representations of a sword-dance is a painting by Peter Breugel the Elder, dating from around 1600, titled *The Fair of St George's Day*.

Images of dragons are an integral part of European apotropaic building design. Romanesque architecture especially employs the dragon on entrances and roofs. It was a period when the cultural traditions of northern Paganism were integrated with Christian culture, and set the custom for dragon carvings and paintings to appear in churches not as defeated beasts but also in their own right. They did so until the advent of the Modern

Runestone from Ardre, Gotland, Sweden, with symmetrical interlaced dragons.

Dragon portal from the IIth century stave church at Stedje, Norway, 19th century engraving by Sörensen.

Medieval church furniture from Hittersdal church, Norway, with the lion and serpent motif, and what may be Ragnar-Lodbrok in the snake-pit. 19th century engraving by H.C. Olsen.

Style of architecture in the twentieth century condemned all but geometrical symbolism in building into a hibernation that lasted for more than fifty years.

Dragons appear right across Europe, but among the most notable are those on Norwegian churches. Carved in wood, they have suffered the ravages of time and fire, but enough are extant to demonstrate the richness of the tradition. The west portal of Borgund church and that from Stedje, owned by Bergen Museum, show how two dragons flank and protect the door at the sides and above, their tails forming a dense interlace with foliage that emerges from dragons' heads at the base. Dragons' heads also protect the gable ends of several ancient Stave Churches in Norway. They appear identical with those used on the prows of Scandinavian, English and Norman ships of the period. The famed church at Kilpeck in Herefordshire and the Abbey tower at Bury St Edmunds in Suffolk have remarkable stone dragons' heads of the same period. Clearly, they have the function of warding off all harm that might assail the building. In central Europe, from medieval to Baroque times, it was customary to make water-spouts from the roofs of buildings in the form of dragons' heads, a clear continuation of the tradition. In British buildings erected today, the curly metal pieces inserted at the end of sloping roof-ridges are called Dragons' Heads.

In parts of Germany, it is common to see serpents carved on the right and left doorposts of timber-framed farmhouses, rather in the manner of the Norwegian church portals, but far less ornate. Finally, the dragon is guardian of the inner fire, and in East Frisia in north-west Germany, there is the tradition of making serpentine kettle-cranes that suspended the pot or kettle over the fire in the hearth. These are in the form of a serpent, often with a small ball in the mouth. One of the best examples was made for Scloss Lütetsburg near Norden in Ostfriesland.

Chapter 7

Dragon Signs and Emblems

National Symbols

The Welsh Dragon is a ubiquitous emblem in Wales to-day, and so it may be assumed to be of great antiquity. In 1906, in her notes to the *Mabinogion*, Lady Charlotte Guest wrote; "*the red dragon has long been the national standard of the Welsh*". Its origin in Roman battle-standards has been discussed earlier, but the date at which it became recognised is a matter of dispute. Early references to the dragon are ambiguous because of the repeated use by the Bards of the word 'dragon' to describe a warlord or general. In feudal tradition, the allusions to dragons in *The Prophecies of Merlin* are more likely to refer to individual leaders in combat rather than the post-Enlightenment idea of abstract nations symbolised by red and white dragons. The idea that the red dragon represents Wales or the Welsh people is backed up occasionally by those who quote the writings of the Bard Iolo Goch. In 1385, Roger Mortimer, Earl of March, a descendent of Llewellyn the Great, was recognised as the heir to the throne of England. Then, Iolo Goch composed a praise-song that looked forward to the crowning of a Welshman as king of England:

> "*Gwaid y ddraig goch*
> *yw'r sinobr y sy ynoch.*"
> ("The red that is in you is the blood of the Red Dragon").

The 'red dragon' here is interpreted sometimes by nationalists as meaning the Welsh nation, but it seems more probable that it is an allusion to Mortimer's descent from Llewellyn the Great as 'dragon' of the Welsh. Roger Mortimer never became king, as Richard II outlived him.

The first unambiguous reference to the use of the dragon standard by a Welsh leader comes from 1401. During the siege of Caernarfon on All Souls' Day, 1401, Owain Glyndwr set up his standard, which, according to the chronicler Adam of Usk, was a golden dragon on a white field. His great seal, however, was not a dragon, but four lions rampant, the old royal arms of Gwynedd. But in 1404, as Prince of Wales, he commissioned another great seal, which depicted him mounted wearing a helm crested with a wyvern, as was his horse. His coat-of-arms was supported by a lion and a dragon.

Welsh power waned after the death of Owain Glyndwr, but Welsh aspirations were kept alive by the Bards, and expressed in dragon terminology. The Bard Dafydd Nanmor, for example, prophesied that soon the white dragon of the Saxons would be overthrown by the golden dragon of Britain. But even as late as the fifteenth century, it is uncertain whether the poets are referring to the dragons as representing nations or individual leaders. Once Henry Tudor became king of England by killing the rightful monarch, Richard III, in battle at Bosworth in 1485, the dragon became a popular emblem in Wales. Henry had three standards at Bosworth. One was the arms of St George, another "*a Baner of Tarteron bett wyth a dun cowe*" and the third, "*a red firye dragon beaten upon white and grene sarcenet*". When he assumed the crown as King Henry VII, he had the three standards blessed at St Paul's cathedral in London. When he became king, within the College of Heralds, Henry Tudor instituted the new office called *Rouge Dragon* ('Red Dragon').

Despite the long historical use of dragons in Wales, the red dragon only became the official royal emblem in 1807, when it

143

was established that "a red dragon passant standing on a mound should be the king's badge for Wales". In the 1890s, during an upsurge in regionalism and local nationalism that included calls for autonomy or independence for Ireland, Wales and East Anglia, Welsh societies approached the Crown in an attempt to alter the Royal Standard to include the red dragon in place of one of the fields of golden leopards. Early in the twentieth century, King Edward VII assigned the arms of the Prince of Wales to be the royal red dragon, differenced with a silver label. Later, in 1910, Welsh local authorities again petitioned the king to bring the dragon into the Royal Standard, and onto the coins of the realm. This was not done.

In 1953, Her Majesty Queen Elizabeth II decreed that a motto should be added to the royal red dragon badge:

> *"Y ddraig goch ddyry cychwyn"*
> ('The Red Dragon advances').

This was to be placed on a white field and flown over government buildings on festal occasions. But this new royal emblem was not popular among members of the Gorsedd of Bards of Wales, who in 1958 petitioned Her Majesty to recognise the red dragon on a green and white field to be the flag of Wales. In 1959, it was decreed that *"Only the Red Dragon on a green and white flag should be flown on Government buildings in Wales and in London, where appropriate"*. Thus the red dragon flag of Wales remains a royal banner, the prerogative of the monarch of the United Kingdom.

In Britain, the dragon is not just a symbol of Wales. The Wessex dragon is of equal antiquity with the Welsh dragon. According to Geoffrey of Monmouth, Uther Pendragon, King Arthur's father, placed a dragon in the cathedral at Winchester. Perhaps this is not a reference to the city in sub-Roman times under British rule, but another standard, that of the West Saxons, that hung there in later times, when

144

Winchester was England's capital city. First mentioned by Henry of Huntingdon as the battle-standard at the Battle of Burford in 752 CE, the Wessex Dragon is now a symbol of regional identity in the heartland of southern England. The seal of Roger de Quincey, Earl of Winchester, who died in 1264, shows that he wore a wyvern as the crest on his helm.

In his works on early British heraldry, the Jacobean antiquary and map-maker John Speed identified a red dragon as the emblem of the Pagan West Saxons. Later antiquaries described ancient artifacts with dragons as representing the West Saxon nation, "*the cognizance of the Kingdom of Wessex*", and by the late nineteenth century, the Dragon of Wessex was mentioned in school history books. The county arms of some of the subdivisions of Wessex now bear dragons. The escutcheon of Somerset bears a dragon rampant, whilst that of Dorset is supported by two dragons. In 1935, the Wessex Dragon became the military badge of the Wessex Infantry Division. Since then, the dragon has become the emblem of the (unofficial) Province of Wessex, a symbol of local pride.

Inn Signs

In Europe, it is traditional that inns are named after something or somebody. It is a very ancient tradition. Inn signs were compulsory in England from a very early period. In 1393, a publican, Florence North, was prosecuted at Chelsea for failing to put up her sign. In Cambridge, an Act of Parliament (9 Hen. VI, C.X.) of 1430-31 stated: "*Whosoever shall brew ale in the town of Cambridge with intention of selling it, must hang out a sign, otherwise he shall forfeit his ale*". When an innkeeper's license was revoked, his or her sign was pulled down.

Among inn names, fabulous beasts seem to have existed as long as any other. Many are heraldic in origin, not least the red Lion, which is still one of the most plentiful of public house

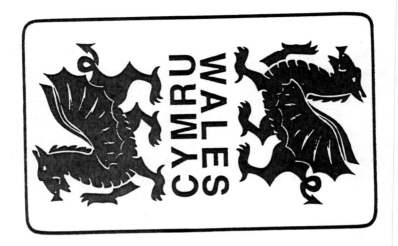

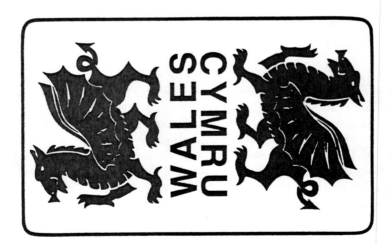

Patriotic contemporary Welsh playing card backs.

names. The dragon was the standard of many nobles and princes, and the Green Dragon was the most popular inn sign. In his *Travels Through London*, Taylor, the Water Poet, listed all of the taverns in London, including seven named after the Green Dragon. In his *The Rape of Lucrece*, (London, 1608) Thomas Heywood wrote a song based on London inn-signs, with their appropriate clientele. Although he does not mention the dragon, green or otherwise, he tells us that the Punk (prostitute) goes to the Cockatrice. In the style of Heywood, the 'Roxburgh Ballad', *London's Ordinarie*, or, *Every Man in His Humour* lists the inns of London. One verse goes:

> *"The Saddlers will dine at the Saddle,*
> *The Painters will go to the Green Dragon,*
> *The Dutchmen will go to the Froe,*
> *Where each man will drink his Flagon".*

A good version of the whole of this ballad can be heard (along with almost every other significant English songs in praise of beer and ale) on the recording *The Tale of Ale* (Free Reed Music, 1977, reissued 1993).

One of the most notable public houses in Cambridge is the *Fort St. George in England* on Midsummer Common next to the River Granta. It has a tall flagpole, on which the flag of England, the Cross of St George, is always flown. Downstream, about a mile distant, and also near the river, is the Green Dragon at Chesterton. St George and the dragon are kept far apart in Cambridge.

Perhaps because of the name of public houses, the dragon has been connected with ale. In 1996, the Campaign For Real Ale in Norwich used the dragon as its emblem, and on St George's Day, April 23, 1997, *Dragon Slayer* beer was being served in *The George* at Fenstanton in Old Huntingdonshire as a 'special'. *Dragon Slayer* was made by Taylor and Banks of Shefford, in Bedfordshire, and used a logo of St George killing the dragon. Specialist food shops all over England and Wales

147

In 1996, the 19th Norwich Beer Festival sported an inn-sign of a dragon.

sell *Dragon's Breath* mustard, which is very hot - but not as hot as their brand called *Devil's Revenge!*

Dragon Weather Vanes

Although the weathercock and flag-shaped weathervane have always been in the great majority, dragon-shaped weather vanes have been made for many centuries. The most celebrated dragon weather vane in England is on the steeple of the church of St Mary le Bow in Cheapside, London. Designed by Sir Christopher Wren after the Great Fire of London, the church replaces a medieval one that had been burnt down like much of the city. The dragon was made by the coppersmith Robert Bird, who on September 25, 1679, was paid £38 for making it. It measures 2.44 metres in length, and was made because the dragon is the bearer of the coat of arms of the City of London. Other notable dragon weather vanes on churches include those on St Margaret's at Upton in Norfolk, St Michael's at Sittingbourne in Kent, St George's at Orleton, Herefordshire, Christchurch in Bristol, Chelmsford Cathedral and the church of St Mary at Latton, in Harlow, Essex.

What might be the oldest British dragon weather-vane can be seen at Newark Park, Ozleworth in Gloucestershire, dating from the sixteenth century. Dating from the 1740s is the dragon vane that tops out the chapel of Sir William Turner's Hospital at Kirkleatham, near Redcar on Teesside. The University College of Wales at Cardiff has a fine dragon surmounted by a crown and the Prince of Wales's feathers. It was made in 1907. Another notable Welsh dragon vane surmounts the Washington Hotel on the sea front at Llandudno. Haddenham in Buckinghamshire has a curious nexus of dragons. Close to a lane called Dragon Tail is the Green Dragon public house, and close by is Dragon Cottage, complete with a dragon weather vane.

149

Emblems

The dragon appears frequently in heraldic charges, both of nobility and royalty, and also civic and company heraldry. In some cases, the dragons are associated with family or civic legends of dragonslaying. The Danish noble family of Drage, which died out in 1536, had a shield with a wyvern, which was also the crest used on parade helmets. The town of Lindenhardt in Bavaria has a dragon emblem that goes back at least to 1567. The ancient arms of the City of London include two dragons as bearers, whilst those of the City of Brussels depict the archangel Michael overcoming a dragon-like Devil. In England, before 1923, the Midland Railway Company used a dragon as its crest. A fine example can be seen on the old Midland Hotel in Manchester. The successor to the Midland, the London, Midland and Scottish Railway Company, had a dragon's wing in its crest.

Orders, Medals, Seals and Coins

Because St George and St Michael are the patron saints of chivalry, they have appeared on the medals and emblems of Orders of Chivalry. The most illustrious order in the United Kingdom is the English Order of the Garter, more properly called The Most Noble Order of the Garter. This was founded by King Edward III in 1348 as a noble fraternity comprising the monarch and 25 Knights Companion. Members of the royal family are included as Royal Knights Companions, and foreigners are Extra Knights. Only Christians are admitted. It is the highest civil and military honour of the United Kingdom.

The collar of the Order has an enamelled pendant emblem of St George, lance in hand, mounted on a white steed, piercing a green dragon with red spits upon it. The badge of the Order is in gold, with a more Classical St George within a garter with the Order's French motto: "*Honi Soit Qui Mal Y Pense*" upon it ("*Dishonour be to him who thinks evil of it*"). The day of the

150

Order is St George's Day, April 23, when a special service is held at St George's Chapel in Windsor Castle.

The Order of St Michael and St George has as its collar a pendant with a seven-pointed star within which is a representation of a winged St Michael overcoming the Satanic dragon. The badge of the Order has St Michael on one side, and on the other, St George killing the dragon. The Order was founded in 1818 by King George III to reward the inhabitants of Malta and the Ionian Islands, who had just come under British sovereignty. It was awarded first to British citizens who had performed meritorious duties in the Mediterranean region. Later, it was extended to diplomats and members of the British Foreign Service.

The George Cross, instituted in September 1940 by King George VI, recognises valour and outstanding gallantry for civilians of the British Commonwealth. It is a cross at the centre of which is a depiction of St George and the Dragon, surrounded by the inscription, "*For Gallantry*". The George Medal, which was instituted on the same occasion, is a lower rank, but it, too, depicts St George and the Dragon. In Greece, the Order of St George and St Constantine was instituted in 1936 by King George II. The badges do not depict a dragon.

In addition to Orders and medals, dragons have appeared occasionally on seals and coins. The seal of the Earl of Winchester has already been mentioned. Another seal, that of Thomas, Earl of Lancaster, 1301, shows the lord's helm surmounted by a wyvern. A seal of Murnau, in Bavaria, also dating from the fourteenth century, shows a Lindwurm, which remains the town's heraldic sign to this day. An 18th century trade token from Holborn, London, shows the 'White Dragon' of England, pierced by an arrow. The reverse side of the standard gold sovereign, first issued by the Bank of England in 1817, shows the mounted St George, by Benedetto Pistrucci, is in Greek classical style, naked except for crested helmet, cloak and boots. He wields a short sword of Greek type and tramples

151

An entrance ticket for the Cretan Folklore Museum at Agios Georgios, Lassithi, Crete, with medallion of St George and the Dragon.

the dragon under his horse's hooves. This design is still produced to-day on current sovereign coins, which are not in general circulation.

Dragons in National Romantic and Fantasy Art

During the nineteenth century, historians all over Europe who formerly had concentrated on ancient Greece and Rome, rediscovered the tales, legends and myths of their own lands, and called it folk-lore. Among the wonderful things that emerged into national consciousness was the dragon. Better-known legends, too, like those of Ragnar Lodbrok, Lord Lambton, Hu Gadarn, Wolfdietrich, Thidrek, Siegfried and Gilles de Chin, were re-told in lavishly illustrated books for adults and children. The dragon took on a new lease of life in central Europe in the nineteenth century as the result of this dissemination of heroic tales and folklore researches, especially those by the Grimm brothers.

Later, the influence of the operas of Richard Wagner and the designers of his stage sets at Beyreuth, such as Georg Dollmann, popularised a neo-medieval approach to life that was nevertheless not a revival of something past, but a creative new manifestation of ancient tradition according to correct principles. In Bavaria, heroic sculptures and illustrations of St George and the dragon were made for Wagner's patron, King Ludwig II in his capacity as grand master of the Order of St George in Munich. Everywhere that a dragon tradition was recognised, a monument appeared, as if the *anima loci* were re-manifesting. A bridge in Ljubljana, then in the Austro-Hungarian Empire, and now the capital city of Slovenia, built in 1888, is guarded by four fine bronze dragons that allude to a local dragonslaying legend similar to that in Klagenfurt.

Hallingdansen.

Norwegian engraving, by Waldemar Olsen in the Dragon Style, showing the remarkable athletic folk-dance of Hallingen.

154

During the nineteenth century, the same process took place in Great Britain. Awareness of local legends in England led to the creation of many dragon and serpent images on civic buildings and structures. The fine painted cast-iron dragons that guard the entrances to the City of London are among the most impressive. Sheffield City Hall has an Arts and Crafts-style carving of an unmounted knight killing a dragon. It is said to represent the demise of the Wantley Dragon at the hands of More of More-Hall. The Serpent's Well at Cawthorne, near Barnsley in south Yorkshire is recalled by a stone cross dating from 1866 that stands in Church Street (formerly Maypole Hill). Carved upon it are twining serpents biting each others' tails.

The Norwegian style of art called 'Dragon Style' was very popular around the turn of the twentieth century. Parallelling the National Romantic styles of Russia and Finland, the Celtic Revival of Scotland and Ireland, and having links to Art Nouveau and Jugendstil in other northern European countries, the Norwegian 'Dragon Style' used historical motifs, especially dragons, in a decorative way, applying them in ways that had not been done before. The illustration of traditional Norwegian *Hallingdansen* by Waldemar Olsen reproduced here is a typical example of the 'Dragon Style'. Some of the art- and craft-work produced in this style is stunning, though little known outside Scandinavia.

Many fine artists of the nineteenth and twentieth centuries have turned to the dragon as a theme for paintings and illustrations. Arthur Rackham (1867-1939) drew dragons for illustrated works based on Wagner's masterpieces, in *The Rhinegold* and *The Valkyrie* (London, 1910), he illustrated *"Horrible the dragon, O swallow me not! Spare the life of poor Loge"*, whilst in *Siegfried and The Twilight of the Gods*, he showed Siegfried killing the dragon Fafnir. Sidney Sime (1867-1941) drew fantastic atmospheric illustrations for magazines like *The Sketch* and especially the works of Lord Dunsany, which, though based clearly upon archetypal mythology, were

155

Drachenwäsche

The dragon-washer, ink drawing by Julius Diet from the journal Jugend, Germany, 1902.

not of any tradition, but new, creative, literature. Sime used fabulous beasts and the dragon motif as part of the fantasy worlds they created. Most notable as an archetype is Sime's Dragon of the Eclipse, that attempts to swallow 'the golden ball' of the sun ('Inzana Calls Up The Thunder', in *Time and the Gods*, London 1906). This is a motif that recalls the East Frisian kettle-holders. Following in the footsteps of Lord Dunsany, but based solidly in the European tradition, J.R.R. Tolkien's rendering of the dragon Smaug in *The Hobbit* (London, 1937) is a classical example of the dragon of the Northern Tradition sitting in its lair on a hoard of gold. Since the runaway success of *The Hobbit* and later *The Lord of the Rings*, dragons have become a staple of fantasy literature and art. Many fine dragons have been made by modellers for fantasy role-playing games, carrying on the tradition in the contemporary world.

'Georgian' the Dragon, who accompanies the Chanctonbury Ring morris
dancers on their outings in the Sussex region of southern England.

Chapter 8

Mummers, Guisers, Morris and Dragon Pageantry

English and Welsh Theatrical and Festal Dragons

To-day, dragons appear occasionally in village and town celebrations, in continuity of tradition. These are not all the same, for there are several ways of making festal dragons. The most common are simply heads worn as all-over masks by human beings who are dressed in some appropriate dragon-like costume. They are most common among Morris dance sides, where, so as not to impede dancing, the dragons have no tail. In the summer in Norfolk, the dragons of the King's Men of King's Lynn and Kemp's Men of Norwich can be seen dancing out. Elsewhere, in Sussex, the Chanctonbury Ring Morris dancers have a fine red-and-green dragon made in 1967.

A number of other English Morris sides also have dragons, and it is not intended to list them all here. The Hampshire Morris sides of Bourne River and Cuphill dance out with dragons as do Croxley Green in Hertfordshire. The Welsh dragon connection is remembered in the English borderlands with the Forest of Dean Morris Men and in Wales proper by the Cardiff and Conwy Morris teams. There is also a Morris team called Green Dragon at Bury St Edmunds, Suffolk.

The larger dragons paraded to-day in England and Belgium are of the 'tourney beast' type. In construction, this is allied to the larger versions of the hobby-horse, where the operator walks and dances inside the beast, with his or her feet protruding from the bottom. The body of the animal is suspended by straps from the shoulders of the operator.

Guilds and Festivals

Because St George is the patron saint of England, he has appeared regularly in English plays and pageants since the Middle Ages. Plays of St George and the Dragon continue to be performed by Mummers' teams, and we know that dragons were part of the properties of professional theatres as far back as Shakespeare's time. An *Inventory* of March 10th, 1598, of the property of Philip Henslowe, included "*Mercury's wings and dragons, 1 chain of dragons*". Henslowe was the leading theatrical promoter of his day, who built the Fortune Theatre in London and ran the company called *Lord Admiral's Men*.

In parallel with the English cultus of St George, the accession of the Tudor king, Henry VII, in 1485 was another spur to dragon performance. Dragons appeared at various royal occasions in Tudor England, beginning with the coronation of Henry VII, when his queen, Elizabeth of York, processed along the river from Greenwich to the Tower of London in one of a flotilla of barges that included "*a great red dragon spewing flames of fire into the Thames*".

The close relationship between the Hobby Horse and the Dragon can be seen to-day in England and Belgium. Not surprisingly, dragons are most associated with the St George's Day festivities on April 23, though, in former times, dragons were also brought out on May Eve and, in more recent times in Norwich, for the Lord Mayor's parade, now held in July. Dragon-pageantry was very widespread, and not confined to any specific locality. In the fifteenth century, amid other pageantry, it is recorded that a dragon made of canvas on a wooden frame was paraded in Newcastle-upon-Tyne. At Burford in Oxfordshire, a dragon and a giant were paraded on Midsummer Eve. The medieval guilds of Chester, Lostwithiel in Cornwall, Little Walsingham in Norfolk and Stratford-upon-Avon all had dragons at one time or another, whilst the guilds specifically dedicated to St George at Canterbury, Leicester and Norwich used dragons as part of their festal pageantry.

In 1555 at York, a dragon appeared in the St George's Day celebrations. In 1564 in Chester, the Midsummer celebrations of the craft and trade guilds mustered a bevy of guisers who carried or personated four giants, a unicorn, two camels, a lynx, and six hobby-horses in addition to the dragon. As befitting the capital city, St George pageantry was strong in old London. A major triumph was held in 1415 to welcome back the victorious King Henry V after his decisive defeat of the French army at Agincourt. The London Midsummer Watch, a parade of the city militia in a pageant, was held annually between 1504 and 1545. The parade took place every June 24, being repeated on June 29. Hobby horses and other beasts are mentioned in accounts, so it is likely that dragons featured at least sometimes. A London pageant planned for Midsummer Eve in 1541, was to have featured Morris dancers, Mummers, religious tableaux and a dragon with *aqua vitae* burning in its mouth. Sadly, politics prevented the Drapers' Company, which had arranged the show, from proceeding with it. But fortunately it was not the last time that dragons had a chance to strut the streets of London.

Attached to certain dragon legends is the story that after the beast was killed, its skin was stuffed and hung up in the local church or some other prominent place. Some of them were crocodiles, brought from north Africa by travellers, but it is possible that some of them are memories of festal dragons being stored in the local church when they were not being used. At Hutton Rudby in north Yorkshire, the 'skin' of a dragon was hung in the church over the pews of the hamlet of

Sexhowe, where the dragon was reputedly killed. In 1578, the Hughenden Dragon near High Wycombe in Buckinghamshire was supposedly stuffed with straw and hung up outside the house of the woman who 'killed it'. In later years the Norwich dragons were hung up in public houses and a shop entrance, just as they hang now in the Castle Museum. In the early 19th century, the historian Robert Surtees reported that as a boy at Old Lambton he saw a relic of the Lambton Worm, a piece of skin resembling bull's hide.

In contemporary England, dragons often appear at festivals commemorating special days in the yearly round. The Hal-an-Tow play performed each May at Helston in Cornwall includes a combat between a dragon and St George. This dragon is not a man in costume like those used by various Morris dance sides around England. Teams of Mummers occasionally perform St George and the Dragon plays, especially around the Christmas season. A resplendent dragon appeared in 1996 at Wembley Stadium in London along with a mounted 'St George' at the official opening of the European football championship finals. But the place where dragon parades have the greatest continuity is in 'The Athens of the North', the fine city of Norwich.

Norwich, the Dragon City

The Norwich dragon tradition is an instance of remarkable continuity that flourishes to-day. It has its origins in the Guild of St George, a religious body founded in 1385 for charitable and social reasons. Its main public event was the celebration each year of St George's Day, when the members of the guild paraded through the streets of the city from the Guildhall to the Cathedral, where Mass was said in the Chapel of St George there. The dragon appears to have been part of the parade from the earliest times. The oldest surviving notice of the dragon is in the records of the Guild Assembly for 1408, when the members voted to provide copes for the priests, "*and the George shall go in procession and make conflict with the Dragon"*. The way for the parade was cleared through the crowds of onlookers by sword-bearing whifflers. An official bearer of the ceremonial sword of King Henry V headed the procession, which included the dragon, St George, the musicians of the City Waits, priests and guild members. The early Norwich dragons were spectacular: in 1429, the snapdragon breathed fire and smoke produced by gunpowder, and the man operating it was paid danger money.

From 1385 until 1417, the Guild of St George was just one of the many religious and trade associations in the City of Norwich. But in the latter year, King Henry V awarded the Guild of St George a Royal Charter in recognition of the bravery of the guild members who had fought with him at the Battle of Agincourt in 1415. Empowered by its Royal Charter, the Guild of St George became the most prominent and powerful organisation in the city. Theoretically, it was possible for anyone to join the guild, but in practice, the high membership fees excluded all but knights, wealthy ladies and the more prosperous merchants and clerics. At the height of its power, the guild numbered around 200 members, including the most influential citizens of Norwich. After the Royal Charter was granted, the city's guilds engaged in a political power-struggle, which culminated in 1430 with the members of the Guild of St George being accused of attempting to rig the election of the Lord Mayor in their favour.

Further attempts by the guild to take over the city were thwarted, but in 1452, in a legal ruling known as Yelverton's Mediation, the Guild of St George was linked legally with the city's administration. After this ruling, the Aldermen of Norwich were automatically members of the guild, whilst the past Lord Mayor became Alderman (president) of the Guild of St George. The lesser members of the civic body were also encouraged to join the guild, and so the guild effectively became the city government. The guild's power was emphasised by the fact that, unlike most religious and trade

163

associations, the Guild of St George did not own or need its own guildhall. In 1486, it took over the upper chamber of the City Guildhall as its headquarters, consolidating its power over the city. The annual parade of the guild was indisting-uishable from the city government, and the dragon was its symbol.

In 1532, the parade saw a new figure added to the entourage of the dragon, St George, the whifflers and standard-bearers. It was a woman, described variously as The Margaret, The Maid or The Lady. But in 1547, the Protestants were in charge, and King Edward VI's Parliament passed an Act that suppressed all religious guilds, brotherhoods and fraternities. All over England, most civic guilds, as well as welfare organisations, were closed down, and their funds confiscated by the state. But there was a problem in Norwich, because the Guild of St George had a Royal Charter. This meant that it could not be suppressed. However, its property was seized by the state and privatised. Stripped of its Roman Catholic religious connect-ions, the Norwich Guild of St George was re-organised in 1548. The organisation was re-founded as The Company and Citizens of St George. During the brief Catholic revival, under Queen Mary I, the religious traditions re-surfaced, though it was not possible for the Company to recover the property that had been confiscated by the Protestants.

Soon, the Protestants regained power under Queen Elizabeth I, and the status of the Company was in jeopardy once more. But in 1584, the City Assembly decided to amalgamate the St George's Day festival with the inauguration of the new Lord Mayor, which was set as the Tuesday before Midsummer's Eve. This event was celebrated with a festive parade annually from 1585 until 1731. Its highlight was the appearance of the dragon universally known as Snap, who had survived the removal, of St George at the Reformation, according to the resolution that stated: "*There shall neither be Gorge nor Margaret; but, for pastime, the Dragon to come and shew himself as in other years*".

For many years, the Lord Mayor's procession took the following form. It was led by six whifflers, dressed in jackets and breeches of satin, with silk hats bedecked with ribbons and feathers. Each whiffler carried a rapier decorated with ribbons. These they used to part the crowds, and to demonstrate their prowess by throwing them in the air and catching them again. Perhaps they performed a now-forgotten East Anglian sword dance. Along with the whifflers ran the Dick Fools, who taunted the crowds with merry japes. The Dick Fools wore red and yellow canvas coats with serpents painted upon them. They also wore caps with bells, and in their hands, they carried dragon-headed staves. These dragons' heads had morris bells on their ears and a string of bells dangling on ribbons from their mouths. Fox and cat tails hung at the Dick Fools' backs, parallelling the costume of the Fool who attended the Plough Monday ceremonies at Whittlesford in Cambridgeshire in the mid-19th century. There, he was "covered with ribbons and attired in skins with a depending tail". The tail is one of the attributes of traditional English 'Fools' and the multi-coloured character called Hellekin or Harlequin, who sometimes appeared in classical form in English parades.

Other Norwich officials included the richly-liveried Standard-Bearers, who carried banners with the City Arms, the Goddess of Justice and the Standard of England, the red cross of St George. The musician of the City Waits, dressed in blue cloaks and their silver chains of office, played them along the Norwich streets. The dragon, Snap, containing and carried by a strong man, cavorted before the Mayor and other civic dignitaries. When the parade arrived at the Cathedral, the Dragon was not allowed inside, but was left on a special stone that lay next to the west door, the Dragon Stone. After a service of dedication, the parade assembled again, the dragon-carrier got back inside, and the procession began anew.

Of course, because of the relatively fragile nature of the beasts, there has been a succession of snapdragons over the years, the

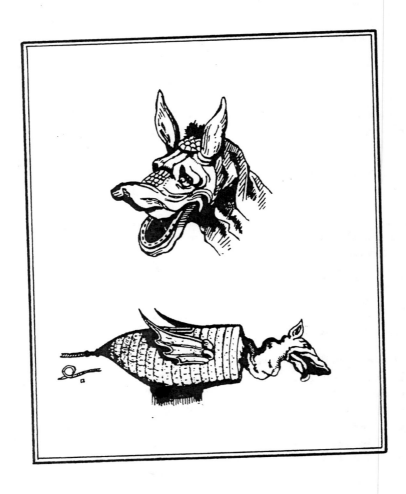

'Old Snap', one of the Norwich festal dragons, as depicted by W. Fairholt in his Gog and Magog (London, 1859).

latest at the time of writing having been made in 1988 by the local artist, John Matthews. However, as far as can be ascertained, the dragons have had the same design, being constructed of a wickerwork frame covered with painted canvas, measuring overall about 15 feet. The oldest extant dragon dates from 1795, and one of the earliest illustrations is an engraving in F.W. Fairholt's book, *Gog and Magog*, published in London in 1859. One of the essential features of these 'tourney beasts', giving it the popular name, is a heavy wooden head with a weighted lower jaw which the operator snaps from time to, time. This is a feature of many beasts in the European mumming tradition, including British Hobby Horses, the Hoodening Horse, and the Old Tup, and elsewhere in Europe, among others, the Scandinavian Julbock, the Austrian Habergeiss and Schnabelpercht and the Tarasque of southern France.

The jaws of the old Norwich snapdragons were weighted with horse-shoes that clashed together when the operator pulled a string. They can be seen in the dragons preserved in Norwich Castle. Fairholt's illustration also shows the horseshoes in the open jaws. Counterbalancing the dragon's heavy wooden head is a long straight tail with a twisted copper pipe at the end which can be altered in shape to alter the centre of gravity, so that the beast is in perfect balance, easing the operator's task. Some Norwich snapdragons had other moving parts. The 1725 dragon could spread and clap its wings. Carrying the heavy dragon, snapping the jaws and flapping the wings, and, on occasion igniting fireworks over a course of more than a mile required both strength and dexterity.

In 1731, after two years' litigation by Alderman William Clarke, the Company of St George was suppressed, and all of its funds, goods and property were passed to the Corporation. The Company of St George had run Norwich for 279 years, a remarkably long period for such an institution to exist. But the institution of the dragon, having already survived the momentous changes from Catholicism to Protestantism and

How the Norwich dragon, 'Snap', is operated.

from a religious to a secular symbol, was more tenacious and outlived the organisation that had given it birth. Municipal dragon parades continued until 1835, when the Municipal Corporations Act abolished many English municipal traditions that had become associated with what was seen as a hopelessly corrupt system of local government.

Even this blow did not mean the end of the Norwich dragon. The citizens of the Dragon City found a way of continuing the tradition. Even before the 1835 Act, the suburbs of the city had set up their own civic guilds and paraded their own dragons. The Pockthorpe Guild, founded in 1772, paraded a dragon that travelled from public house to public house, accompanied by much beery merriment.

The suburban dragon tradition continued for many years, for until the early 20th century, the Pockthorpe Dragon could be seen at various times, parading through the streets, collecting money. The snapping jaws would grab people's hats, which were then ransomed back, to the ditty "Snap, snap, steal a boy's cap; give him a penny, he'll give it back". Another snapdragon belonged to the Costessey Guild, which also processed from pub to pub every Whit Tuesday. Successive 'Mock Mayors of Costessey' and their merry followers continued their dragon parades until 1895.

There are three complete old Norwich dragons currently known to exist. They are all on show in the Castle Museum in the city. The oldest dates from 1795, and is a Municipal Dragon. The others are erstwhile Pockthorpe Snaps, which formerly resided in public houses when not in use. In the 1880s, one of them was acquired by Back and Company's wine and spirit shop close to Norwich Market Place. It hung in the shop's doorway, and the company's advertisements promoted *Old Snap* brand whisky and gin with a colour print of Old Snap standing in front of St Andrew's Hall.

The 1988 'Snap' on the streets of Norwich, accompanied by his two Whifflers in the Lord Mayor's Procession, July 13, 1996.

170

In addition to the three intact dragons in the Castle Museum, there is a detached head from one of the Costessey Dragons. It is believed to be earlier than the whole 1795 dragon.

As with many Old English traditions, there was a hiatus in Norwich dragonry during the first half of the 20th century. The Great War and its aftermath had a devastating effect on indigenous folk-customs. Many were stopped, seemingly never to be performed again. However, like the apparently slain ragged hero of the mummers' plays, the traditions were not dead, for they rose again *"and did amaze them all"*. In 1951, one of the preserved Snaps was paraded through the streets as part of the Festival of Britain celebrations, and after that, a dragon appeared at infrequent intervals. For example, Old Snap made a visit to a costume exhibition at Strangers' Hall in 1959. In the 1980s, a new dragon, made by Lucy Ellis, appeared with the Kemp's Men Morris Dancers, and resumed its rightful place in the Lord Mayor's procession.

Sadly, this dragon was burnt subsequently in a house fire, and so, in 1988, a new one was made by John Matthews to replace it. It was this dragon that appeared in London in 1990 with Kemp's Men at the 90th birthday celebrations of Her Royal Highness Queen Elizabeth the Queen Mother. When it is not in use, the dragon is kept in Dragon Hall in Norwich. It appears each year in the Lord Mayor's parade. In 1996, for the first time since the 1830s, it was accompanied by two sword-bearing whifflers, members of Kemp's Men, dressed in brand-new satin-and-silk costumes made according to ancient tradition. Led by the splendid Town Crier, and followed by the Dragon, the whifflers, and the City sword- and mace-bearers, the Lord Mayor and the Bishop of Norwich; the Lord Mayor's parade is one of the finest in England outside the City of London.

Engraving of the Tarasque of Tarascon, France, in its original six-legged form.

Dragons in Mainland Europe

Another instance of the medieval guising tradition is maintained at Tarascon in Provence in the south of France. It is one of the most colourful of dragon traditions. In the late fifth century CE, Mamert, the Bishop of Vienne, and St Césaire, the Archbishop of Arles, replaced the Pagan ceremonies there with the new Rogationtide rites of the Christian Church. This transition from Paganism to Christianity was symbolised by a dragon called the Tarasque, which in local legend had been overcome by St Marthe (St Martha). William of Tilbury wrote about the dragon in the twelfth century, and in 1474, King René set up a guild to oversee and conduct the ceremonies at Tarascon. They involved parading an effigy of the Tarasque through the streets, accompanied by whifflers from the guild. The Tarasque was a wicker-and-canvas beast similar in construction to the Norwich and Mons dragons. In common with many guilds of mummers and guisers, one of the pleasures of the members was to drink copious quantities of alcoholic beverages. The brotherhood of Tarascaires had the motto, "*Anen Beure*", ('Let Us Drink'). The royal charter stated that the Tarascaires should parade the Tarasque at least seven times each century, on Ascension Day and St Martha's Day, June 29th.

On its first outing in the year, Ascension Day, the Tarasque is a ferocious beast that rampages through the streets of Tarascon, whipping people off their feet with its tail. Flames and smoke burst forth from its snout, produced by fireworks. The Tarasque is accompanied by the Tarascaires, men dressed in white shirts with sashes, white knee-breeches and hats with feathers. The Tarascaires assist the men inside the beast, who carry the Tarasque, snapping its jaws and letting off the fireworks.

On its second outing in the year, the Tarasque is led by a girl dressed in white, personating St Marthe. Like many dragon-leading women, she leads it by a ribbon. Captured by St

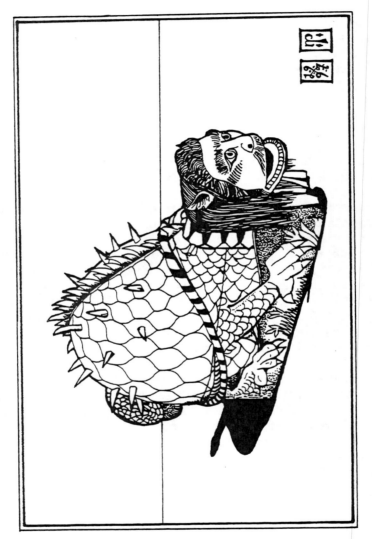

The current Tarasque, which only has four 'legs'.

Marthe, the Tarasque is no longer the ferocious fire-breathing dragon of Ascension Day, but is as docile as a well-trained dog.

In his *Relations de la Course de la Tarasque*, the writer Mouren tells of a parade held on Whit Monday, 1792: "*The Tarascaires were ready to start, the drummers had gathered together by the fountain in the square and were beating out the rhythm of the Farandole and the Rigaudon. Everybody was dancing when the Tarasque was taken and led gently into the square, to the corner next to the Town Hall. There they put two fireworks into his nostrils, and the men squeezed themselves into position.....they danced until Midnight, before the feast was over*". After the festival, the Tarasque was destroyed by being thrown into the River Rhone from the Pont de Jarnegues. Today, the Tarasque is not thrown into the river, but kept at the castle until its next outing. According to a 19th century pilgrim's manual, the Tarasque in use then measured 7 metres in length. It was over 1 metre 20 centimetres in height and 1 metre 50 centimetres wide. The Tarasque has the head of a heraldic lion, a green, scale-painted tortoise-like carapace covered with red spines, six scaly legs and a whippy tail. Old illustrations of the beast, such as that reproduced here, shows it in the process of swallowing a human victim.

At Draguignan, a similar tradition was celebrated with a dragon parade. There, legend tells that St Hermentaire vanquished a dragon. The ceremonials at Draguignan were similar to those at Tarascon, the dragon being accompanied by whifflers and other ceremonial characters.

At Mons in Belgium is another dragon parade, where a tourney beast called Le Lumecon, in structure very similar to Norwich's Old Snap, appears. This ceremony began in the year 1349, some years before the foundation of the Guild of St George in Norwich. In that year, the Black Death was raging unchecked across Europe. In a desperate final attempt to drive away the pestilence, the relics of St Waudru were carried in procession through the streets of Mons. The ritual was

175

19th century broadsheet of the Mons (Belgium) dragon festivities of Le Lumeçon, with St George folk-song.

conducted by members of the Confrerie de Saint-George (The Brotherhood of St George). It was perceived as successful, for the plague began to abate after the ceremony. Votive and expiatory parades of the clergy with saintly relics, or town guilds with their emblems, were common in time of stress in Catholic Europe in medieval times. There are many instances from mainland Europe of guild processions, ceremonial dances and symbolic plays being performed to counter the plague, such as the Drachenstich at Furth in Oberpfalz, Germany, which is described below.

From the event at Mons arose the tradition of parading St George and the Dragon, called Le Lumecon, through the town annually. Traditionally, Le Lumecon is accompanied by Wild Men wielding clubs, hobby horses called Chinchins, and fools who carry bladders with which they strike unsuspecting by-standers. Spectators attempt to grab ribbons from the dragon while it parades through the town. To do successfully brings good fortune for the coming year. At the culmination of the festival, the Mons snapdragon is 'killed' by the man personating St George or alternatively Gilles de Chin, the local dragon-killer. Unusually, the Mons dragonslayer 'kills' Le Lumecon with a shot from a gun. In 1837, it was reported that Le Lumecon measured 7.15 metres in length. The close resemblance of its design and construction to the Norwich snapdragon may indicate a common origin.

According to legend, the dragon-slayer Gilles de Chin, celebrated also at Wasmes by a dragon procession, had the assistance of Our Lady when he killed the dragon in the year 1133. This dating may give an indication of when dragon processions first came into being, for the Tarasque seems to have appeared around that time. The Mons festival is known to date from at least 1349, and the Norwich one probably from 1385. The earliest reference to a dragon parade in Germany of the "*Ludus Draconis*" ('Dragon Game') of Magdeburg, in a text from the year 1416. This was a mimic dragon-fight, using a dragon something like those of Mons and Norwich. The

The 1996 dragon of Fürth-im-Wald, Bavaria, Germany, powered by a motor vehicle.

178

medieval Metzgersprung and Schöfflertanz of Munich included a Mummers' play in which a character called Gretel (Margaret) was rescued by means of songs and play from the jaws of the Plague Dragon.

At Furth im Wald, in Bavaria, half-way between Regensburg and Prague, a Mummers' play was established in the fifteenth century in remembrance of a plague, as at Mons. This was called Der Drachenstich, and it was performed originally on the first Sunday after Corpus Christi each year. The main characters of the play are a king's daughter with her servant, an armed knight, and a wooden dragon, accompanied by two *Burschen* ('Good Old Lads'). The dragon breathes real fire, whilst inside it is a blood-filled bull's bladder. At the appropriate moment in the play, the knight pierces the dragon with his sword, and blood spills onto the ground. At this moment, spectators run forward to dip their handkerchiefs in the 'dragon's blood'. It is customary to lay them on the ground in fields and gardens to promote the fertility of the land. The Drachenstich is performed each year from the second to the third Sunday in August. In 1878, the ceremony was taken over from the former religious society by the citizens of Furth. The present-day dragon is powered by a motor vehicle inside it, and an earlier one is preserved in the local museum.

In the Netherland, a dragon-festival called Draaksteken is held to this day in the town of Beesel. Elsewhere in the Low Countries, dragon festivals were conducted at Brussels and Namur, in present-day Belgium, where the snapdragons had operating jaws like Le Lumecon and Old Snap. An important dragon festival once took place at Metz in France. It was celebrated on April 23, St George's Day, but despite this, commemorated Metz's own two dragon-slayers, not St George. They are both bishops who lived around the fifth century CE, Clemens and Adelphus. The Metz dragon, called Le Graouilli or Le Graully, who was said to date from the year 47 CE, was paraded through the streets, and local bakers made little bread dragons for sale on St George's Day during the festival.

LE GRAULLY

(LÉGENDE MESSINE)

Dragon effroyable, aux proportions gigantesques, qui répandit dans la cité Messine la terreur,
l'épouvante et la mort. Il fut vaincu par saint Clément, Ier Évêque de Metz, en l'an 47 de notre ère.

(Voir la Notice qui se vend au profit du Bureau de Bienfaisance.)

ITINÉRAIRE DU CORTÉGE DU GRAULLY.

Départ de la place Mazelle, à 11 heures du matin.

1. Place Mazelle.
2. Rue d'Asfeld.
3. Place Saint-Thiébault.
4. Rue du Neufbourg.
5. Rue La Salle.
6. Rue de l'Esplanade.
7. Place de la République.
8. Palais de Justice.
9. Rue de la Garde.
10. Rue Sainte-Marie.
11. Rue Pierre-Hardie.
12. Rue Fabert.
13. Place Napoléon.
14. Rue des Jardins.
15. Rue du Pontiffroy.
16. Rempart Belle-Isle.
17. Rue des Bénédictins.
18. Rue Saint-Vincent.
19. Rue Saint-Marcel.
20. Rue du Pont-des-Morts.
21. Rue de la Haye.
22. Rue du Pont-Saint-Marcel.
23. Place de la Comédie.
24. Place de la Préfecture.
25. Pont de la Préfecture.
26. Place de Chambre.
27. Rampe de la Cathédrale.
28. Place de la Cathédrale.
29. Rue de la Cathédrale.
30. Rue du Palais.
31. Rue des Clercs.
32. Place de la République.
33. Rue de l'Esplanade.
34. Place Saint-Martin.
35. Rue Lasalle.
36. Rue de la Fontaine.
37. Rue Nationale.
38. Place Saint-Louis.
39. Rue du Change.
40. Rue Fournirue.
41. Rue Fabert.
42. Rue du Petit-Paris.
43. Rue de la Tête-d'Or.
44. Place Saint-Louis.
45. Rue de la Boche.
46. Rue des Allemands.
47. Rue du Grand-Wad.
48. Rue Mazelle.
49. Place Mazelle.

METZ, TYPOGRAPHIE DEMBOUR ET GANGEL.

19th century poster from Metz, France, showing the route of the
procession of the dragon called Le Graully.

180

The name Le Graouilli resembles the name of the local saint of the Eifel region, St Graulert, who was a dragon-killer.

Dragon Attendants and Ancillaries

In the Mons dragon festival, Wild Men form part of Le Lumecon's entourage. The Wild Man is part of a wider class of guising characters that includes the 'Green George' (St George) of Eastern Europe, the *Zapfenmanndl* and *Verschmanndl* of the Austrian Perchtenlauf and others. According to Central European tradition, wild men (and women) live beneath the earth in caves and crevices in the rocks. In Austria and Switzerland are many caves, mountains and rocky features with names like Wildermannlisloch and Wildermannstein. These are the features in which dragons traditionally make their lairs. In Central Europe, the Wildmannspiel (Wild Man's Game) and Wildmanntanz (Wild Man's Dance) are performed at festivals concerned with driving out the winter, protection against evil spirits and the promotion of fruitfulness.

The St George's plays and dragon processions have exactly the same functions. The old Prussian god of flowers and growth, Latinized as Pergrubius and probably an aspect of Perkunas was mentioned by Bishop Jan Lasicki (1534-1602) as still being worshipped in his day on April 23, St George's Day. The Wild Man is honoured in traditional inn-names in both English and German-speaking lands, as *The Green Man* or *Zum Wilden Mann*. A town in the Harz region of Germany even bears his name - Wildemann. As a symbolic spirit or personification of the earth, the wild man has a similar emblematic role as the dragon does in certain alchemical traditions.

Snapping-jawed beasts are personated by guisers all over Europe. This one was biting people at the Perchtenlauf in St Johann in Pongau, Austria, on January 5, 1997.

Chapter 9

A Gazetteer of Notable Dragons in Great Britain

Many places in Great Britain have dragon legends, some of which have been re-told in ballads and folk-songs, or in embellished form by creative writers. This list does not intend to be comprehensive, but to give some of the major instances of what is a universal folk-motif. Each place has a National Grid reference to assist any would-be traveller who might wish to visit the places listed below.

Avebury, Wiltshire, England, SU 0969. The great stone circle and earthworks at Avebury were seen by early modern Druids as a great serpent temple, where a double row of standing stones ran through the circle, like a serpent and egg, which they recognised as an ancient Druidic symbol. The church font shows a bishop spearing the head of one dragon whilst another bites the hem of his vestments.

Bamburgh, Northumberland, England, NU 1834. The legend of the Laidley Worm is localised at Bamburgh. It was a young woman, turned into a monster by magic, who devastated the countryside. The Childe of Wynde, son of the Northumbrian King, went to kill the wyrm. But the wyrm was his sister, bewitched by the evil queen. It refused to fight him, and then he realised what the wyrm truly was, and this dispelled the spell. The spell being broken, the evil queen was herself transmuted into a toad who still lives in a cave under the castle.

The human imagination knows no bounds when the beastly contents of the world are depicted. The dragon is but one of many.

Baslow, Derbyshire, England, SK 2572. Close to Baslow is Dragon's Cave at a place called Wormstall.

Betws-y-Coed, Gwynedd, Wales, SH 7956. Here dwelt the Wybrant Viper, which terrorised the neighbourhood. An outlaw from Hiraethog went to kill it. But he died a threefold death, by viper-bite, cut throat and drowning.

Bishop Auckland, County Durham, England, NZ 2029. The Pollard Worm spoken of here has an alternative version as a dangerous wild boar, and may be an example of gewurm or 'vermin' rather than the more colourful and attractive dragon.

Brent Pelham, Hertfordshire, England, TL 4330. The church contains the reputed tomb of the dragonslayer Piers Shonkes, who shot the Devil's favourite dragon at Peppsall Field nearby.

Bretforton, Hereford and Worcester, England, SP 0944. Bretforton's church dedicated to the Sussex dragonslaying saint, Leonard, has an image of St Margaret being eaten by a dragon.

Brinsop, Hereford and Worcester, England, SO 4444. A dragon once lived in Duck's Pool Meadow at Brinsop, but like most of them, it was slain by a local knight.

Bromfield, Shropshire, England, SO 4877. In 1344, a destructive dragon at Bromfield was killed magically by an Arab physician. In the dragon's lair was a great treasure, which the Arab did not get. It was taken by Earl Warren, who became a wealthy man.

Bures, Essex, England, TL 9034. A dragon appeared here in 1405, *"vast in body with a crested head, teeth like a saw, and tail extending to an enormous length"*. Archers were sent out to despatch it, but their arrows bounced off its scaly body. It fled, never to be seen again.

185

Burley, Hampshire, England, SU 2103. The Bisterne Dragon lived in the earthworks of Burley Beacon, and demanded a pail of milk a day from the local milkmaids. A brave knight accompanied by two dogs, attacked the dragon. After a bloody fight, the dogs and dragon were dead, and the knight mortally wounded. A lane at Bisterne is called Dragon Lane after this monster.

Castle Neroche, Somerset, England, ST 2622. At Castle Ratch, called by map-making officialdom Castle Neroche, a dragon once guarded the treasure reputed to be buried there.

Cawthorne, South Yorkshire, England, SE 2807. The Serpent's Well here is connected with a flying serpent that sometimes flew from there to Cawthorne Park to the east.

Chipping Norton, Oxfordshire, England, SP 3127. In 1354, near Chipping Norton, someone claimed to have found an unlikely serpent that had two heads, and two faces like those of women.

Crowcombe, Somerset, England, ST 1336. A dragon-slaying legend here is remembered (or prompted) by a carving in the church that shows two naked men spearing a dragon on a background of vines. Unlike most English dragons, but like the Chipping Norton example, the Crowcombe Dragon had two heads.

Dartford, Kent, England, TQ 5474. The church at Dartford, which dates from the 13th century, has a remarkable medieval mural of St George and the dragon, probably the best of its age in any English church.

Deerhurst, Gloucestershire, England, SO 8729. An evil serpent plagued Deerhurst and devoured local cattle. Its depredations became so bad that the King decreed that whosoever should slay the dragon would be rewarded by a great estate. A certain Smith knocked out the dragon with drugged milk, and then beheaded it. He was rewarded duly with the estate.

Dinas Emrys, Snowdonia, Wales, SH 6049. At this Iron-Age hillfort overlooking Llyn Dinas near Beddgelert, King Lludd ab Beli buried the two dragons that fought each May Eve at Oxford. Merlin was discovered here by King Vortigern, who dug up the dragons again.

Dronley, Tayside, Scotland, NO 3437. A Pictish stone here is reputed to mark the place where a knight called Martin killed a maiden-eating dragon. Nearby is the village of Boldragon.

Dunstanburgh, Northumberland, England, NZ 2263. A dragon legend associated with Dunstanburgh Castle may be a literary invention from a ballad first published in 1808, and reinterpreted ever since. Sir Guy the Seeker was the slayer of this wyrm, with a little help from a wizard.

Durham, Co. Durham, England, NZ 2742. In or around the year 1060, an individual named Osulf who was plagued by a supernatural serpent that coiled itself around him. He got rid of it by entering Durham Cathedral and praying for three days and three nights. The Conyers Falchion that reputedly slew the Sockburn Worm is kept in the cathedral treasury and used ceremonially in the rites of inauguration of each Bishop of Durham.

Five Oaks, Jersey, Channel Islands. The megalithic mound called La Hogue Bie, near Five Oaks, is the legendary location of a dragonslaying by the Seigneur de Hanbye, who was murdered immediately afterwards as he rested by a servant who wished to take the credit.

Gunnerton, near Gunnerford, Northumberland, England, NY 9074. A dragon once protected Money Hill here.

The Henham Dragon, from the contemporary broadsheet. Perhaps this was an escaped peacock.

Handale, Yorkshire, England. The Serpent of Handale lived in Scaw Wood and ate young maidens. It was slain by a youth called Scaw, who liberated an earl's daughter and became rich.

Henham, Essex, England, TL 5428. The Henham Dragon is known from a pamphlet of 1699, *The Flying Serpent, Or Strange News Out Of Essex,* that told of a 3-metre long winged dragon seen in a field near the village. It had two rows of teeth and eyes the "bigness of a sheep's eye". It disappeared without trouble. Until the custom was discontinued in World War II, small dragons were sold each July at the Henham Fair, and a special ale called *Snakebite* was brewed in honour of the wyrm.

Highclere, Hampshire, England, SU 4360. One of the more improbable monsters of Britain was the Highclere Grampus that had its nest in a Yew tree. Commonly, a grampus is a killer-whale. Whatever it was, the parish priest exorcised it and banished it to the Red Sea for 1000 years. By ending up in the sea, the beastie in this tale resembles the Norwegian *Lindorm.*

Horsham, Sussex, England, TQ 1730. In 1614, a dragon was reported at Horsham, "nine feet, or rather more" in length. Its neck had a ring of white scales around it. It had poisonous breath which killed two people, and left a trail of slime. This dragon may be counted as part of the recurring dragon legends of St Leonard's Forest (q.v.).

Hutton Rudby, Yorkshire, England, NZ 4606. Near this village lived a dragon that coiled around the mound called Sexhowe. A passing knight killed the dragon, which was later hung up as a relic in the church at Stokesley.

Kellington, Yorkshire, England, SE 5524. The dragon here was killed by Armroyd the shepherd with his crook. In the church is the Kellington Serpent Stone, a grave-slab with a cross and serpent.

Ker Moor, Somerset, England, ST 0243. The dragon here is recorded in *The Life of St Carantoc*. The Celtic saint dragged the dragon out of the marsh by means of his ecclesiastical stole, and brought it to the court of King Arthur. Afterwards, he ordered it to go away and never return, which it did.

Kilve, Somerset, England, ST 1443. A fire-breathing dragon known as Old Ben once occupied Putsham Hill at Kilve. Sometimes, the Devil would take Old Ben to Hell to pull his chariot around the infernal domains. Old Ben died prosaically when he went to the sea to cool himself, and was drowned in the tidal mud. Old Ben is another *lindorm*-like beastie.

King's Lynn, Norfolk, England, TF 6220. The church dedicated to the dragon-killing saint Margaret has a moon-dial which shows high and low tides at Lynn. The pointer is a green dragon.

Kingston, Dorset, England, ST 7509. On a hillside overlooking the hamlet of Ivyton, a man killed a dragon that had been plaguing the land around. He shouted at it, and when it attempted to burn him with its breath, he pushed a boulder down the hill, which rolled into the dragon's mouth and killed it.

Kirkton of Strathmartine, Angus, Scotland, NO 3735. A carved Pictish boulder 3 km to the north of Kirkton is where a dragon was slain by a man called Martin after nine maidens had met their end there.

Linton, Roxburghshire (Borders), Scotland, NT 7726. A hill at Linton once was the home of a wyrm called The Dragon of Wyrmiston that terrorised the surrounding landscape. A local man called Somerville killed it by putting a wheel daubed with pitch on his lance, and setting fire to it. He thrust the blazing wheel down the gullet of the wyrm, thereby finishing it off. Perhaps this is a memory of an old fire-wheel rite once conducted on the hilltop.

Llandeilo Graban, Powys, Wales, SO 0944. The church tower at Llandeilo Graban once held the nest of a dragon. It lived there, terrorising the neighbourhood until a blacksmith made an artificial dragon of iron, which he put in the nest while the real dragon was away. When the dragon returned, it tried to throw the metal dragon out of its nest, but in so doing, it triggered a mechanism that thrust sharp spikes out all over the iron dragon's body, impaling and killing the real dragon.

Llyn Cynwch, Gwynedd, Wales, SH 6511. A fatal serpent once lived in the waters of this lake, leaving it to hunt animals and humans to eat. Like a basilisk, this monster killed with its stare. But it was found asleep by a shepherd, who beheaded it. The place if its death is commemorated by a cairn called Carnedd-y-Wibber, 'The Cairn of the Woman's-milk-fed Serpent'.

Ludham, Norfolk, England, TG 3818. The dragon of Ludham lived in a burrow, and only came out at night, until one fateful occasion when it decided to bask in the sun. The local people then blocked up its hole, so it ran away, disappearing into the ruins of St Benet's Abbey.

Lyminster, Sussex, England, TQ 0204. A deep pool called Knuckler Hole is 150 metres north-west of Lyminster churchyard. In the days when Sussex was a Saxon kingdom, at Lyminster lived a dragon which only ate fair maidens. Finally, as in the St George legend, all the maidens of the land had been eaten, save the daughter of the King of Sussex. The king offered her hand in marriage and half the kingdom to any brave man who could kill the dragon. A fearless knight duly obliged, and the Slayer's Stone, a Norman coffin, remains in the church to attest to the deed.

Middlewich, Cheshire, England, SJ 7066. The church at Middlewich has a chapel dedicated to the Venables family, whose ancestor, Thomas Venables, killed a dragon that lived in Bache Pool at Moston. At the moment when it was about to eat

Medieval dragon carving in a spandrel of the roof of Dragon Hall in Norwich, Norfolk, England. The hall, long thought destroyed, was rediscovered in the 1990s when old walls were pulled down and what had been thought to be several old buildings were revealed as an ancient hall. This dragon was rediscovered at the same time.

a child, he shot it in the eye and then finished it off with other weapons.

Mordiford, Hereford and Worcester, England, SO 5737. The Mordiford Dragon lived in a nest at Haugh Wood, and came out along Serpent Lane at the foot of West Hill to raid the countryside for cows to eat. After everyone else had failed to do away with the dragon, a condemned criminal called Garnstone offered to kill it in return for his freedom. He hid in a cider-barrel furnished with steel spikes, around which the dragon wound its coils, thereby cutting itself to pieces. In former times, the church had a mural of 'the true effigy of that strange prodigious monster'.

Newcastle-upon-Tyne, Tyneside, England, NZ 2464. In 1275, a comet was seen by the terrified inhabitants of Newcastle as a threatening dragon.

Norton Fitzwarren, Somerset, England, ST 1925. A dragon that lived in the ancient earthwork of Norton Camp was generated spontaneously from a huge pile of bodies left there by the Roman general Ostorius after a massacre of Britons. The dragon grew over the centuries, and was finally extirpated in medieval times by a hero from the Fitzwarren family.

Norwich, Norfolk, England, TG 2308. Each year in July, the Lord Mayor's parade contains Old Snap, the tourney-beast dragon, direct descendent of the dragons of the Guild and Company of St George, dating from 1385.

Nunnington, Yorkshire, England, SE 6679. On the south bank of the River Rye, 8 km south-east of Helmsley is Loschy Hill. Here the local hero Peter Loschy, wearing a blade-studded suit of armour, cut apart the dragon that plagued the locality, his dog carrying away the parts so that they could not reassemble themselves. Finally, his dog succumbed to the dragon's poison, and died, but the dragon was dead.

Penmynydd, Anglesey, Wales, SH 5174. Close to the manor farm of Penhesgyn at Penmynydd was the home of a dragon. A wizard foretold that the heir would be brought to death by the dragon, so he was sent to England to escape the prophecy. Another young man killed the dragon by digging a pit in which he placed a polished cauldron. The dragon saw its own reflection and fought it, finally falling exhausted into the cauldron. Then the youth slew the dragon. The heir returned, thinking all was well now the dragon was dead. But he insisted on seeing the carcass, which was exhumed. The heir kicked the dragon's head, but a poisonous fang entered his foot, and he died, fulfilling the wizard's prophecy.

Penshaw, Durham, England, NZ 3253 The legend of the Lambton Worm is located at the castle near the village of Penshaw.

Ramsbury, Wiltshire, England, SU 2771. There is a 9th century Celtic cross-shaft here with a carving of an interlaced dragon.

Renwick, Cumberland, England, NY 5943. When the church was pulled down in 1733, a cockatrice flew out of the foundations. A local man, John Tallantire, armed with a branch of the Rowan tree, attacked the cockatrice and killed it. As a reward, he was exempted from paying taxes for the rest of his life.

Saffron Walden, Essex, England, TL 5438. A cockatrice once lived near Saffron Walden. It was slain by a knight who wore armour of crystal glass, whose purity prevented the venom from harming the warrior.

Saint Leonard's Forest, east of Horsham, Sussex, England, TQ 2532. In the sixth century, the Sussex forest was infested by serpents and a dragon that only the French Christian hermit St Leonard could deal with. Leonard was wounded by the dragon, and where the saint's blood fell, lilies-of-the-valley sprang up. As well as killing the dragon, St Leonard emulated St Patrick and St Columba by ridding the forest of serpents and nightingales, the latter having disturbed his prayers. In 1614, another dragon, "a strange and monstrous serpent" was seen there, and although it was said to have killed a man and a woman, it was not hunted. In the south-west of the forest is a place called Dragon's Green.

Shervage Wood, Crowcombe, Somerset, England, ST 1336. A great wyrm, measuring greater than three oak trees' girth, lived in Shervage Wood in North Devon. It behaved in the normal manner of such legendary beasts, venturing into farmland to take sheep and ponies.

After two gypsies and a shepherd disappeared in the wood, no local person would go there. An old woman who made her living making bilberry pies, asked a travelling woodsman to go there to pick some berries for her. When the wyrm came to him to steal his lunch of bread, cheese and cider, the woodsman cut the beast up with his axe.

Slingsby, Yorkshire, England, SE 6974. A dragon was killed here by the local hero Wyvill and his dog.

Sockburn, County Durham, England, NZ 0285. In the 14th century, the destructive Sockburn Worm was slain by Sir John Conyers, who used a special weapon, the Conyers Falchion. This very weapon is used to-day in the inauguration ritual of the Bishops of Durham.

Tanfield, Yorkshire, England, NZ 1855. A holy well dedicated to St Michael, between Well and Tanfield, 11 km north of Ripon is the locus of a fight where the local hero Latimer slew a dragon.

Trull, near Taunton, Somerset, England, ST 2122. At Trull, south of Taunton, a dragon that "took great toll of human life" was slain at Wormstall Field by an unnamed

The Trull Dragon meeting its end. Engraving from an old broadsheet.

196

"valiant knight". In its death throes, the dragon tore a gully in the side of Castleman's Hill, which is still there to-day.

Uffington, Oxfordshire, England, SU 3089. Below the hill on which is the chalk-cut hill-figure of the Uffington White Horse, is Dragon Hill, one of the reputed places where St George killed the dragon. On top of the hill, where the dragon's blood fell, contrary to the usual notions of dragon's blood being highly fertile, the grass does not grow, and there is barren white chalk. Some see the stylised Celtic hill figure as not a horse at all, but the dragon.

Wells, Somerset, England, ST 5445. Named after the seven holy springs next to which a Christian cathedral was built, Wells is the place where Bishop Jocelyn drove off a dragon which had been harassing the local inhabitants.

Wherwell, Hampshire, England, SU 3840. Hatched by a toad sitting on a cock's egg in the crypt of Wherwell Priory, the Wherwell Cockatrice grew into a human-devouring monster. It killed several knights who came to kill it, but finally a local labourer took a mirror into the monster's crypt. When the cockatrice saw itself, it fell dead at its own reflection. The cockatrice weather-vane which once topped the church of St Peter and Holy Cross at Wherwell is now preserved in Andover Museum.

Windsor, Berkshire, England, SU 9676. St George's Chapel in Windsor Castle is the sacred place of the Most Noble Order of the Garter, the highest Order of Chivalry of England, under the patronage of St George. The chapel contains the earliest heraldic enamel with the Helm of Awe.

Wiveliscombe, Somerset, England, ST 0827. A dragon, St Andrew and the Devil all appeared in this village in 1827, according to local lore. When the church was being rebuilt, the Devil appeared, riding on a green dragon, and began to toss rocks at the church. In response to this Satanic attack, there

197

was then an epiphany of St Andrew, who repulsed both Devil and dragon with his cross.

Wormingford, Essex, England, TL 9332. Around the year 1400, a dragon appeared at a ford on the River Stour here, and killed wayfarers. According to one account, it was killed by Sir Bertram de Haye, who felled a tree on top of the beast. Another version tells how the wyrm was fed on young maidens, until it was slain by Sir George Marney, wielding a lance.

Wormhill, Miller's Dale, Derbyshire, England, SK 1353. The place-name is self-apparent, and the church has a carving of St Margaret and the Dragon. To the east, the hill called Knotlow has terraces that recall the wyrm that coiled around it.

The dragon of light and the dragon of darkness. Drawing by Call Silk 1997.

Postscript

The dragon has appeared at many places in the West, and remains one of the enduring mythic images of our age. We may encounter dragons anywhere from traditional performance on the street to computer-generated movies and advertising. The protean guise of the dragon enables it to appear in forms that are suited perfectly to the places and times at which it makes itself manifest. Carl Jung saw the dragon as representing, at least on certain occasions, the 'devouring' aspect of the mother-figure. In his view, the battle between the hero and the dragon can be seen as the symbolic expression of the process of growing up. The 'damsel in distress' who is often the captive, and intended dragon's dinner, is the anima, the 'eternal feminine' which must be freed from domination. The dragon is a fresh symbol for each age, representing the fears, failures and triumphs particular to the time that people must undergo in their lives. Because each new thing is unprecedented, it can only be understood, albeit imperfectly, in symbolic terms. Because every dragon that has ever existed has come from within us, the future of the dragon species is forever bound up with the fate of humankind. Doubtless, there will be new roles for the dragon in the future. In ways as yet inconceivable, the dragon will symbolise ways of being that are yet to emerge.

The dragon in the vesica, symbol of eternal female power.

Bibliography

Adéline, J. and Adéline, C.: *Les sculptures grotesques et symboliques*. Rouen, 1879.
Allen, Judy, and Griffiths, Jeanne: *The Book of the Dragon*. London, 1979.
Andrews, W. (ed.): *Bygone Norfolk*. London, 1898.
Andrews, W. (ed.): *Bygone Durham*. London, 1898.
Aspelin, J.R.; Hamkens, Haye; Sieber, Siegfried, and Mössinger, Friedrich: *Trojaburgen*. Bar Hill and Benfleet, 1982.
Barber, R., and Riches, A.: *A Dictionary of Fabulous Beasts*. London, 1971.
Börtsch, Albert: *Holz Masken. Fastnachts- und Maskenbrauchtum in der Schweiz, in Süddeutschland und Österreich*. Aarau, 1993.
Bastian, H.: *Mummenschanz. Sinneslust und Gefühlsbeherrschung im Fastnachtsspiel des 15. Jahrhunderts*. Frankfurt, 1983.
Behrend, Michael: *The Girton Hobby Horse and Others*. Albion 1, 4-9, 1978.
Behrend, Michael: *The Dragon as Crocodile. Journal of Geomancy*, Volume 4, No. 1 (1979), 15 - 20.
Bett, Henry: *English Legends*. London, 1950.
Blackburne, Harry, and Bond, Maurice: *The Romance of St George's Chapel, Windsor Castle*. Windsor, 1971.
Briggs, Katherine M.: *A Dictionary of British Folk Tales*. London 1970-71.
Bromwich, R.: *Trioedd Ynys Prydein*. Cardiff, 1979.
Bucknell, Peter A.: *Entertainment and Ritual 600 - 1600*. London, 1979.
Burke, Peter: *Popular Culture in Early Modern Europe*. London, 1978.
Burland, C.A.: *The Arts of the Alchemists*. London, 1967.
Campbell, J.F.: *The Celtic Dragon Myth*. Edinburgh, 1911.
Cawte, E.G.: *Ritual Animal Disguise*. London, 1978.
Cinotti, Mia: *The Complete Paintings of Bosch*. London, 1966.
Clarke, David, and Reeder, Phil: *The Wantley Dragon*. Northern Earth Mysteries 33, 11-17, 1987.
Cobb, Gerald: *The Old Churches of London*. London, 1942.
Coggeshall, Ralph of: *Chronicon Anglicanum*. London, 1875.
Cohn, Norman: *Cosmos, Chaos and the World to Come*. London, 1993.

Corrsin, Steve: *Sword Dancing in Europe: A History*. Rattle Up My Boys, Series 4, No.2 (1993), 6 - 7.

Cysat, Leopold: *Beschreibung des berthmter Lucerner oder Vier-Waldstätter See*. Luzern, 1611.

Davies, D.J.: *'Baner y Ddraig Goch'*, Y Fflam, 6, 1948.

Deghaye, P.: *La Doctrine Esoterique de Zinzendorf* (1700-1760). Paris, 1969.

Devizes, Richard of: *De Rebus Gestis Ricardi Primi*. London, 1866.

Devlin, James Dacres: *The Mordiford Dragon*. London, 1848.

Dontenvill, H.: *La France Mythologique*. Paris, 1966.

Dumant, L.: *La Tarasque*. Paris, 1951.

Dunsany, Lord: *Time and the Gods*. London, 1906.

Elliott Smith, G.: *The Evolution of the Dragon*. Manchester, 1919.

Elworthy, Frederick Thomas: *The Evil Eye*. London, 1895.

Evans, Howell T.: *Wales and the Wars of the Roses*. Cambridge, 1915.

Ewing, W.C.: *Notices and Illustrations of the costume, procession, pageantry etc.* formerly displayed by the Corporation of Norwich. Norwich, 1850.

Fairholt, F.W.: *Gog and Magog*. London, 1859.

Fontenrose, Joseph: *Python. A Study of Delphic Myth and its Origins*. Berkeley, 1959.

Frampton, George: *Whittlesey Straw Bear*. Peterborough, 1990.

Fulcanelli: *Le Mystère des Cathédrales*. Sudbury, 1971.

Gammon, Vic (compiler, writer and arranger): *The Tale of Ale*. Free Reed Records, FRMC 23, Belper, 1993.

Gombrich, E.R.: *Symbolic Images*. London, 1972.

Green, Martin: *Curious Customs*. London, 1993.

Grieve, M, ed. Leyel, C.F.: *A Modern Herbal*. London, 1994.

Guest, Lady Charlotte (trans.): *The Mabinogion*. London, 1906.

Gueusquin, M-F.: *Le Mois des Dragons*. Paris, 1987.

Gwynn Jones, T.: *Welsh Folk-Lore and Folk-Custom*. London, 1930.

Hackwood, Frederick W.: *Inns, Ales and Drinking Customs of Old England*. London, 1987.

Hakluyt, Richard: *The Principall Navigations, Voiages and Discoveries of the English Nation*. London, 1589.

Halseloff, Gunther: *Kunststile des Frhen Mittelalters*. Stuttgart, 1979.

Hammond, Wayne G., and Scull, Christina: *J.R.R. Tolkien, Artist and Illustrator*. London, 1995.

Harland, John, and Wilkinson, T.T.: *Lancashire Folk-Lore*. London, 1867.

Harper, Charles G.: *Queer Things about London*. London, 1931.

Harper, Clive: *The Hughendon Dragon*. High Wycombe, 1985.

Harrison, J.: *Prolegomena to the Study of Greek Religion*. Camrbridge, 1903.

Harte, Jeremy: *The Dragon of Wessex*. Earth Giant, N.S. 3, 3-6, 1982.

Harte, Jeremy: *Dragons of the Marches*. Mercian Mysteries 20, 1-7, 1994.
Hartmann, M.R.: *St Beatushählen*. Sundlauenen, n.d.
Heaword, Rose: *Snap the Dragon*. Albion 2, 12-23, 1978.
Helm, Alex: *The Mummers' Play*. Ipswich, 1981.
Henderson, C.W.: *Folk-Lore of the Northern Counties*. London, 1879.
Henken, Elissa R.: *Traditions of the Welsh Saints*. Bury St Edmunds, 1987.
Heydon, John: *Theomagia*. London, 1664.
Hieronymussen, Paul: *Orders, Medals and Decorations of Britain and Europe*. London, 1967.
Hogarth, Peter, and Clery, Val: *Dragons*. London, 1979.
Hole, Christina: *A Dictionary of British Folk Customs*. Oxford, 1995.
Hoult, Janet: *Dragons, their History and Symbolism*. Glastonbury, 1990.
Hughes, Meirion, and Evans, Wayne: *Rumours and Oddities from North Wales*. Llanwrst, 1986.
Hughes, Thomas: *The Scouring of the White Horse*. London, 1857.
Hulme, F.E.: *Mythland*. London, 1886.
Huntingdon, Henry of: *Historia Anglorum*. London, 1879.
Hutton, Ronald: *The Stations of the Sun*. Oxford, 1996.
Huxley, Francis: *The Dragon*. London, 1979.
Hyltén-Cavallius, Gunnar Olof: *Om draken eller lindormen*. Wexjö, 1942.
Johnson, Kenneth Rayner: *The Fulcanelli Phenomenon*. Sudbury, 1980.
Jones, Francis: *The Holy Wells of Wales*. Cardiff, 1954.
Jones, Prudence, and Pennick, Nigel: *A History of Pagan Europe*. London, 1997.
Jones, T. Gwyn: *Welsh Folklore and Welsh Custom*. London, 1930.
Kihnau, R.: *Schlesische Sagen*. Leipzig, 1910-1913.
Larwood, Jacob and Hotten John Camden: *English Inn Signs*. London, 1951.
Ledbury, John: *The Historical Evidence for Sword Dancing in Britain*. Rattle Up My Boys, Series 4, No. 3 (1993).
Leibbrand, J.: *Speculum Bestialitatis. Die Tiergestalten der Fastnacht und des Karnevals im Kontext christlicher Allegorese*. Munich, 1987.
Lofmark, Carl (ed. Wells, G.E.): *A History of the Red Dragon*. Llanwrst, 1995.
L'tolf, Alois: Sagen, Brauche, *Legenden aus den Fünf Orten*. Luzern, 1862.
Mackerell, Benjamin: *An Account of the Company of St George in Norwich*.
Massingham, H.J.: *Fe, Fi, Fo, Fum: The Giants of England*. London, 1926.
Norfolk Archaeolgy, III, 315-374.
Matthäus, Hartmut: *Der Arzt in Rämischer Zeit*. Aalen, 1987.

McCall, A.: *The Medieval Underworld*. London, 1979.

McLauchlan, T.: ed. and trans. *The Dean of Lismore's Book*. Edinburg, 1866.

Meaney, A.L.: *Anglo-Saxon Amulets and Curing Stones*. London, 1981.

Meurger, Michel: *Lake Monster Traditions: A Cross-Cultural Analysis*. London, 1988.

Michell, John: *The View Over Atlantis*. London, 1969.

Mockridge, Patricia and Mockridge, Philip: *Weathervanes of Great Britain*. London, 1990.

Mota, Jordi, and Infiesta, Maria (eds.): *Das Werk Richard Wagners im Spiegel der Kunst*. Tibingen, 1995.

Newman, Paul: *The Hill of the Dragon*. London, 1979.

Obermayr, August, and Wegner, Josef: *Bajuwaren zwischen Inn und Salzach*. Freilassing, 1977.

Olrik, Axel: *Ragnarök: die sagen vom Weltuntergang*. Berlin, 1922.

Olrik, Axel: *Danish Legends*. London, 1928.

Parke, H.W.: *A History of the Delphic Oracle*. Oxford, 1939.

Paulsen, Peter: *Drachenkämpfer, Löwenritter und die Heinrichssaga*. Köln, 1966.

Pegg, Bob: *Rites and Riots: Folk Customs of Britain and Europe*. London, 1981.

Pennick, Nigel: *The Mysteries of King's College Chapel*. Cambridge, 1974.

Pennick, Nigel: *The Ancient Science of Geomancy*. London, 1979.

Pennick, Nigel: *The Cosmic Axis*. Bar Hill, 1987.

Pennick, Nigel: *Mazes and Labyrinths*. London, 1990.

Pennick, Nigel: *The Oracle of Geomancy*. Chieveley, 1995.

Pennick, Nigel: *The Inner Mysteries of the Goths*. Chieveley, 1995.

Pennick, Nigel: *Celtic Sacred Landscapes*. London, 1996.

Pennick, Nigel: *Secret Signs, Symbols and Sigils*. Chieveley, 1996.

Pennick, Nigel: *The Celtic Saints*. London, 1997.

Pennick, Nigel: *The Celtic Cross*. London, 1997.

Pennick, Nigel: *Earth Harmony*. Chieveley, 1997.

Pennick, Nigel: *Ley Lines*. London, 1997.

Pennick, Nigel, and Devereux, Paul: *Lines on the Landscape*. London, 1989.

Petrie, Sir Flinders: *Decorative Patterns of the Ancient World*. London, 1930.

Porter, Enid: *The Folklore of East Anglia*. London, 1969.

Prost, A.: *Etudes sur l'Histoire de Mets*. Metz, 1897.

Renard, L.: *La Tarasque*. Paris, 1991.

Roberts, Anthony: *Atlantean Traditions in Ancient Britain*. Brighton, 1974.

Roob, Alexander: *Alchemie und Mystik*. Cologne, 1996.

Russett, Vince: *The Dragons of Quantock*, Picwinnard 8, 19-24, 1979.

Salverte, E.: *Des dragons et des serpentes monstreueux qui figurent dans un grand nombre de récits fabuleux et historiques*. Paris, 1826.

Salzle, K.: *Tier und Mensch, Gottheit und Dämon*. Mìnchen, 1965.

Schwilgué, C.: *Description abrégée de l'horloge de la cathédrale de Strasbourg*. Strasbourg, 1843.

Seymour, John: *Pictures From the Past: Rural Life*. Devizes, 1993.

Screeton, Paul: *The Lambton Worm and Other Northumbrian Dragon Legends*. London, 1978.

Shortt, Hugh: *The Giant and Hob-Nob*. Salisbury, 1972.

Shuttleworth, Ron: *Constructing a Hobby Animal - mainly for Morris dancers*. Coventry, 1994.

Silberer, Herbert: *Hidden Symbolism of Alchemy and the Occult Arts*. New York, 1971.

Simpson, Jacqueline: *The Folklore of Sussex*. London, 1973.

Simpson, Jacqueline: *British Dragons*. London, 1980.

Simpson, Jacqueline: *European Mythology*. London, 1987.

Spence, Lewis: *The Mysteries of Britain*. London, 1928.

Spence, Lewis: *The Minor Traditions of British Mythology*. London, 1948.

Swoboda, O.: *AlpenlÜndisches Brauchtum im Jahreslauf*. Munich, 1979.

Tatham, Canon: *Dragon Folklore in Sussex*. Sussex County Magazine, Volume 5, 662.

Tatlock, J.S.P.: *The Dragons of Wessex and Wales*, Speculum 8, 223-235, 1933.

Tolkien, J.R.R.: *The Hobbit, or There and Back Again*. London, 1937.

Trevelyan, Marie: *Folk-Lore and Folk-Stories of Wales*. London, 1909.

Van Genlles, A.: *Le Folklore de la Flandres et du Hainaut*. Paris, 1936.

Von der Au, Hans: *Das Volktanzgut in Rheinfränkischen*. Berlin, 1939.

Von Harless, G.C.A.: *Jacob Böhme und die Alchymisten*. Berlin, 1882.

Von Zaborsky, Oskar: *Urväter-Erbe in deutsche Volkskunst*. Berlin, 1936.

Wales, Tony: *We Wunt Be Druv - Songs and Stories From Sussex*. London, 1976.

Watkins, Alfred: *The Old Straight Track*. London, 1922.

Weever, John: *Funeral Monuments of Great Britain*. London, 1631.

Weir, Anthony, and Jerman, James: *Images of Lust: Sexual Carvings on Medieval Churches*. London, 1986.

Whitlock, Ralph: *Here be Dragons*. London, 1983.

Wildhaber, R.: *Masken und Maskenbrauchtum aus Ost- und Sıdosteuropa*. Basel, 1968.

Witzchel, A.: *Sagen aus Thuringen*. Wien, 1878.

Yates, Frances A.: *The Rosicrucian Enlightenment*. London, 1972.

Index

Nwyvre, 11, 133, 135

Obby Oss, 5
Olaf Tryggvason, 83-85
Old Ben, 190
Orouboros, 111
Oseberg ship, 81
Owain ap Urien, 76

Padstow Day Song,, 91
Pan, 33
Peacock, 5, 29, 190
Peter Loschy, 59-60, 192
Piers Shonks, 61-65
Pliny, 1, 25
Pollard Worm of Bishop
   Auckland, 15
Pope Sylvester I, 105
Prose Edda, 25
Pytho, 34
Python, 34-35, 117, 119, 129,
   203
Péiste, 23

Ragnar Lodbrok, 24, 42-43,
   45, 137, 155
Regin, 41-42
Richard I, 78
Saemundr's Edda, 15
Salamander, 3, 7-8, 10, 13, 55
Salamander's wool, 7
Seigneur de Hanbye, 187
Serpens, 119
Serpent's egg, 25
Shakespeare, 7, 93, 161
Sigurd Fafnirsbane, 41
Sir Guy the Seeker, 187

Sir John Conyers, 59-60, 110,
   196
Sir Perceval, 9, 23, 46-47, 85-
   86, 113
Snowdonia, 23, 51-52, 187
Sockburn Worm, 59, 187, 196
Sol, 116-117, 128
St Beatus, 67-68, 105, 109
St Bertrand, 29
St Cain, 107
St Columba, 107, 109, 197
St Donatus, 105
St George, 5, 13, 19, 42, 63,
   65, 70-72, 79, 88-93, 95, 99-
   101, 141, 144, 149-153, 155,
   160-164, 166, 168, 175-176,
   178, 180, 182, 186, 191-192,
   196, 202, 204
St Graulert, 183
St Hermentaire, 176
St Hilarion, 105
St Hilda of Whitby, 107
St Mangold, 109
St Margaret, 31, 101-103,
   150, 185, 198
St Martha, 103-104, 172
St Michael, 11, 98-101, 126,
   150-151, 153, 196
St Patrick, 107, 109, 196
St Samson, 105, 107
St Waudru, 176
Strathmartin dragon, 70

Tarasque, 103-104, 107, 169,
   172-174, 176, 178, 203, 205
Thor, 19, 21-23, 72
Thora, 43, 45
Tree of the Gods, 23

Typhon, 29, 33-34

Uther Pendragon, 76-77, 145

Volsunga Saga, 17, 41

Wantley Dragon, 3, 65-66,
    157, 203
Welsh Dragon, 74-77, 143,
    145, 150, 159
Wessex, 77, 145, 147, 203,
    206
Wherwell Cockatrice, 198
Whifflers, 163-164, 166, 170-
    172, 176
Wibber, 9, 11, 15
Wild Huntress of Westphalia,
    103
Woden, 70, 72
Wybrant Viper, 186
Wyvern, 3, 5-7, 29, 59, 63, 79,
    98, 113, 125, 133, 144, 147,
    151, 153

Zaltys, 11
Zeus, 33-35, 37, 74

FREE DETAILED CATALOGUE

Animals, Mind Body Spirit & Folklore

Angels and Goddesses - Celtic Christianity & Paganism by Michael Howard
Arthur - The Legend Unveiled by C Johnson & E Lung
Auguries and Omens - The Magical Lore of Birds by Yvonne Aburrow
Book of the Veil The by Peter Paddon
Caer Sidhe - Celtic Astrology and Astronomy by Michael Bayley
Call of the Horned Piper by Nigel Jackson
Cats' Company by Ann Walker
Celtic Lore & Druidic Ritual by Rhiannon Ryall
Compleat Vampyre - The Vampyre Shaman: Werewolves & Witchery by Nigel Jackson
Crystal Clear - A Guide to Quartz Crystal by Jennifer Dent
Earth Dance - A Year of Pagan Rituals by Jan Brodie
Earth Harmony - Places of Power, Holiness and Healing by Nigel Pennick
Earth Magic by Margaret McArthur
Enchanted Forest - The Magical Lore of Trees by Yvonne Aburrow
Familiars - Animal Powers of Britain by Anna Franklin
Healing Homes by Jennifer Dent
Herbcraft - Shamanic & Ritual Use of Herbs by Susan Lavender & Anna Franklin
In Search of Herne the Hunter by Eric Fitch
Inner Space Workbook - Developing Counselling & Magical Skills Through the Tarot
Kecks, Keddles & Kesh by Michael Bayley
Living Tarot by Ann Walker
Magical Incenses and Perfumes by Jan Brodie
Magical Lore of Cats by Marion Davies
Magical Lore of Herbs by Marion Davies
Masks of Misrule - The Horned God & His Cult in Europe by Nigel Jackson
Mysteries of the Runes by Michael Howard
Oracle of Geomancy by Nigel Pennick
Patchwork of Magic by Julia Day
Pathworking - A Practical Book of Guided Meditations by Pete Jennings
Pickingill Papers - The Origins of Gardnerian Wicca by Michael Howard
Psychic Animals by Dennis Bardens
Psychic Self Defence - Real Solutions by Jan Brodie
Runic Astrology by Nigel Pennick
Sacred Animals by Gordon MacLellan
Sacred Grove - The Mysteries of the Forest by Yvonne Aburrow
Sacred Geometry by Nigel Pennick
Sacred Lore of Horses The by Marion Davies
Sacred Ring - Pagan Origins British Folk Festivals & Customs by Michael Howard
Seasonal Magic - Diary of a Village Witch by Paddy Slade
Secret Places of the Goddess by Philip Heselton
Talking to the Earth by Gordon Maclellan
Taming the Wolf - Full Moon Meditations by Steve Hounsome
The Goddess Year by Nigel Pennick & Helen Field
West Country Wicca by Rhiannon Ryall
Witches of Oz The by Matthew & Julia Phillips